How to
Start
a
Business
in
Georgia

Fifth Edition

Hon. Charles T. Robertson II

and

Mark Warda
Attorneys at Law

SPHINX® PUBLISHING
AN IMPRINT OF SOURCEBOOKS, INC.®
NAPERVILLE, ILLINOIS
www.SphinxLegal.com

Fifth Edition, 2008

Published by: **Sphinx® Publishing, An Imprint of Sourcebooks, Inc.®**

Naperville Office
P.O. Box 4410
Naperville, Illinois 60567-4410
630-961-3900
Fax: 630-961-2168
www.sourcebooks.com
www.SphinxLegal.com

This publication is designed to provide accurate and authoritative information in regard to the subject matter covered. It is sold with the understanding that the publisher is not engaged in rendering legal, accounting, or other professional service. If legal advice or other expert assistance is required, the services of a competent professional person should be sought.

From a Declaration of Principles Jointly Adopted by a Committee of the American Bar Association and a Committee of Publishers and Associations

This product is not a substitute for legal advice.

Disclaimer required by Texas statues.

Library of Congress Cataloging-in-Publication Data

Robertson, Charles T.
    How to start a business in Georgia / by Charles T. Robertson II and Mark Warda.-- 4th ed.
        p. cm.
    Includes index.
    ISBN 1-57248-642-2 (pbk. : alk. paper)
    1. Business enterprises--Law and legislation--Georgia--Popular works. 2. Business enterprises--Law and legislation--Georgia--Forms. 3. Business law--Georgia. I. Warda, Mark. II. Title.

    KFG205.Z9R63 2005
    346.758'065--dc22

                                                    2005027272

Printed and bound in the United States of America.
SB — 10 9 8 7 6 5 4 3 2 1

Contents

Using Self-Help Law Books

Before using a self-help law book, you should realize the advantages and disadvantages of doing your own legal work and understand the challenges and diligence that this requires.

The Growing Trend

Rest assured that you will not be the first or only person handling your own legal matter. For example, in some states, more than 75% of the people in divorces and other cases represent themselves. Because of the high cost of legal services, this is a major trend, and many courts are struggling to make it easier for people to represent themselves. However, some courts are not happy with people who do not use attorneys and refuse to help them in any way. For some, the attitude is, "Go to the law library and figure it out for yourself."

We write and publish self-help law books to give people an alternative to the often complicated and confusing legal books found in most law libraries. We have made the explanations of the law as simple and easy to understand as possible. Of course, unlike an attorney advising an individual client, we cannot cover every conceivable possibility.

Cost/Value Analysis

Whenever you shop for a product or service, you are faced with various levels of quality and price. In deciding what product or service to buy, you make a cost/value analysis on the basis of your willingness to pay and the quality you desire.

When buying a car, you decide whether you want transportation, comfort, status, or sex appeal. Accordingly, you decide among choices such as a Neon, a Lincoln, a Rolls Royce, or a Porsche. Before making a decision, you usually weigh the merits of each option against the cost.

When you get a headache, you can take a pain reliever (such as aspirin) or visit a medical specialist for a neurological examination. Given this choice, most people, of course, take a pain reliever, since it costs only pennies, whereas a medical examination costs hundreds of dollars and takes a lot of time. This is usually a logical choice because it is rare to need anything more than a pain reliever for a headache. But in some cases, a headache may indicate a brain tumor, and failing to see a specialist right away can result in complications. Should everyone with a headache go to a specialist? Of course not, but people treating their own illnesses must realize that they are betting, on the basis of their cost/value analysis of the situation, that they are taking the most logical option.

The same cost/value analysis must be made when deciding to do one's own legal work. Many legal situations are very straightforward, requiring a simple form and no complicated analysis. Anyone with a little intelligence and a book of instructions can handle the matter without outside help.

But there is always the chance that complications are involved that only an attorney would notice. To simplify the law into a book like this, several legal cases often must be condensed into a single sentence or paragraph. Otherwise, the book would be several hundred pages long and too complicated for most people. However, this simplification necessarily leaves out many details and nuances that would apply to special or unusual situations. Also, there are many ways to interpret most legal questions. Your case may come before a judge who disagrees with the analysis of our authors.

Therefore, in deciding to use a self-help law book and to do your own legal work, you must realize that you are making a cost/value analysis. You have decided that the money you will save in doing it yourself outweighs the chance that your case will not turn out to your satisfaction. Most people handling their own simple legal matters never have a problem, but occasionally people find that it ended up costing them more to have an attorney straighten out the situation than it would have if they had hired an attorney in the beginning. Keep this in mind while handling your case, and be sure to consult an attorney if you feel you might need further guidance.

Local Rules   The next thing to remember is that a book that covers the law for the entire nation, or even for an entire state, cannot possibly include every procedural difference of every jurisdiction. Whenever possible, we provide the exact form needed; however, in some areas, each county, or even each judge, may require unique forms and procedures. In our state books, our forms usually cover the majority of counties in the state or provide examples of the type of form that will be required. In our national books, our forms are sometimes even more general in nature but are designed to give a good idea of the type of form that will be needed in most locations. Nonetheless, keep in mind that your state, county, or judge may have a requirement, or use a form, that is not included in this book.

You should not necessarily expect to be able to get all the information and resources you need solely from within the pages of this book. This book will serve as your guide, giving you specific information whenever possible and helping you to find out what else you will need to know. This is just like if you decided to build your own backyard deck. You might purchase a book on how to build decks. However, such a book would not include the building codes and permit requirements of every city, town, county, and township in the nation; nor would it include the lumber, nails, saws, hammers, and other materials and tools you would need to actually build the deck. You would use the book as your guide, and then do some work and research involving such matters as whether you need a permit of some kind, what type and grade of wood is available in your area, whether to use hand tools or power tools, and how to use those tools.

Before using the forms in a book like this, you should check with your court clerk to see if there are any local rules of which you should be aware or local forms you will need to use. Often, such forms will require the same information as the forms in the book but are merely laid out differently or use slightly different language. They will sometimes require additional information.

Changes in the Law   Besides being subject to local rules and practices, the law is subject to change at any time. The courts and the legislatures of all fifty states are constantly revising the laws. It is possible that while you are reading this book, some aspect of the law is being changed.

In most cases, the change will be of minimal significance. A form will be redesigned, additional information will be required, or a waiting period will be extended. As a result, you might need to revise a form, file an extra form, or wait out a longer time period. These types of changes will not usually affect the outcome of your case. On the other hand, sometimes a major part of the law is changed, the entire law in a particular area is rewritten, or a case that was the basis of a central legal point is overruled. In such instances, your entire ability to pursue your case may be impaired.

Introduction

Welcome to the fifth edition of *Start a Business in Georgia*. There have been tremendous fundamental changes in business and in the financial environments of the country since the first edition was published ten years ago. You will find many changes in this edition, some substantial, some philosophical. The heady days of the technology boom have been replaced by corporate downsizing. Many of you are reading this book for information as you start over in a new career, many are looking for supplements to retirement, and some are starting their economic paths fresh from high school or college. For many, self-employment and small business are the only answers to the problems you face, and this book is designed to help guide you through the maze.

No matter what your circumstances are, your goal is to run your own business. Be your own boss, and be as successful as you dare to be. But if you do not follow the laws of the state, your progress can be slowed or stopped by government fines, civil judgments, or even criminal penalties.

This book is intended to give you the framework for legally opening a business in Georgia. It also includes information on where to find special rules for each type of business. If you have problems not covered by this book, you should seek out an attorney who can be available for your ongoing needs.

In order to cover all the aspects of any business you are thinking of starting, you should read through this entire book, rather than skipping to the parts that look most pertinent. There are many laws that may not sound like they apply to you but have provisions that will affect your business.

In recent years, government bureaucracies have been amending and lengthening their forms. The forms included in this book were the most recent available at the time of publication. It is possible that some may be revised at the time you read this book, but in most cases, previous versions of the forms will still be accepted.

chapter 1

Deciding to Start a Business

If you are reading this book, then you have probably made a serious decision to take the plunge and start your own business. Hundreds of thousands of people make the same decision each year, and many of them become very successful. A lot of them also fail. Knowledge can only help your chances of success. You need to know why some succeed while others fail. Some of what follows may seem obvious, but to someone wrapped up in a new business idea, some of this information is occasionally overlooked.

KNOW YOUR STRENGTHS

The last thing a budding entrepreneur wants to hear is that he or she is not cut out for running his or her own business. Those *do you have what it takes* quizzes are ignored with the fear that the answer might be one the entrepreneur does not want to hear. But even if you lack some skills, you can be successful if you know where to get them.

You should consider all the skills and knowledge that running a successful business needs and decide whether you have what it takes. If you do not, it does not necessarily mean you are doomed to be an employee all your life. Perhaps you just need a partner who has the skills you lack, or perhaps you can hire someone with the skills you need. You can structure your business to avoid areas where you are weak. If those options do not work, maybe you can learn those skills.

For example, if you are not good at dealing with employees (either you are too passive and get taken advantage of or are too tough and scare them off), you can:

- handle product development yourself and have a partner or manager deal with employees;

- take seminars in employee management; or,

- structure your business so that you do not need employees (keep it small or use independent contractors).

Here are some of the factors to consider when planning your business.

- If it takes months or years before your business turns a profit, do you have the resources to hold out? Businesses have gone under or have been sold just before they were about to take off. Staying power is an important ingredient to success.

- Are you willing to put in a lot of overtime to make your business a success? Owners of businesses do not set their own hours; the businesses set them for the owners. Many business owners work long hours, seven days a week. However, many take great joy in running their businesses.

- Are you willing to do the dirtiest or most unpleasant work of the business? Emergencies come up and employees are not always dependable. You might need to mop up a flooded room, spend a weekend stuffing 10,000 envelopes, or work Christmas if someone calls in sick.

- Do you know enough about the product or service? Are you aware of the trends in the industry and what changes new technology might bring?

- Do you know enough about accounting and inventory to manage the business? Do you have a good head for business? Some people naturally know how to save money and do things profitably. Others are in the habit of buying the best and the most expensive of everything. The latter can be fatal to a struggling new business.

- ✪ Are you good at managing employees?

- ✪ Do you know how to sell your product or service? You can have the best product on the market, but people will not beat a path to your door if you do not know how to sell it. If you are a wholesaler, shelf space in major stores is hard to get, especially for a new company without a record, a large line of products, or a large advertising budget.

- ✪ Do you know enough about getting publicity? The media receives thousands of press releases and announcements each day, and most are thrown away. Do not count on free publicity to put your name in front of the public.

KNOW YOUR BUSINESS

Not only do you need to know the concept of a business, you also need the experience of working in a business. Maybe you always dreamed of running a bed and breakfast or having your own pizza place, and now you think it is time to use your savings to fulfill your dream. Have you ever worked in such a business? If not, you may have no idea of the day-to-day headaches and problems of the business. For example, do you really know how much to allow for theft, spoilage, and unhappy customers?

You might feel silly taking an entry level job at a pizza place when you would rather start your own, but it might be the most valuable preparation you could have. A few weeks of seeing how a business operates could mean the difference between success and failure.

Working in a business as an employee is one of the best ways to be successful at running such a business in the future. New people with new ideas working in old industries have been known to revolutionize them with obvious improvements that no one before dared to try.

DO THE MATH

Conventional wisdom says you need a business plan before committing yourself to a new venture. But lots of businesses are started successfully without the owners even knowing what a business plan is. They have a great concept, put it on the market, and it takes off. But you at least need to do some basic calculations to see if the business can make a profit. Here are some examples.

○ If you want to start a retail shop, figure out how many people are close enough to become customers, and how many other stores will be competing for those customers. Visit some of those other shops and see how busy they are. Without giving away your plans to compete, ask employees some general questions like "How's business?" and maybe they will share their frustrations or successes.

○ Whether you sell a good or a service, do the math to find out how much profit is in it. For example, if you plan to start a house painting company, find out what you will have to pay to hire painters; what it will cost you for all the insurance, bonding, and licensing you will need; and what the advertising will cost you. Figure out how many jobs you can do per month and what other painters are charging. In some industries, depending on where in the state you plan to operate, there may be a large margin of profit, or there may be almost no profit.

○ Find out if there is a demand for your product or service. Suppose you have designed a beautiful new kind of candle, and your friends all say you should open a shop because "everyone will want them." Before making a hundred of them and renting a store, bring a few to craft shows or flea markets and see what happens.

○ Figure out what the income and expenses would be for a typical month of running your new business. List monthly expenses such as:

  • rent;

  • salaries;

- utilities;

- insurance;

- taxes;

- supplies;

- advertising;

- services; and,

- other overhead.

Then figure out how much profit you will average from each sale. Next, figure out how many sales you will need to cover your overhead, and divide that by the number of business days in the month. Can you reasonably expect that many sales? How will you get those sales?

Most types of businesses have trade associations with figures on how profitable their members are. Some even have start-up kits for people wanting to start businesses. One good source of information on such organizations is the *Encyclopedia of Associations* published by Thomson Gale. It is available in many library reference sections. Producers of products to a trade often give assistance to small companies getting started to win their loyalty. Contact the largest suppliers of the products your business will be using and see if they can help.

SOURCES FOR FURTHER GUIDANCE

There are many things to consider as you prepare to start your own business. Most likely, you will have numerous questions that need to be answered before opening your doors for the first time. Luckily, there are many resources available for help. The sources discussed in this section offer free or low-cost guidance for new businesses.

The *Service Corps of Retired Executives* (SCORE) is a nonprofit organization of people who are glad to give free guidance to new businesses.

Educational programs for small businesses are offered through the *Small Business Development Centers* (SBDC) at many Georiga colleges and universities. You should see if they have any that could help you in any areas in which you are weak.

chapter 2

Choosing and Starting a Form of Business

Proprietorship A *proprietorship* is one person doing business in his or her own name or under a fictitious name.

Advantages. Simplicity is a proprietorship's greatest advantage. There is also no organizational expense and no extra tax forms or reports.

Disadvantages. The proprietor is personally liable for all debts and obligations. There is also no continuation of the business after death. All profits are directly taxable, which is certainly a disadvantage for the proprietor, and business affairs are easily mixed with personal affairs.

General Partnership A *general partnership* involves two or more people carrying on a business together to share the profits and losses.

Advantages. Partners can combine expertise and assets. A general partnership allows liability to be spread among more persons. Also, the business can be continued after the death of a partner if bought out by a surviving partner.

Disadvantages. Each partner is liable for the acts of other partners within the scope of the business. This means that if your partner harms a customer or signs a million-dollar credit line in the partnership's name, you can be personally liable. Even if you leave all profits in the business, those profits are taxable. Control is shared by all parties, and the death of a partner may result in liquidation. In a general partnership, it is often hard to get rid of a bad partner.

Limited Partnership

A *limited partnership* has characteristics similar to both a corporation and a partnership. There are general partners who have the control and personal liability, and there are limited partners who only put up money and whose liability is limited to what they paid for their share of the partnership (like corporate stock). A new type of limited partnership, a limited liability partnership, allows all partners to avoid liability.

Advantages. Capital can be contributed by limited partners who have no control of the business or liability for its debts.

Disadvantages. A great disadvantage is high start-up costs. Also, an extensive partnership agreement is required because general partners are personally liable for partnership debts and for the acts of each other. (One solution to this problem is to use a corporation as the general partner.)

Limited Liability Company

The IRS originally approved the concept of a *limited liability company* (LLC) in 1988, and Georgia followed the rest of the nation in allowing them. An LLC is like a limited partnership without general partners. It has characteristics of both a corporation and a partnership. None of the members have liability and all can have some control, and LLCs may be exempt from Georgia corporate income tax.

Advantages. The limited liability company (LLC) is an incredibly flexible ownership option. If there is only one member, it can be taxed on a Schedule C of your personal taxes. It can also elect to be taxed as a partnership or a corporation. It may have different classes of ownership, an unlimited number of members, and the members can even be foreigners. An LLC can be filed online, in just a few minutes, with the Georgia Secretary of State's office at **http://corp.sos. state.ga.us/business** for about $100 ($125 if you reserve the name).

Disadvantages.   Because they are so easy, they are very easy to abuse. It is pretty common for people to forget they are using an LLC and use their own checking accounts instead of company funds, to co-mingle assets and accounts and to generally not treat it with any level of seriousness. I assure you, however, it is VERY serious. There are some situations in which LLCs would pay Social Security tax on all profits (up to a limit), whereas S corporation profits are exempt from Social Security tax.

NOTE: *One way that high-end accountants and lawyers take advantage of the relative benefits of LLCs and corporations is what I have heard called a "nested S corp" (your accountant or lawyer may have other names). This strategy sets up an LLC for each business venture, but the LLC (or it could be several LLCs) is owned by a sub-S corporation. The LLC then pays a management fee to the sub-S. That strategy manages to marry the benefits of a sub-S with the advantages of an LLC.*

Limited Liability Partnership

The *limited liability partnership* is like a general partnership without personal liability. It was devised to allow partnerships to limit their personal liability without losing their partnership structure. This was important because converting to an LLC could have tax consequences, and some states do not allow professionals to operate as LLCs. Both general and limited partnerships can register as LLPs.

Advantages. The limited liability partnership offers the flexibility and tax benefits of a partnership with the protection from liability of a corporation.

Disadvantages. Start-up and annual fees are higher than for a corporation. Also, the law requires the partnership to maintain certain minimum insurance.

START-UP PROCEDURES

Except for a sole proprietorship, you must prepare some paperwork to start your business, and for some types, you must file the paperwork and pay a registration fee.

Sole Proprietorship   In a sole proprietorship, all accounts, property, and licenses are taken in the name of the owner. (See Chapter 3 for using a fictitious name.)

Partnership   To form a partnership, a written agreement should be prepared to spell out the rights and obligations of the parties. In most cases, licenses can be in either the name of the partnership or in the names of the partners. (See Chapter 3 for using a fictitious name.)

Corporation   Since a corporation is not an individual, a name must be chosen. If the name is important to you, and you believe that someone else might take it or think of it, a name may be reserved prior to filing. A reservation fee of $25 must accompany the request. Alternately, you can simply request a name when you file and provide a couple acceptable alternatives and save the $25. The reservation may be made at the Corporations Division website at www.georgiacorporations. org. Look at the drop-down box under "Online Services and Registration," and select "File a Name Reservation." The form will ask for a name, and then charge you $25 on your credit card. The office will respond to a request by return email within twenty-four hours or less and give you a number that remains in effect for thirty days. Place the number on the Transmittal Form 227 that is filed with the ARTICLES OF INCORPORATION (see form 4, p.235). Reservations are not available by telephone. Filings are accepted without a name reservation.

Forming a simple corporation is neither difficult nor expensive. The Georgia Secretary of State's office is responsible for processing the paperwork. Choose and register your corporate name and file the form along with the Articles of Incorporation. It costs $100 in filing fees with the secretary of state to form your corporation, and another $40 to publish notice of incorporation in the county legal newspaper in the county in which the business will be located. The secretary of state will send you a formal notice of incorporation for your business, and you can use that notice to help you open, for example, a checking account. Be careful not to begin any company business without completing the incorporation. In some instances, obligations that were incurred before a corporation was completely formed will be the personal responsibility of the person making them.

Each Georgia corporation must file an initial annual registration that lists three principal officers with the secretary of state within ninety days of incorporation. The fee increased recently to $30. The registration can be filed online at **www.georgiacorporations.org**. Corporations that form between October 2 and December 31 file the initial registration between January 1 and April 1 of the following year. Changes to the corporation address and/or officers throughout the year are made by filing another registration and paying the $30 fee. A corporation that does not submit its annual registration is subject to administrative dissolution. There is a $100 fee, plus past due registration fees, to reinstate an administratively dissolved corporation.

Limited Liability Partnership

A written limited partnership agreement must be drawn up and registered with the clerk of the Superior Court, and a lengthy disclosure document should be given to all prospective limited partners. Because of the complexity of securities laws and the criminal penalties for violation, it is advantageous to have an attorney organize a limited partnership. Two or more persons may form a limited liability partnership by filing a *Statement of Registration of Georgia Registered Limited Liability Partnership* with the secretary of state in Atlanta. Licenses and accounts are in the name of the company.

Limited Liability Company

LLCs are increasing in popularity. Like a corporation, an LLC is not an individual, and a name must be chosen. If the name is important to you, and you believe that someone else might take it or think of it, a name may be reserved prior to filing Articles of Organization with the secretary of state. A reservation fee of $25 must accompany the request. Alternately, you can simply request a name when you file and provide a couple of acceptable alternatives and save the $25. The reservation may be made at the Corporations Division website at **www.georgiacorporations.org**. Reservations are not available by telephone. Filings are accepted without a name reservation.

One or more persons may form a limited liability company by filing Articles of Organization with the secretary of state online, or in the Atlanta offices, along with $100 in filing fees. LLCs do not require the same types of meetings that corporations require. LLCs, interestingly, are not legally required to file notices of publication; however, most people follow the processes used by corporations anyway.

Each Georgia LLC must file an initial annual registration that lists three principal officers with the secretary of state within ninety days of organizing. The fee increased recently to $30. The registration can be filed online at **www.georigacorporations.org**. Look at the drop down box under "Online Services and Registration," and select "File a Name Reservation." The form will ask for a name, and then charge you $25 on your credit card. LLCs that form between October 2 and December 31 file the initial registration between January 1 and April 1 of the following year. Changes to the corporate address and/or officers throughout the year are made by filing another registration and paying the $30 fee. An LLC that does not submit its annual registration is subject to administrative dissolution. There is a $100 fee, plus past due registration fees, to reinstate an administratively dissolved LLC.

START-UP BASICS

Each of these issues will be addressed more fully in later chapters, but for quick reference, see the chart on the following page.

An Employee Identification Number (EIN) will be needed. It is obtained from the Internal Revenue Service (IRS). Call 866-816-2065 or visit the IRS website at:

www.irs.ustreas.gov

The Georgia Department of Revenue (DOR) should be contacted regarding compliance with state tax laws. Income and net worth tax information may be obtained by calling 404-417-2409. Sales and withholding tax information may be obtained by calling 404-417-2311 or by visiting the DOR's website:

www.dor.ga.gov

Many limited liability companies will be required to obtain workers' compensation insurance. Workers' compensation information may be obtained by calling 800-533-0682 or 404-656-3818.

Many limited liability companies will be subject to the unemployment tax requirements of the "Georgia Employment Security Law."

Information may be obtained from the Georgia Department of Labor at 404-232-3001 or on its website:

www.dol.state.ga.us

BUSINESS COMPARISON CHART

	Sole Proprietorship	General Partnership	Limited Partnership	Limited Liability Co.	Corporation C or S	Nonprofit Corporation
Liability Protection	No	No	For limited partners	For all members	For all shareholders	For all members
Taxes	Pass through	Pass through	Pass through	Pass through	S corps. pass through / C corps. pay tax	None on income / Employees pay on wages
Minimum # of Members	1	2	2	1	1	3
Start-Up Fee	None	None	$100	$100	$100	$100
Annual Fee	None	None	$30	$30	$30	$30
Diff. Classes of Ownership	No	Yes	Yes	Yes	S corps. No / C corps. Yes	No ownership Diff. classes of membership
Survives after Death	No	No	Yes	Yes	Yes	Yes
Best for	1 person low-risk business or no assets	Low-risk business	Low-risk business with silent partners	All types of businesses	All types of businesses	Educational

BUSINESS START-UP CHECKLIST

❏ Make your plan
   ❏ Obtain and read all relevant publications on your type of business
   ❏ Obtain and read all laws and regulations affecting your business
   ❏ Calculate whether your plan will produce a profit
   ❏ Plan your sources of capital
   ❏ Plan your sources of goods or services
   ❏ Plan your marketing efforts
❏ Choose your business name
   ❏ Check other business names and trademarks
   ❏ Register your name, trademark, etc.
❏ Choose the business form
   ❏ Prepare and file organizational papers
   ❏ Prepare and file tradename if necessary
   ❏ Choose a domain name and set up a website
❏ Choose the location
   ❏ Check competitors
   ❏ Check zoning
❏ Obtain necessary licenses
   ❏ City   ❏ State
   ❏ County   ❏ Federal
❏ Choose a bank
   ❏ Checking
   ❏ Credit card processing
   ❏ Loans
❏ Obtain necessary insurance
   ❏ Workers' compensation   ❏ Automobile
   ❏ Liability   ❏ Health
   ❏ Hazard   ❏ Life/Disability
❏ File necessary federal tax registrations
❏ File necessary state tax registrations
❏ Set up a bookkeeping system
❏ Plan your hiring
   ❏ Obtain required posters
   ❏ Obtain or prepare employment application
   ❏ Obtain new hire tax forms
   ❏ Prepare employment policies

❏ Determine compliance with health and safety laws
❏ Plan your opening
    ❏ Obtain all necessary equipment and supplies
    ❏ Obtain all necessary inventory
    ❏ Do all necessary marketing and publicity
    ❏ Obtain all necessary forms and agreements
    ❏ Prepare your company policies on refunds, exchanges, and returns

Registering Your Business Name

Naming a business can be confusing because many businesses operate under different names than their owners. For example, "Precision Tune" is a nationally known chain of automobile tune-up shops, but each shop is independently owned by individuals and corporations who have licensed the right to use the name. When the name of a business is different from that of the owner, it is refered to as either a *tradename*, a *d/b/a* (doing business as), or a *fictitious name*.

Before deciding upon a name for your business, you should be sure that it is not already in use by someone else. Many business owners have spent thousands of dollars on publicity and printing only to throw it all away because another company owned the name. A company that owns a name can take you to court and force you to stop using that name. It can also sue you for damages if it thinks your use of the name cost it a financial loss.

If you will be running a small local shop with no plans for expansion, you should at least check out whether the name has been trade-marked. If someone else is using the same name anywhere in the country and has registered it as a federal trademark, he or she can sue you. If you plan to expand or to deal nationally, you should do a thorough search of the name.

Researching a Business Name

The first places to look are the phone books and official records of your county. Next, you should check with the secretary of state's office in Atlanta to see if someone has registered a fictitious name or corporate name the same as, or similar to, the one you have chosen. The secretary of state's office keeps a computerized list of names at:

www.sos.state.ga.us/corporations/corpsearch.htm

National Search

To do a national search, you should check trade directories and phone books of major cities. These can be found at the library and are usually reference books that cannot be checked out. *Companies and Their Brands* and *Brands and Their Companies* is a two-volume set of names compiled from many sources published by Thomson Gale.

Internet Search

You can use the Internet to search all the Yellow Pages listings in the United States at a number of sites. The website, **http://go.com**, offers free searches of Yellow Pages for all states at once. You can also search the Georgia corporation names at the secretary of state's website:

www.sos.state.ga.us/corporations/corpsearch.htm

Trademark Search

To be sure that your use of the name does not violate someone else's trademark rights, you should have a trademark search done of the mark in the United States Patent and Trademark Office (USPTO). In the past this required a visit to the USPTO offices or the hiring of an expensive search firm. Now, the USPTO puts its trademark records online and you can search them at:

www.uspto.gov

Search Firms

If you do not have access to the Internet, you might be able to do research at a public library or to have one of its employees order an online search for you for a small fee. If this is not available to you, you can have the search done through a firm. One such firm is Government Liaison Services, Inc. It also offers searches of 100 trade directories and 4,800 phone books.

No matter how thorough your search is, there is no guarantee that there is not a local user somewhere with rights to the mark. If, for example, you register a name for a new chain of restaurants and later find out that someone in Tucumcari, New Mexico, has been using the name longer than you, that person will still have the right to use the name, but just in his or her local area. If you do not want that restaurant to cause confusion with your chain, you can try to buy him or her out. Similarly, if you are operating a small business under a unique name, and a law firm in New York writes and offers to buy the right to your name, you can assume that some large corporation wants to start a major expansion under that name.

The best way to make sure a name you are using is not already owned by someone else is to make up a name. *Xerox*, *Kodak*, and *Exxon* are made-up names that did not have any meaning prior to their use.

NOTE: *There are millions of businesses and even something you make up may already be in use. Do a search anyway.*

TRADENAMES

In Georgia, as in most states, unless you do business in your own legal name, you must register the name you are using. If you are not using your own name, the name you are using is probably called a *tradename*.

Individuals often use tradenames. For example, if your name is John Doe and you are operating a masonry business, you may operate your business as *John Doe, Mason* without registering it. But any other use of the name must be registered. Any variation such as these would have to be registered:

Doe Masonry	Doe Masonry Company
Doe Company	Georgia Peach Masonry

Businesses also use tradenames. For example, Jan's Manicure Salon and Tanning Beds, Inc. may prefer to be called "Hands and Tans" (or United Parcel Service, Inc. may wish to be called "UPS"), and this process is also accomplished through registration of a tradename.

Businesses have one more special reason for being sure their names are registered. If a business owner operates a business under a different name, without registering it to the business, then the business owner could be personally liable for any losses or damages from the business even though he or she intended to operate through his or her company.

The laws regarding ownership and use of tradenames is well beyond the level of this instructional guide, but in general, you are far better off registering than not registering.

Registration   Registering a tradename is pretty simple. There is one form for individuals (sole proprietorships) and another for businesses (corporations, LLCs, etc.). These forms, called **AFFIDAVITS TO REGISTER TRADE NAME** (see form 1, p.229, and form 2, p.231), are included in the appendix.

To complete the **AFFIDAVIT TO REGISTER TRADE NAME—INDIVIDUALS** (form 1, p.229), type in the county name in the top left-hand corner, the name of the applicant in the first blank and the signature block, the business address in the second blank, and the tradename you wish to use in the third blank. In the last blank, type the general nature of the business (such as "auto repair," "Amway distributorship," or "nuclear research"). Have your application notarized, and take it to the Superior Court Clerk of the county in which the applicant resides. Usually, the Superior Court Clerk is in the county courthouse. A list of all the clerks can be found at **www.gsccca.org/clerks**. The clerk will charge you about $25 to file your application and another $50 (approximately) to run an announcement in the local legal newspaper for two weeks. You then have secured your rights to that name in your county from anyone who would try to take your name to steal your business.

The **AFFIDAVIT TO REGISTER TRADE NAME—BUSINESS** (form 2, p.231) would be filled out in a similar fashion, but an officer or director must make the application and sign it. The applicant must put his or her name in the first blank, then his or her title, the legal name of the business followed by its location, the tradename he or she wishes to use, and the general nature of the business. The filing process is the same for businesses and individuals.

As discussed previously, you should do some research to see if the name you intend to use is already in use by anyone else. Even persons who have not registered a name can acquire some legal rights to the name through mere use.

CORPORATE NAMES

A corporation does not have to register a fictitious name because it already has a legal name. The name of a corporation must contain one of the following words:

Incorporated	Inc.	Corporation	Corp.
Company	Co.	Limited	Ltd.

If the name of the corporation does not contain one of the above words, it will be rejected by the secretary of state. It will also be rejected if the name is already taken or is similar to the name of another corporation. There are also forbidden words such as "Bank" or "Trust" that can only be used by a corporation in that industry and must be approved by the regulatories of the industry. To check on a name, use the secretary of state's Internet corporate search site at:

www.sos.state.ga.us/corporations/corpsearch.htm

If a name you pick is taken by another company, you may be able to change it slightly and have it accepted. For example, if there is already a Tri-City Upholstery, Inc., and it is in a different county, you may be allowed to use Tri-City Upholstery of Liberty County, Inc. However, even if this is approved by the secretary of state, you might get sued by the other company if your business is close to theirs or if there is a likelihood of confusion.

Do not have anything printed with your business name on it until you have final approval. If you register online, you will get an email approval that the articles are filed. If you file by mail, you should wait until you receive the copy back with the filing date stamped on it.

If a corporation wants to do business under a name other than its corporate name, it can register a fictitious name, such as "Doe Corporation d/b/a Doe Industries." However, if the name leads people to believe that the business is not a corporation, the right to limited liability may be lost. If you use such a name, it should always be accompanied by the corporate name.

PROFESSIONAL CORPORATIONS

Professionals such as attorneys, doctors, dentists, life insurance agents, and architects can form corporations or limited liability companies in which to practice. Professionals in Georgia cannot insulate themselves from malpractice liability through a corporation, but they may be able to protect themselves from business liability and the malpractice liability of partners through a *professional corporation*.

Under Georgia law, a professional corporation cannot use the usual corporate designations Inc., Corp., or Co., but must use the words *professional corporation*, or the abbreviation, *P.C.* In some states, professional corporations are called *professional associations* (P.A.s), but P.C. is the proper description in Georgia.

DOMAIN NAMES

With the Internet changing so rapidly, all the rules for Internet names have not yet been worked out. Originally, the first person to reserve a name owned it, and enterprising souls bought up the names of most of the Fortune 500 corporations. Then a few of the corporations went to court and the rule was developed that if a company had a trademark for a name, that company could stop someone else from using it if the other person did not have a trademark. More recently, Congress made it illegal for cybersquatters to register the names of famous persons and companies. Once you have a valid trademark, you will be safe using it for your domain name.

In recent years, several new top-level domains (TLDs) have been created. TLDs are the last letters of the URL (uniform resource locator), such as ".com," ".org," and ".net." Now you can also register names with the following TLDs.

.biz   .pro

.cc   .aero

.info   .coop

.name   .museum

To find out if a domain name is available, go to **www.whois.net**.

One of the best places to register a domain name is **www. registerfly.com**. If your name is taken, the site automatically suggests related names that might work for you, and its registration fees are lower than most other sites.

If you wish to protect your domain name, the best thing to do at this point is to get a trademark for it. To do this, you would have to use it on your goods or services. The following section gives some basic information about trademarks.

TRADEMARKS

As your business builds goodwill, its name will become more valuable, and you will want to protect it from others who wish to copy it. To protect a name used to describe your goods or services, you can register it as a trademark (for goods) or a service mark (for services), with either the secretary of state of Georgia or with the United States Patent and Trademark Office.

You cannot obtain a trademark for the name of your business, but you can trademark the name you use on your goods and services. In most cases you use your company name on your goods as your trademark, so it, in effect, protects your company name. Another way to protect your company name is to incorporate. A particular corporate name can only be registered by one company in Georgia.

Georgia Registration
State registration would be useful if you only expect to use your trademark within the state of Georgia. Federal registration would protect your mark anywhere in the country. The registration of a mark gives you exclusive use of the mark for the types of goods for which you register it. The only exception is a person who already uses the mark. You cannot stop people who have been using the mark prior to your registration.

The process for trademarks and service marks is fairly simple. The Georgia Secretary of State's office provides the form. (see form 3, p.233.) Sample, filled-in forms and their instructions are in Appendix C. The filing fee is $15 and the process takes about a week or two. The secretary of state provides a good question-and-answer website regarding trademarks at:

www.sos.georiga.gov/corporations/trademarks.htm

Federal Registration   For federal registration, the procedure is a little more complicated. You will use one of two applications depending upon whether you have already made actual use of the mark or whether you merely have an intention to use the mark in the future. For a trademark that has been in use, you must file an application form along with specimens showing actual use and a drawing of the mark, which complies with all the rules of the United States Patent and Trademark Office. For an *intent to use* application, you must file two separate forms: one when you make the initial application, and the other after you have made actual use of the mark, as well as the specimens and drawing. Before a mark can be entitled to federal registration, the use of the mark must be in interstate commerce or in commerce with another country. The fee for registration is $335, but if you file an intent to use application, there is a second fee of $100 for the filing after actual use.

Preparing a Business Plan

Not everyone needs a business plan to start a business, but if you have one it might help you avoid mistakes and make better decisions. For example, if you think it would be a great idea to start a candle shop in a little seaside resort, you might find out after preparing a business plan that considering the number of people who might stop by, you could never sell enough candles to pay the rent.

A business plan lets you look at the costs, expenses, and potential sales, and see whether or not your plan can be profitable. It also allows you to find alternatives that might be more profitable. In the candle shop example, you might find that if you chose a more populous location or if you sold something else in addition to the candles, you would be more likely to make a profit.

ADVANTAGES AND DISADVANTAGES OF A BUSINESS PLAN

Other than helping you figure out if your business will be profitable, a business plan would also be useful if you hope to borrow money or have investors buy into your business. Lenders and equity investors always require a business plan before they will provide money to a business.

If your idea is truly unusual, a business plan may discourage you from starting your business. A business idea might look like a failure on paper, but if in your gut you know it would work, it might be worth trying without a business plan.

Example:

When Chester Carlson invented the first photocopy machine, he went to IBM. They spent $50,000 to analyze the idea and concluded that nobody needed a photocopy machine because people already had carbon paper—which was cheaper. However, he believed in his machine and started Xerox Corporation, which became one of the biggest and hottest companies of its time.

However, even with a great concept, you need to at least do some basic calculations to see if the business can make a profit.

- ✪ If you want to start a retail shop, figure out how many people are close enough to become customers and how many other stores will be competing for those customers. Visit some of those other shops and see how busy they are. Without giving away your plans to compete, ask employees some general questions like "How's business?" and maybe they will share their frustrations or successes.

- ✪ Whether you sell a good or a service, do the math to find out how much profit is in it. For example, if you plan to start a house painting company, find out what you will have to pay to hire painters, what it will cost you for all the insurance, what bonding and licensing you will need, and what the advertising will cost you. Figure out how many jobs you can do per month and what other painters are charging. In some industries, in different areas of the state there may be a large margin of profit, while in other areas there may be almost no profit.

- ✪ Find out if there is a demand for your product or service. Suppose you have designed a beautiful new kind of candle and your friends all say you should open a shop because "everyone will want them." Before making a hundred of them and renting a store, bring a few to craft shows or flea markets and see what happens.

- ✪ Figure out what the income and expenses would be for a typical month of your new business. List monthly expenses, such as rent, salaries, utilities, insurance, taxes, supplies, advertising, services, and other overhead. Then, figure out how much profit you will average from each sale. Next, figure out how many sales you will need to cover your overhead and divide by the number of business days in the month. Can you reasonably expect that many sales? How will you get those sales?

Most types of businesses have trade associations, which often have figures on how profitable its members are. Some even have start-up kits for people wanting to start businesses. One good source of information on such organizations is the *Encyclopedia of Associations* published by Thomson Gale, available in many library reference sections. Suppliers of products to the trade often give assistance to small companies getting started, to win their loyalty. Contact the largest suppliers of the products your business will be using and see if they can be of help.

OUTLINE FOR YOUR BUSINESS PLAN

While you may believe that you do not need a business plan, conventional wisdom says you do and it only makes good business sense to have one. A typical business plan has sections that cover topics such as the following:

- ✪ executive summary;

- ✪ product or service;

- ✪ market;

- ✪ competition;

- ✪ marketing plan;

- ✪ production plan;

- ✪ organizational plan;

- ✪ financial projections;

- ✪ management team; and,

- ✪ risks.

The following is an explanation of each.

Executive Summary

The *executive summary* is an overview of what the business will be and why it is expected to be successful. If the business plan will be used to lure investors, this section is the most important, since many might not read any further if they are not impressed with the summary.

Product or Service

This is a detailed description of what you will be selling. You should describe what is different about it and why people would need it or want it.

Market

The market section should analyze who the potential buyers of your product or service are. Describe both the physical location of the customers and their demographics. For example, a bodybuilding gym would probably mostly appeal to males in the 18–40 age bracket in a ten- to twenty-mile radius, depending on the location.

If you will sell things from a retail shop, you might also want to sell from mail order catalogs or over the Internet if your local customer base would not be large enough to support the business. Describe what you will be doing for those ventures.

If you are manufacturing things, you should find out who the wholesalers and distributors are, and what their terms are. This information should also be included in this section.

Competition   Before opening your business, you should know who and where your competitors are. If you are opening an antique shop, you might want to be near other antique shops so more customers come by your place, since antiques are unique and do not really compete with other antiques. However, if you open a florist shop, you probably do not want to be near other florist shops since most florists sell similar products and a new shop would just dilute the customer base.

If you have a truly unique way of selling something, you might want to go near other similar businesses to grab their existing customer base and expand your market share. However, if they could easily copy your idea, you might not take away the business for long and end up diluting the market for each business. (see Chapter 6.)

Marketing Plan   Many a business has closed just a few months after opening because not enough customers showed up. How do you expect customers to find out about your business? Even if you get a nice write-up in the local paper, not everyone reads the paper, many people do not read every page, and lots of people forget what they read.

Your marketing plan describes how you will advertise your business. List how much the advertising will cost, and describe how you expect people to respond to the advertising.

Production Plan   The production plan needs to address and answer questions such as the following.

- If you are manufacturing a product, do you know how you will be able to produce a large quantity of it?

- Do you know all the costs and the possible production problems that could come up?

- If Wal-Mart orders 100,000 of the product, could you get them made in a reasonable time?

The production plan needs to anticipate the normal schedule you intend to use, as well as how to handle any changes, positive or negative, to that schedule.

If you are selling a service and will need employees to perform those services, your production plan should explain how you will recruit and train those employees.

Organizational Plan

If your business will be more than a mom-and-pop operation, what will the organizational plan be? How many employees will you need and who will supervise whom? How much of the work will be done by employees and how much will be hired out to other businesses and independent contractors? Will you have a sales force? Will you need manufacturing employees? Will your accounting, website maintenance, and office cleaning and maintenance be contracted out or done by employees?

Financial Projections

Tying all the previously discussed topics together is what your financial plan will discuss. You should know how much rent, utilities, insurance, taxes, marketing, and product costs or wages for labor will cost you for the first year. Besides listing known, expected expenses, you should calculate your financial well-being under a number of different possible scenarios. Some of the questions to think about and answer will be: *How long would you be in business if you have very few customers the first few months?* and *If Wal-Mart does order 100,000 of your products, could you afford to manufacture them, knowing you won't be paid for months?*

Management Team

If you will be seeking outside funding, you will need to list the experience and skills of the management of the business. Investors want to know that the people have experience and know what they are doing.

Risks

A good business plan weighs all the risks of the new enterprise. Is new technology in the works that will make the business obsolete? Would a rise in the price of a particularly needed supply eliminate all your profits? What are the chances of a new competitor entering the market if you show some success, and what are you going to do about it? Part of your analysis should be to look at all the possible things that could happen in the field you chose and to gauge the likelihood of success.

Gathering Information

Some of the sections of your business plan require a lot of research. People sometimes take years to prepare them. Today, the Internet puts a nearly infinite amount of information at your fingertips, but you might also want to do some personal research.

Sometimes the best way to get the feel for a business is to get a job in a similar business. At a minimum, you should visit similar businesses and perhaps sit outside of one, and see how many customers they have and how much business they do. There are start-up guides for many types of businesses, which can be found at Amazon.com, your local bookstores, and library. Your local chamber of commerce, business development office, or SCORE office might also have materials to help your research.

Sample Business Plan

The following plan is one for a simple one-person business that will use its owner's assets to start. Of course, a larger business, or one that needs financing, will need a much longer and more detailed plan.

You can find sixty sample business plans and information on business plan software at **www.bplans.com**.

Executive Summary. This is the plan for a new business, Reardon Computer Repair, LLC, by Henry Reardon, to be started locally and then expanded throughout the state and perhaps further if results indicate this is feasible.

The mission of Reardon Computer Repair (RCR) is to offer fast, affordable repairs to office and home computers. The objective is to become profitable within the first three months and to grow at a quick but manageable pace.

In order to offer customers the quickest service possible, RCR will rely on youthful computer whizzes who are students and have the time and expertise to provide the service. They will also have the flexibility to arrive quickly and the motivation to show off their expertise.

To reach customers, we will use limited advertising, but primarily the Internet and word of mouth from happy customers.

With nearly every business and family having several computers and the lack of fast service currently available, it is expected this business could be successful quickly and could grow rapidly.

Product or Service. The company will offer computer repair services both at its shop and at customers' offices and homes. It will sell computer parts as necessary to complete the repairs and it will also carry upgrades, accessories, and peripherals, which will most likely be of value to customers needing repairs.

Market. The market would be nearly every business and family at every address in the city, state, and country, since today nearly everyone has a computer. Figures show nearly 250 million computers in use in America, and that number is expected to grow to over 300 million in five years.

The market for the initial shop would be a 15-mile radius, which is a reasonable driving distance for our employees. The population in that area is 300,000 people, which would mean 240,000 potential customers, based on the current level of 800 computers per 1,000 people.

The market would not include new computers, which typically come with a one-year guarantee. It would also not include people who bought extended guarantees.

The growth trend for the industry is 8%–10% for the next decade.

Competition. The competition would be the authorized repair shops working with the computer manufacturers. While these have the advantage of being authorized, research and experience have shown that they are slow and do not meet customers' need for an immediate repair.

There is one computer repair shop within a 10-mile radius of the proposed shop and two more within a 25-mile radius. Average wait time for a dropped off repair is one week. The two closest repair services offer no on-site repair. Shipping a computer to a dealer for repair takes one to two weeks. Most customers need their computers fixed within a day or two.

One potential source for competition would be from employees or former employees who are asked to work for customers "on the side" at a reduced rate. To discourage this, the company will have a contract with employees with a noncompete agreement that specifies that they will pay the company three times what they earn. Also, agreements with customers will include a clause that they have the option to hire away one of our employees for a one-time $2,000 fee.

Marketing Plan. The business will be marketed through networking, Internet marketing, advertising, and creative marketing.

Networking will be through the owner's contacts and local computer clubs and software stores. Some local retailers do not offer service, and they have already indicated that they would promote a local business that could offer fast repairs.

A website would be linked to local businesses and community groups, and to major computer repair referral sites.

Advertising would include the Yellow Pages and local computer club newsletters. Studies have shown that newspaper and television advertising would be too expensive and not cost effective for this type of business.

Creative advertising would include vinyl lettering on the back window of the owner's vehicle.

Production Plan. The company will be selling the services of computer technicians and computer parts. The owner will supply most of the services in the beginning and then add student technicians as needed.

The parts will all be purchased ready-made from the manufacturers, except for cables, which can be made on an as-needed basis and are much cheaper than ready-made ones.

Employees. The employees will be students who are extremely knowledgeable about computers. Some would call them computer "geeks"—in a nice way. They have extensive knowledge of the workings of computers, have lots of free time, need money, and would love to show off how knowledgeable they are.

As students, they already have health insurance and do not need full-time work. They would be available as needed. The company would pay them $12 an hour plus mileage, which is more than any other jobs available to students, but is not cost prohibitive, considering the charge to customers of $50 per hour.

Financial Projections. The minimum charge for a service call will be $75 on-site and $50 in-shop, which will include one hour of service. The parts markup will be the industry standard of 20%. The average customer bill will be estimated to be $100 including labor and markup.

The labor cost is estimated to be $30 per call including time, taxes, insurance, and mileage. The owner will be estimated to handle 75% of the work the first six months and 50% the second six months.

Rent, utilities, insurance, taxes, and other fixed costs are estimated to be $3,000 per month.

Advertising and promotion expenses are expected to be $3,000 per month.

Estimated number of customers will be:

First three months   10 per week

Second three months   20 per week

Third three months   35 per week

Fourth three months   50 per week

Estimated monthly revenue:

First three months $4,000

Second three months $8,000

Third three months $14,000

Fourth three months $20,000

Monthly income and expense projection:

First three months:

Income $4,000

Labor $300

Fixed costs $3,000

Advertising $3,000

Net $2,300 loss per month

Second 3 months:

Income $8,000

Labor $600

Fixed costs $3,000

Advertising $3,000

Net $1,400 profit per month

Third 3 months:

Income	$14,000
Labor	$2,100
Fixed costs	$3,000
Advertising	$3,000
Net	$5,900 profit per month

Fourth 3 months:

Income	$20,000
Labor	$3,000
Fixed costs	$3,000
Advertising	$3,000
Net	$11,000 profit per month

Organizational Plan. The business will start with the owner, Henry Reardon, and three students who are experts at computer repair and available as part-time workers on an as-needed basis.

The owner will manage the business and do as many repairs as possible with the time remaining in the week.

One of the students, Peter Galt, will work after school in the shop, and the others, Dom Roark and Howard Taggert, are willing to work on an on-call basis, either at the shop or at customers' homes.

As business grows, the company will recruit more student employees through the school job placement offices and at computer clubs.

Management Team. The owner, Henry Reardon, will be the sole manager of the company. He will use the accounting services of his accountant, Dave Burton. The owner anticipates being able to supervise up to ten employees. When there are more than ten, the company will need a manager to take over scheduling and some of the other management functions.

Risks. Because the business does not require a lot of capital, there will be a low financial risk in the beginning. The biggest reason for failure would be an inability to get the word out that the company exists and can fill a need when it arises. For this reason, the most important task in the beginning will be marketing and promotion.

As the company grows, the risk will be that computers will need fewer repairs, become harder to repair, and become so cheap they are disposable. To guard against this possibility, the company will add computer consulting services as it grows so that it will always have something to offer computer owners.

Financing Your Business

The way to finance your business is determined by how fast you want your business to grow and how much you are willing to risk. Letting the business grow with its own income is the slowest but safest way to grow. Taking out a personal loan against your house to expand quickly is the fastest but riskiest way to grow.

GROWING WITH PROFITS

Many successful businesses have started out with little money and used the profits to grow bigger and bigger. If you have another source of income to live on (such as a job or a spouse), you can invest all the income of your fledgling business into growth.

Some businesses start as hobbies or part-time ventures on the weekend while the entrepreneur holds down a full-time job. Many types of businesses start this way. Even some multimillion dollar corporations, such as Apple Computer, began in this manner.

Starting slow allows you to test your idea with little risk. If you find you are not good at running that type of business, or the time or location was not right for your idea, all you lose is the time you spent and your start-up capital.

However, a business can only grow so big from its own income. In many cases, as a business grows, it gets to a point in which the orders are so big that money must be borrowed to produce the desired product. With this kind of order, there is the risk that if the customer cannot pay or goes bankrupt, the business will also go under. At such a point, a business owner should investigate the credit worthiness of the customer and weigh the risks. Some businesses have grown rapidly, some have gone under, and others have decided not to take the risk and stayed small. You can worry about that down the road.

USING YOUR SAVINGS

The best source of money when starting your business is savings. You will not have to pay high interest rates, and you will not have to worry about paying someone back.

Home Equity

If you have owned your home for several years, it is possible that the equity has grown substantially, and you can get a second mortgage to finance your business. Some lenders will make second mortgages that exceed the equity if you have been in the home for many years and have a good record of paying your bills. Just remember, if your business fails, you may lose your house.

Retirement Accounts

Be careful about borrowing from your retirement savings. There are huge tax penalties for borrowing from or against certain types of retirement accounts. Your future financial security may be lost if your business does not succeed.

Having Too Much Money

It probably does not seem possible to have too much money when starting a business, but many businesses have failed for that reason. With plenty of start-up capital available, a business owner does not feel so much pressure to watch expenses and can become wasteful. Employees get used to lavish spending. Once the money runs out, and the business must run on its own earnings, it fails.

Starting with the bare minimum forces a business to watch its expenses and be frugal. It necessitates finding the least expensive solutions to problems that crop up and discovering creative ways to be productive.

BORROWING MONEY

It is extremely tempting to look to others to get the money to start a business. The risk of failure is less worrisome and the pressure is lower, but that is the problem with borrowing. Using the money of others will not motivate you to succeed the way putting everything on the line will.

You should, however, be even more concerned when using the money of others. Your reputation should be more valuable than the money itself, which can always be replaced. Yet that is not always the case. How many people borrow again and again from family for failed business ventures?

Family Depending on how much money your family can spare, it may be the most comfortable or most uncomfortable source of funds for you. If you have been assured a large inheritance and your parents have more funds than they need to live, you may be able to borrow against your inheritance without worry. It will be your money anyway, and you need it much more now than you will ten or twenty or more years from now. If you lose it all, it is your own loss anyway.

However, if you are borrowing your widowed mother's source of income, asking her to cash in a CD to finance your get-rich-quick scheme, you should have second thoughts about it. Stop and consider all the reasons your business might not succeed, and what your mother would do without the income.

Friends Borrowing from friends is like borrowing from family members. If you know they have the funds available and could survive a loss, you may want to risk it, but if they would be loaning you their only resources, do not chance it.

Financial problems can be the worst thing for a relationship, whether it is a casual friendship or a long-term romantic involvement. Before you borrow from a friend, try to imagine what would happen if you could not pay the loan back, and how you would feel if debt caused the end of your relationship.

The ideal situation would be if your friend were a coventurer in your business and the burden to see how funds were spent was not totally yours. Still, realize that such a venture will put extra strain on the relationship.

Bank
In a way, a bank can be a more comfortable party from which to borrow because you do not have a personal relationship with it as with a friend or family member. If you fail, the bank will write your loan off rather than disown you. But a bank can also be the least comfortable party to borrow from because it will demand realistic projections and put pressure on you to perform. If you do not meet its expectations, the bank may call your loan just when you need it most.

The best thing about a bank loan is that it will require you to do your homework. You must have plans that make sense to a banker. If your loan is approved, you know that your plans are at least reasonable.

Bank loans are not cheap or easy. You will be paying interest, and you will have to put up collateral. If your business does not have equipment or receivables, a bank may require you to put up your house and other personal property to guarantee the loan.

Banks are easier to deal with when you get a *Small Business Administration* (SBA) loan. That is because the SBA guarantees that it will pay the bank if you default on the loan. SBA loans are obtained through local bank branches. Go to **www.sba.gov** for more information on how the SBA can help.

Credit Cards
Borrowing against a credit card is one of the fastest growing ways of financing a business, but it can be one of the most expensive. The rates can go higher than 20%, but many cards offer lower rates, and some people are able to get numerous cards. Some successful businesses have used the partners' credit cards to get off the ground or weather a cash crunch. However, if the business does not begin to generate the cash to make the payments, you could soon end up bankrupt. A good strategy is to only use credit cards for long-term assets like a computer or something that will quickly generate cash, like buying inventory to fill an order. Do not use credit cards to pay expenses that are not generating revenue.

A RICH PARTNER

One of the best business combinations is a young entrepreneur with ideas and ambition and a retired investor with business experience and money. Together they can supply everything the business needs.

How do you find such a partner? Be creative. You should have investigated the business you are starting and know others who have been in such businesses. Have any of them had partners retire over the last few years? Are any of them planning to phase out of the business?

SELLING SHARES OF YOUR BUSINESS

Silent investors are the best source of capital for your business. You retain full control of the business, and if it happens to fail, you have no obligation to them. Unfortunately, few silent investors are interested in a new business. You will be able to attract such investors only after you have proven your concept to be successful and built up a rather large enterprise.

The most common way to obtain money from investors is to issue stock to them. For this, the best type of business entity is the corporation. It gives you almost unlimited flexibility in the number and kinds of shares of stock you can issue.

A directory of Georgia venture capital sources can be found at:

www.cfol.com
or
www.nfsn.com

SECURITIES LAWS

There is one major problem with selling stock in your business—all the federal and state regulations with which you must comply. Both the state and federal governments have long and complicated laws dealing with the sales of *securities*. There are also hundreds of court cases attempting to explain what these laws mean. A thorough explanation of this area of law is beyond the scope of this book.

Basically, securities have been held to exist in any case in which a person provides money to someone with the expectation of obtaining a profit through the efforts of that person. This can apply to any situation in which someone buys stock in, or makes a loan to, your business. What the laws require is disclosure of the risks involved, and in some cases, registration of the securities with the government.

There are some *exemptions*, such as for small amounts of money and for limited numbers of investors.

Over and above regulations imposed by the federal government, the offer or sales of securities in Georgia are subject to state regulation under the *Georgia Securities Act*. Under the law, unless the security is subject to a properly recorded registration statement, or the security or transaction is exempt, you cannot offer or sell any security in Georgia.

When you think "securities" you are probably thinking stock in the New York Stock Exchange. However, Georgia and U.S. laws also apply to limited partnership interests, certificates of interest, general partnerships, and business borrowings, including bonds, debentures, or participation in any profit-sharing agreement and (possibly evidence of indebtedness).

Before you panic, certain securities transactions are exempted from registration requirements if they comply with the following conditions.

❂ No offer for sale is made by means of publicly disseminated advertisements or sales literature.

❂ Any certificates representing securities issued or offered for sale under the exemption are clearly marked for a period of one year from the date of issuance or sale to indicate that they were issued or sold in reliance on the exemption.

❂ No more than fifteen novice purchasers of securities from the issuer in Georgia during the twelve-month period ending on the date of issuance. Generally, people who acquired securities that are not subject to the Georgia Securities Act are exempt under other provisions of the act.

✪ Each Georgia purchaser signs a statement showing securities issued or offered for sale under the exemption have been purchased for investment for his or her own account. If he or she holds securities for one year past the date on which the securities were fully paid by that individual, then he or she is presumed to have purchased the securities for investment.

✪ Securities cannot be sold or transferred except under specific circumstances.

The sales of securities must comply with both state and federal laws; however, keep in mind that the state and federal laws are not identical. Compliance under state law will not necessarily constitute compliance under federal law. Some transactions are, however, exempt from federal securities laws under the federal law *Regulation D*, with some restrictions. For example, no commission, finder's fee, or similar remuneration can be paid to any unregistered securities dealer or salesperson in connection with the issue. Also, all reports, notices, and fees must be filed in a timely manner. The total number of unaccredited purchasers cannot exceed thirty-five purchasers in Georgia during any twelve-month period.

There are also some exemptions for certain types of securities, such as promissory notes, which mature within nine months from the date of issuance and are not offered for sale by public advertisements. Other exemptions may be available, depending upon the facts and circumstances of the particular transactions. If an exemption is not available for a particular issue, then the issue must be registered.

The filing of registration statements can be very complicated and expensive. Specific information and documentation concerning the details of the offering and the participants must be given to both the potential investors and the state. Other small issue rules apply to offerings that do not exceed $500,000 in total, or involve fifty or fewer purchasers, but that do not qualify for exemption. Small issues still require informational filings under the act, but the filing requirements are not as cumbersome as the general registration requirements.

Exempt from registration or not, there is no exemption from the fraud protections of the act. Anyone who participates in a scheme to defraud or deceive a security purchaser or seller can be in violation of the Georgia Securities Act. No one selling a security, or participating in an offering, can mislead a purchaser in speech or writing regarding the offer or sale of a security. Nor can one omit a material fact when such an omission would be misleading.

Violations of the Georgia Securities Act may make the seller liable to the purchaser for the amount the purchaser paid for the security, plus interest from the date of purchase. If the purchaser disposed of the security, the recovery is then the difference between the original purchase price of the security and the selling price, plus interest from the date of purchase. Finally, every director, officer, partner, the seller, or any dealer or salesperson involved in the sale may be liable to the purchaser for damages.

Willful violation of any provision of the securities act can be a felony. The punishment is a fine of up to $500,000 or a one- to five-year imprisonment—or both.

USING THE INTERNET TO FIND CAPITAL

The Internet does have some sources of capital listed. The following sites may be helpful.

BusinessFinance
www.businessfinance.com

U.S. Small Business Administration (SBA)
www.sba.gov/financing

NVST
www.nvst.com/pnvHome.asp

The Capital Network
www.thecapitalnetwork.org

Before attempting to market your company's shares on the Internet, be sure to get an opinion from a securities lawyer.

Locating Your Business

The right location for your business will be determined by what type of business it is and how fast you expect to grow. For some types of businesses, the location will not be important to your success or failure. In others, it will be crucial.

WORKING OUT OF YOUR HOME

Many small businesses get started out of the home. Chapter 7 discusses the legalities of home businesses. This section discusses the practicalities.

Starting a business out of your home can save you the rent, electricity, insurance, and other costs of setting up at another location. For some people this is ideal. They can combine their home and work duties easily and efficiently. For other people it is a disaster. Spouses, children, neighbors, television, and household chores can be so distracting that no other work gets done.

Since residential telephone rates are usually lower than business lines, many people use their residential telephone line to conduct business or add a second residential line. However, if you wish to be listed in the Yellow Pages, you will need to have a business line in your home. If you are running two or more types of businesses, you can probably add their names as additional listings on the original number and avoid paying for another business line.

You also should consider whether the type of business you are starting is compatible with a home office. For example, if your business mostly consists of calling clients, then the home may be an ideal place to run it. If your clients need to visit you or if you will need daily pickups and deliveries by truck, then the home may not be a good location. (This is discussed in more detail in Chapter 7.)

CHOOSING A RETAIL SITE

For most types of retail stores, the location is of prime importance. Such things to consider are how close it is to your potential customers, how visible it is to the public, and how easily accessible it is to both automobiles and pedestrians. The attractiveness and safety should also be considered.

Location would be less important for a business that was the only one of its kind in the area. For example, if you were the only moped parts dealer or Armenian restaurant owner in a metropolitan area, people would have to come to wherever you are if they want your products or services. However, even with such businesses, keep in mind that there is competition. People who want moped parts can order them by mail, and restaurant customers can choose another type of cuisine.

Look up all the businesses similar to the one you plan to run in the phone book and mark them on a map. For some businesses, such as a cleaners, you would want to be far from the others. For other businesses, such as antique stores, you would want to be near those that are similar. (Antique stores usually do not carry the same things, therefore they do not compete, and people like to go to an *antique district* and visit all the shops.)

CHOOSING OFFICE, MANUFACTURING, OR WAREHOUSE SPACE

If your business will be the type in which customers will not come to you, then locating it near customers is not as much of a concern. You can probably save money by locating away from the high-traffic central business districts. However, you should consider the convenience for employees and not locate in an area that would be unattractive to them or too far from where they would likely live.

For manufacturing or warehouse operations, consider your proximity to a post office, trucking company, or rail line. Where several sites are available, you might consider which one has the earliest or most convenient pickup schedule for the carriers you plan to use.

LEASING A SITE

A lease of space can be one of the biggest expenses of a small business, so do a lot of homework before signing one. There are a lot of terms in a commercial lease that can make or break your business. These are the most critical.

Zoning

Before signing a lease, be sure that everything your business will need to do is allowed by the zoning of the property. Your county zoning board can explain what is and is not allowed in regard to how your property is zoned.

Restrictions

In some shopping centers, existing tenants have guarantees that other tenants do not compete with them. For example, if you plan to open a restaurant and bakery, you may be forbidden to sell carry-out baked goods if the supermarket next door has a bakery and a noncompete clause.

Signs

Business signs are regulated by zoning laws, sign laws, and property restrictions. If you rent a hidden location with no possibility for adequate signage, your business will have a much smaller chance of success than with a more visible site or much larger sign.

ADA Compliance

The *Americans with Disabilities Act* (ADA) requires that reasonable accommodations be made to make businesses accessible to the handicapped. When a business is remodeled, many more changes are required than if no remodeling is done. When renting space, you should be sure that it complies with the law or that the landlord will be responsible for compliance. Be aware of the full costs you will bear.

Expansion   As your business grows, you may need to expand your space. The time to find out about your options is before you sign the lease. Perhaps you can take over adjoining units when those leases expire.

Renewal   Location is a key to success for some businesses. If you spend five years building up a clientele, you do not want someone to take over your locale at the end of your lease. Therefore, you should have a renewal clause on your lease. This usually allows an increase in rent based on inflation.

Guarantee   Most landlords of commercial space will not rent to a small corporation without a personal guarantee of the lease. This is a very risky thing for a new business owner to do. The lifetime rent on a long-term commercial lease can be hundreds of thousands of dollars. If your business fails, the last thing you want is to be personally responsible for five years of rent.

Where space is scarce or a location is hot, a landlord can get the guaranties he or she demands, and there is nothing you can do about it (except perhaps set up an asset protection plan ahead of time). But where several units are vacant or the commercial rental market is soft, you can often negotiate out of the personal guarantee. If the lease is five years, maybe you can get away with a guarantee of just the first year. Possibly, you can agree with the landlord to limit the amount of the guarantee to a dollar figure you can live with. We all expect to be successful, but remember that sometimes bad things happen to good people and you may want to consider some preservation planning.

Duty to Open   Some shopping centers have rules requiring all shops to be open certain hours. If you cannot afford to staff it the whole time required or if you have religious or other reasons that make this a problem, negotiate it out of the lease or find another location.

Sublease   At some point you may decide to sell your business, and in many cases, the location is the most valuable aspect of it. For this reason, you should be sure that you have the right to either assign your lease or to sublease the property. If this is impossible, one way around a prohibition is to incorporate your business before signing the lease, and then when you sell the business, sell the stock. Some lease clauses prohibit the transfer of *any* interest in the business, so read the lease carefully.

BUYING A SITE

If you are experienced with owning rental property, you will probably be more inclined to buy a site for your business. If you have no experience with real estate, you should probably rent and not take on the extra cost and responsibility of property ownership.

One reason to buy your site is that you can build up equity. Rather than pay rent to a landlord, you can pay off a mortgage and eventually own the property.

Separating the Ownership

One risk in buying a business site is that if the business gets into financial trouble, the creditors may go after the building as well. For this reason, most people who buy a site for their business keep the ownership out of the business.

Example:
The business will be a corporation, and the real estate will be owned personally by the owner or by a trust unrelated to the business.

Expansion

Before buying a site, consider the growth potential of your business. If it grows quickly, will you be able to expand at that site or will you have to move? Might the property next door be available for sale in the future if you need it? Can you get an option on it?

If the site is a good investment whether or not you have your business, then by all means, buy it. But if its main use is for your business, think twice.

Zoning   Some of the concerns when buying a site are the same as when renting. You will want to make sure that the zoning permits the type of business you wish to start or that you can get a variance without a large expense or delay. Be aware that just because a business is now using the site does not mean that you can expand or remodel the business at that site. Check with the zoning department and find out exactly what is allowed.

Signs   Signs are another concern. Some cities have regulated signs and do not allow new or larger ones. Some businesses have used these laws to get publicity. A car dealer who was told to take down a large number of American flags on his lot filed a federal lawsuit, and the community rallied behind him.

ADA Compliance   ADA compliance is another concern when buying a commercial building. Find out from the building department if the building is in compliance or what needs to be done to put it in compliance. If you remodel, the requirements may be more strict.

> **NOTE:** *When dealing with public officials, keep in mind that they do not always know what the law is or do not accurately explain it. They occasionally try to intimidate people into doing things that are not required by law. Read the requirements yourself and question the officials if they seem to be interpreting it wrong. Seek legal advice if officials refuse to re-examine the law or move away from an erroneous position.*
>
> *Also consider that keeping them happy may be worth the price. If you are already doing something they have overlooked, do not make a big deal over a little thing they want changed, or they may subject you to a full inspection or audit.*

CHECKING GOVERNMENT REGULATIONS

When looking for a site for your business, investigate the different government regulations in your area. For example, a location just outside the city or county limits might have a lower licensing fee, a lower sales tax rate, and less strict sign requirements.

Licensing Your Business

The federal and state legislatures and local governments have an interest in protecting consumers from bad business practices. Therefore, in order to ensure that consumers are protected from unscrupulous businesspeople, and to require a minimum level of service to the public, the federal, state, and local governments have developed hundreds of licensing requirements that cover occupations and services ranging from attorneys to barbers to day care providers and hundreds of others.

This arena is also becoming a favorite hunting ground for government tax authorities. It is common now in Georgia to not renew business and professional licenses if all taxes (including property taxes!) are not current. Be very careful to keep your taxes up to date. A friend of mine found out the hard way when a government agency refused to renew his restaurant's liquor license on December 31, and he was out of business in a matter of days.

OCCUPATIONAL LICENSES AND ZONING

Some Georgia counties and cities require you to obtain an *occupational license*. If you are in a city, you may need both a city and a county license. Businesses that do work in several cities, such as builders, must obtain a license from each city in which they do work.

This does not have to be done until you actually begin a job in a particular city.

County occupational licenses can be obtained from the tax collector in the county courthouse. City licenses are usually available at the city hall. Be sure to find out if zoning allows your type of business before buying or leasing property. The licensing departments will check the zoning before issuing your license.

If you will be preparing or serving food, you will need to check with the local health department to be sure that the premises comply with their regulations. In some areas, if food has been served on the premises in the past, there is no problem getting a license. If food has never been served on the premises, then the property must comply with all the newest regulations, which can be very costly.

Home Business

Problems occasionally arise when someone attempts to start a business in his or her home. New small businesses cannot always afford to pay rent for commercial space, and cities often try to forbid business in residential areas. Getting a county occupational license or advertising a fictitious name often gives notice to the city that a business is being conducted in a residential area.

Some people avoid the problem by starting their businesses without occupational licenses, figuring that the penalties are less expensive than the cost of office space. Others get the county license and ignore the city rules. If a person has commercial trucks and equipment all over his or her property, there will probably be complaints from neighbors and the city will probably take legal action. But if a person's business consists merely of making phone calls out of the home and keeping supplies there, the problem may never come up.

If a problem does arise regarding a home business that does not disturb the neighbors, a good argument can be made that the zoning law that prohibits the business is unconstitutional. But court battles with a city are expensive and probably not worth the effort for a small business. The best course of action is to keep a low profile. Using a post office box is sometimes helpful in diverting attention away from the residence.

STATE-REGULATED PROFESSIONS

Many professions require special state licenses. You will probably be called upon to produce such a license when applying for an occupational license.

If you are in a regulated profession, you should be aware of the laws that apply to your profession. The following is the main address and phone number of the Licensing Boards Division.

Secretary of State
Professional Licensing Boards Division
237 Coliseum Drive
Macon, GA 31217
478-207-2440

Businesses that sell food or groceries need a license from:

Georgia Department of Agriculture
Consumer Protection Division
19 Martin Luther King Jr. Drive, SW
Atlanta, GA 30334
404-656-3627

Businesses selling alcoholic beverages must obtain a license from their city or county.

Businesses that are engaged in activities that are considered *in the public interest* (such as nurseries, schools, transportation companies, financial institutions, and securities dealers) need special permits. To find out which agency covers your business, call the State of Georgia Information Line at 404-656-2000.

FEDERAL LICENSES

Few businesses require federal registration. If you are in any of the types of businesses in the following list, you should check with the federal agency connected with it.

✪   Radio or television stations or manufacturers of equipment emitting radio waves:

Federal Communications Commission
445 12th Street, SW
Washington, DC 20554
www.fcc.gov

✪   Manufacturers of alcohol, tobacco, or firearms:

Bureau of Alcohol, Tobacco, Firearms, and Explosives
Office of Public and Governmental Affairs
99 New York Avenue, NE
Mail Stop 5S144
Washington, DC 20226
www.atf.treas.gov

✪   Securities brokers and providers of investment advice:

SEC
100 F Street, NE
Washington, DC 20549
www.sec.gov

✪   Manufacturers of drugs and processors of meat:

Food and Drug Administration
5600 Fishers Lane
Rockville, MD 20857
www.fda.gov

✪   Interstate carriers:

Surface Transportation Board
395 E Street, SW
Washington, DC 20423
www.stb.dot.gov

✪   Exporters:

Bureau of Industry and Security
U.S. Department of Commerce
14th Street & Constitution Avenue, NW
Washington, DC 20230
www.bis.doc.gov

Contract Laws

As a business owner, you will need to know the basics of forming a simple contract for your transactions with both customers and vendors. There is a lot of misunderstanding about what the law is and people may give you erroneous information. Relying on it can cost you money. This chapter gives you a quick overview of the principles that apply to your transactions and the pitfalls to avoid. If you face more complicated contract questions, consult a law library or an attorney familiar with small business law.

TRADITIONAL CONTRACT LAW

One of the first things taught in law school is that a contract is not legal unless three elements are present: an *offer*, *acceptance*, and *consideration*. The rest of the semester dissects exactly what may be a valid offer, acceptance, and consideration.

For your purposes, the important things to remember are as follows.

- ✪ If you make an offer to someone, it may result in a binding contract, even if you change your mind or find out it was a bad deal for you.

✪   Unless an offer is accepted and both parties agree to the same terms, there is no contract.

✪   A contract does not always have to be in writing. Some laws require certain contracts to be in writing, but as a general rule an oral contract is legal. The problem is in proving that the contract existed.

✪   Without *consideration* (the exchange of something of value or mutual promises), there is not a valid contract.

The most important rules for the business owner are as follows.

✪   An advertisement is not an offer. Suppose you put an ad in the newspaper offering new IBM computers for $1,995, but there is a typo in the ad and it says $19.95? Can people come in and say, *I accept, here's my $19.95*, creating a legal contract? Fortunately, no. Courts have ruled that the ad is not an offer that a person can accept. It is an invitation to come in and make offers, which the business can accept or reject.

✪   The same rule applies to the price tag on an item. If someone switches price tags on your merchandise, or if you accidentally put the wrong price on it, you are not required by law to sell it at that price. However, many merchants honor a mistaken price, because refusing to do so would constitute bad will and probably lose a customer. If you intentionally put a lower price on an item, intending to require a buyer to pay a higher price, you may be in violation of bait and switch laws.

✪   When a person makes an offer, several things may happen. It may be accepted, creating a legal contract. It may be rejected. It may expire before it has been accepted. Or, it may be withdrawn before acceptance. A contract may expire either by a date made in the offer (e.g., *This offer remains open until noon on January 29, 2005*) or after a reasonable amount of time. What is *reasonable* is a legal question that a court must decide. If someone makes you an offer to sell goods, clearly you cannot come back five years later and accept. Can you accept a week later or a month later and create a legal contract? That depends on the type of goods and the circumstances.

- ✪ A person accepting an offer cannot add any terms to it. If you offer to sell a car for $1,000 and the other party says they accept as long as you put new tires on it, there is no contract. An acceptance with changed terms is considered a rejection and a counteroffer.

- ✪ When someone rejects your offer and makes a counteroffer, a contract can be created by your acceptance of the counteroffer.

These rules can affect your business on a daily basis. Suppose you offer to sell something to one customer over the phone and five minutes later another customer walks in and offers you more for it. To protect yourself, you should call the first customer and withdraw your offer before accepting the offer of the second customer. If the first customer accepts before you have withdrawn your offer, you may be sued if you sell the item to the second customer.

Exceptions   There are a few exceptions to the basic rules of contracts. They are as follows.

- ✪ *Consent* to a contract must be voluntary. If it is made under a threat, the contract is not valid. If a business refuses to give a person's car back unless he or she pays $200 for changing the oil, the customer could probably sue and get the $200 back.

- ✪ Contracts to do *illegal* acts or acts *against public policy* are not enforceable. If an electrician signs a contract to put some wiring in a house that is not legal, the customer could probably not force him or her to do it because the court would refuse to require an illegal act. Recently, the surge in popularity of gambling has made this an important little rule. Gambling debts are not only NOT ENFORCEABLE in Georgia, but there are some laws that let bounty hunters sue for money spent on gambling—scary stuff if you run the neighborhood game! This will not help if you lose money in Las Vegas, then come to Georgia, though—since gambling *is* legal in Vegas and that is where the contract was entered.

○ If either party to an offer *dies*, then the offer expires and cannot be accepted by the heirs. If a painter is hired to paint a portrait and dies before completing it, his wife cannot finish it and require payment. However, a corporation does not die, even if its owners die. If a corporation is hired to build a house and the owner dies, his or her heirs may take over the corporation, finish the job, and require payment.

○ Contracts made under *misrepresentation* are not enforceable. For example, if someone tells you a car has 35,000 miles on it and you later discover it has 135,000 miles, you may be able to rescind the contract for fraud and misrepresentation.

○ If there was a *mutual mistake*, a contract may be rescinded. For example, if both you and the seller thought the car had 35,000 miles on it and both relied on that assumption, the contract could be rescinded. However, if the seller knew the car had 135,000 miles on it, but you assumed it had 35,000 and did not ask, you probably could not rescind the contract.

STATUTORY CONTRACT LAW

The previous section discussed the basics of contract law. These are not usually stated in the statutes, but are the legal principles decided by judges over hundreds of years. In recent times the legislatures have made numerous exceptions to these principles. In most cases, these laws have been passed when the legislature felt that traditional law was not fair. The important laws that affect contracts are as follows.

Statute of Frauds   The *Statute of Frauds* states when a contract must be in writing to be valid. In Georgia, some of the contracts that must be in writing, and the applicable statute sections, are as follows:

○ promises by an executor, administrator, or guardian for personal payment (O.C.G.A., Section 13-5-30.);

○ sales of any interest in real estate (O.C.G.A., Section 13-5-30.);

- ✪ guarantees of debts of another person (O.C.G.A., Section 13-5-30.);

- ✪ sales of goods of over $500 (O.C.G.A., Section 11-2-201.);

- ✪ sales of personal property of over $5,000 (O.C.G.A., Section 11-1-206.);

- ✪ agreements that take over one year to complete (O.C.G.A., Section 13-5-30.);

- ✪ sales of securities (O.C.G.A., Section 11-8-319.);

- ✪ leases over $1,000 (O.C.G.A., Section 11-2A-201.);

- ✪ prenuptial agreements (O.C.G.A., Section 13-5-30.); and,

- ✪ any commitment to lend money (O.C.G.A., Section 13-5-30).

Because of alleged unfair practices by some types of businesses, laws have been passed controlling the types of contracts they may use. Most notable among these are health clubs and door-to-door solicitations. The laws covering these businesses usually give the consumer a certain time to cancel the contract. These laws are described in Chapter 12.

PREPARING YOUR CONTRACTS

Before you open your business, you should obtain or prepare the contracts or policies you will use in your business. In some businesses, such as a restaurant, you will not need much. Perhaps you will want a sign near the entrance stating *Shirt and shoes required* or *Diners must be seated by 10:30 p.m.*

However, if you are a building contractor or a similar business, you will need detailed contracts to use with your customers. If you do not clearly spell out your rights and obligations, you may end up in court and lose thousands of dollars in profits.

The best way to have an effective contract is to have one prepared by an attorney who is experienced in the subject. However, since this may be too expensive for your new operation, you may want to go elsewhere. Sources for the contracts you will need could be other businesses like yours, trade associations, and legal form books. Obtain as many different contracts as possible, compare them, and decide which terms are most comfortable for you.

Insurance Laws

Remember from Chapter 2 that a corporation or LLC may protect you from personal liability for losses exceeding your insurance coverage. If you have elected to operate without a corporation, or have a corporation and still have personal liability or personal guarantees, there are a number of strategies that you could use to limit your exposure. These strategies are as simple as not going into business with any interest in any property at all (perhaps all assets are owned by a parent or spouse). They can also be as complex as offshore corporations loaning money to U.S. shell corporations with offices in Delaware owned by Nevada corporations. This discussion encompasses practical, financial, moral, and ethical decisions that are beyond the scope of this book. However, an investigation into asset protection through your attorney, CPA, or trade association is never a bad idea.

Be aware that there can be a wide range of prices and coverage in insurance policies. You should get at least three quotes from different insurance agents and ask each one to explain the benefits of his or her policy. Good general information is contained in the booklet *First Stop Business Guide,* available from the following address:

First Stop Business Information Center
2 Martin Luther King Jr. Drive
West Tower
Suite 315
Atlanta, GA 30334
404-656-7061
or
800-656-4558

WORKERS' COMPENSATION

If you have three or more employees, you are required by law to carry workers' compensation insurance. In exchange, injured employees generally cannot sue their employers.

The term *employee* is specifically defined in the O.C.G.A., Section 34-9-1. You should read this law carefully if you think you need to comply with it. For example, part-time employees, students, aliens, or illegal workers can count as employees. However, under certain conditions, volunteers, real estate agents, musical performers, taxi cab or limo drivers, officers of a corporation, casual workers, and persons who transport property by vehicle are not considered employees. Neither are independent contractors considered employees, but the definition of independent contractors is adjusting rapidly. Even if you are not required to have workers' compensation insurance, you may still wish to carry it because it can protect you from litigation.

This insurance can be obtained from most insurance companies and, at least for low-risk occupations, is not expensive. If you have such coverage, you are protected against potentially ruinous claims by employees or their heirs in case of accident or death.

For high-risk occupations such as roofing, it can be very expensive, sometimes 30¢ to 50¢ for each dollar of payroll. For this reason, construction companies try to become exempt through means such as hiring independent contractors or only having a few employees who are also officers of the business. However, the requirements for the exemptions are strict, so anyone intending to obtain an exemption should first check with an attorney specializing in workers' compensation to be sure to do it right.

Failure to provide workers' compensation insurance when required is considered serious. If a person is injured on a job, even if another employee caused it or the injured person contributed to his or her own injury, you, along with other officers, may be required to pay for all resulting losses personally.

There are other requirements of the *Workers' Compensation Law*, such as reporting any on-the-job deaths of workers within twenty-four hours.

This law has been subject to frequent change lately so you should check with the State Board of Workers' Compensation for the latest requirements. Contact them at:

State Board of Workers' Compensation
270 Peachtree Street, NW
Atlanta, GA 30303
404-656-3875
or
800-533-0682

Note: *The Georgia rules regarding employees are different from the federal rules. Under federal law, contractors are, for the most part, exempt from unemployment taxes as 1099 sub-contractors. Recent Georgia cases have held that subs CAN BE COUNTED as employees, regardless of the terms of employment. Be careful! A smart thing to do, since unemployment insurance is only on the first $8,500 and is cheap, is to pay unemployment insurance in Georgia for your subcontractors, but continue to treat them as 1099 contractors for federal tax purposes.*

LIABILITY INSURANCE

In most cases, you are not required to carry liability insurance. Liability insurance can be divided into two main areas: coverage for injuries on your premises or by your employees, and coverage for injuries caused by your products.

Asset Protection

Coverage for the first type of injury is usually very reasonably priced. Injuries in your business or by your employees (such as in an auto accident) are covered by standard premises or auto policies. But coverage for injuries by products may be harder to find and more expensive.

If insurance is unavailable or unaffordable, you can go without and use a corporation and other asset protection devices to protect yourself from liability. As discussed in Chapter 2, a properly formed and maintained LLC or corporation can provide personal protection for the principals for obligations of the company. Keep in mind, though, that there are a number of potential pitfalls in simply relying on your corporation or LLC. Sometimes people forget to maintain them. Other times obligations are *personally guaranteed* by the principals—sometimes in the fine print of contracts.

Umbrella Policy

The best way to find out if insurance is available for your type of business is to check with other businesses. If there is a trade group for your industry, its newsletter or magazine may contain ads for insurers.

As a business owner, you will be more visible as a target for lawsuits, even if there is little merit to them. Lawyers know that a *nuisance suit* is often settled for thousands of dollars. Because of your greater exposure, you should consider getting a personal *umbrella policy*. This is a policy that covers you for claims of up to a certain dollar amount (possibly even two or five million) and is very reasonably priced.

HAZARD INSURANCE

One of the worst things that can happen to your business is a fire, flood, or other disaster. Due to lost customer lists, inventory, and equipment, many businesses have been forced to close after such a disaster.

The premium for hazard insurance is usually reasonable and could protect you from losing your business. You can even get business interruption insurance, which will cover your losses while your business is getting back on its feet.

HOME BUSINESS INSURANCE

There is a special insurance problem for home businesses. Most homeowner and tenant insurance policies do not cover business activities. In fact, under some policies, you may be denied coverage if you use your home for a business.

You probably will not have a problem and will not need extra coverage if you merely use your home to make business phone calls and send letters. If you own equipment or have dedicated a portion of your home exclusively to the business, you could have a problem. Check with your insurance agent for the options that are available to you.

If your business is a sole proprietorship and you have a computer that you use both personally and for your business, it would probably be covered under your homeowners' policy. But if you incorporate your business and bought the computer in the name of the corporation, coverage might be denied. It is possible to get a special insurance policy in the company name covering just the computer if it is your main business asset. One company that offers such a policy is Safeware. It can be reached at 800-800-1492. Other specialty insurance may be found on the Internet.

AUTOMOBILE INSURANCE

If you or any of your employees will be using an automobile for business purposes, be sure to have this use covered. Sometimes a policy may contain an exclusion for business use. Check to be sure your liability policy covers you if one of your employees causes an accident while running a business errand.

HEALTH INSURANCE

While new businesses can rarely afford health insurance for their employees, the sooner they can obtain it, the better chance they will have to find and keep good employees. Those starting a business usually need insurance for themselves, and they can sometimes receive a better rate if they obtain a small business package.

EMPLOYEE THEFT

If you fear employees may be able to steal from your business, you may want to have them bonded. This means that you pay an insurance company a premium to guarantee employees' honesty, and if they cheat you the insurance company pays you damages. This can cover all existing and new employees.

SALES TAX BONDS

For some businesses, the Georgia Department of Revenue will require a bond to guarantee payment of sales taxes. This can be obtained from your insurance agent.

Your Business and the Internet

The Internet has opened up a world of opportunities for businesses. It was not long ago that getting national visibility cost a fortune. Today, a business can set up a web page for a few hundred dollars, and with some clever publicity and a little luck, millions of people around the world will see it.

This new world has new legal issues and new liabilities. Not all of them have been addressed by laws or by the courts. Before you begin doing business on the Internet, you should know the existing rules and the areas where legal issues exist.

DOMAIN NAMES

A domain name is the address of your website. For example, **www.apple.com** is the domain name of Apple Computer, Inc. The last part of the domain name, the ".com" (or "dot com") is the top-level domain, or TLD. Dot com is the most popular, but others are currently available in the United States, including ".net" and ".org." (Originally, ".net" was only available to network service providers and ".org" only to nonprofit organizations, but regulations have eliminated those requirements.)

It may seem like most words have been taken as a dot-com name, but if you combine two or three short words or abbreviations, a nearly unlimited number of possibilities are available. For example, if you have a business dealing with automobiles, most likely someone has already registered automobile.com and auto.com. You can come up with all kinds of variations, using adjectives or your name, depending on your type of business:

autos4u.com	joesauto.com	autobob.com
myauto.com	yourauto.com	onlyautos.com
greatauto.com	autosfirst.com	usautos.com
greatautos.com	firstautoworld.com	4autos.com

When the Internet first began, some individuals realized that major corporations would soon want to register their names. Since the registration was easy and cheap, people registered names they thought would ultimately be used by someone else.

At first, some companies paid high fees to buy their names from the registrants. One company, Intermatic, filed a lawsuit instead of paying. The owner of the domain name it wanted had registered numerous domain names, such as britishairways.com and ussteel.com. The court ruled that since Intermatic owned a trademark on the name, the registration of its name by someone else violated that trademark, and that Intermatic was entitled to it.

Since then, people have registered names that are not trademarks, such as CalRipkin.com, and have attempted to charge the individuals with those names to buy their domains. In 1998, Congress passed the *Anti-Cybersquatting Consumer Protection Act*, making it illegal to register a domain with no legitimate need to use it.

This law helped a lot of companies protect their names, but then some companies started abusing it and tried to stop legitimate users of names similar to theirs. This is especially likely against small companies. An organization that has been set up to help small companies protect their domains is the Domain Name Rights Coalition. Its website is **www.netpolicy.com**. Some other good information on domain names can be found at **www.bitlaw.com/internet/domain.html**.

Registering a domain name for your own business is a simple process. There are many companies that offer registration services. For a list of those companies, visit the site of the Internet Corporation for Assigned Names and Numbers (ICANN) at **www.icann.org**. You can link directly to any member's site and compare the costs and registration procedures required for the different top-level domains.

WEB PAGES

There are many new companies eager to help you set up a website. Some offer turnkey sites for a low, flat rate, while custom sites can cost tens of thousands of dollars. If you have plenty of capital, you may want to have your site handled by one of these professionals. However, setting up a website is a fairly simple process, and once you learn the basics, you can handle most of it in-house.

If you are new to the Web, you may want to look at **www.learnthenet.com** and **www.webopedia.com**, which will familiarize you with the Internet jargon and give you a basic introduction to the Web.

Site Setup   There are seven steps to setting up a website: site purpose, design, content, structure, programming, testing, and publicity. Whether you do it yourself, hire a professional site designer, or employ a college student, the steps toward creating an effective site are the same.

Before beginning your own site, you should look at other sites, including those of major corporations and of small businesses. Look at the sites of all the companies that compete with you. Look at hundreds of sites and click through them to see how they work (or do not work).

Site purpose. To know what to include on your site, you must decide what its purpose will be. Do you want to take orders for your products or services, attract new employees, give away samples, or show off your company headquarters? You might want to do several of these things.

Site design. After looking at other sites, you can see that there are numerous ways to design a site. It can be crowded, or open and airy, it can have several windows (frames) open at once or just one, and it can allow long scrolling or just click-throughs.

You will have to decide whether the site will have text only; text plus photographs and graphics; or, text plus photos, graphics, and other design elements, such as animation or Java script. Additionally, you will begin to make decisions about colors, fonts, and the basic graphic appearance of the site.

Site content. You must create the content for your site. For this, you can use your existing promotional materials, new material just for the website, or a combination of the two. Whatever you choose, remember that the written material should be concise, free of errors, and easy for your target audience to read. Any graphics (including photographs) and written materials not created by you require permission. You should obtain such permission from the lawful copyright holder in order to use any copyrighted material. Once you know your site's purpose, look, and content, you can begin to piece the site together.

Site structure. You must decide how the content (text plus photographs, graphics, animation, etc.) will be structured—what content will be on which page, and how a user will link from one part of the site to another. For example, your first page may have the business name and then choices to click on, such as "about us," "opportunities," or "product catalog." Have those choices connect to another page containing the detailed information, so that a user will see the catalog when he or she clicks on "product catalog." Your site could also have an option to click on a link to another website related to yours.

Site programming and setup. When you know nothing about setting up a website, it can seem like a daunting task that will require an expert. However, programming here means merely putting a site together. There are inexpensive computer programs available that make it very simple.

Commercial programs such as Microsoft FrontPage, Dreamweaver, Pagemaker, Photoshop, MS Publisher, and PageMill allow you to set up web pages as easily as laying out a print publication. These programs will convert the text and graphics you create into HTML, the programming language of the Web. Before you choose web design software and design your site, you should determine which web hosting service you will use. Make sure that the design software you use is compatible with the host server's system. The web host is the provider who will give you space on its server and who may provide other services to you, such as secure order processing and analysis of your site to see who is visiting and linking to it.

If you have an America Online (AOL) account, you can download design software and a tutorial for free. You do not have to use AOL's design software in order to use this service. You are eligible to use this site whether you design your own pages, have someone else do the design work for you, or use AOL's templates. This service allows you to use your own domain name and choose the package that is appropriate for your business.

If you have used a page layout program, you can usually get a simple web page up and running within a day or two. If you do not have much experience with a computer, you might consider hiring a college student to set up a web page for you.

Site testing. Some of the website setup programs allow you to thoroughly check your new site to see if all the pictures are included and all the links are proper. There are also websites you can go to that will check out your site. Some even allow you to improve your site, such as by reducing the size of your graphics so they download faster. Use a major search engine listed on page 76 to look for companies that can test your site before you launch it on the Web.

NOTE: *Many web authoring programs let you copy a page from the Internet as a template. Then you can change colors, styles, or content to your personal preferences. If you do, MAKE SURE IT IS NOT COPYRIGHTED! Look for the copyright notice on the page. If there is not a notice, the author has left it pretty much fair game; however, even without a copyright notice, do not just steal other people's intellectual property. Use it as a starting point to build your own.*

Site publicity. Once you set up your website, you will want to get people to look at it. Publicity means getting your site noticed as much as possible by drawing people to it.

The first thing to do to get noticed is to be sure your site is registered with as many *search engines* as possible. These are pages that people use to find things on the Internet, such as Yahoo and Google. They do not automatically know about you just because you created a website. You must tell them about your site, and they must examine and catalog it.

For a fee, there are services that will register your site with numerous search engines. If you are starting out on a shoestring, you can easily do it yourself. While there are hundreds of search engines, most people use a dozen or so of the bigger ones. If your site is in a niche area, such as genealogy services, then you would want to be listed on any specific genealogy search engines. Most businesses should be mainly concerned with getting on the biggest ones.

By far the biggest and most successful search engine today is Google (**www.google.com**). Some of the other big ones are:

www.altavista.com	www.hotbot.com
www.excite.com	www.lycos.com
www.fastsearch.com	www.metacrawler.com
www.go.com	www.northernlight.com
www.goto.com	www.webcrawler.com

Getting Your Site Known Most of these sites have a place to click to "add your site" to their system. Some sites charge hundreds of dollars to be listed. If your site contains valuable information that people are looking for, you should be able to do well without paying these fees.

A *meta tag* is an invisible subject word added to your site that can be found by a search engine. For example, if you are a pest control company, you may want to list all the scientific names of the pests you control and all the treatments you have available, but you may not need them to be part of the visual design of your site. List these words as meta tags when you set up your page so people searching for those words will find your site.

Some companies thought that a clever way to get viewers would be to use commonly searched names, or names of major competitors, as meta tags to attract people looking for those big companies. For example, a small delivery service that has nothing to do with UPS or FedEx might use those company names as meta tags so people looking for them would find the smaller company. While it may sound like a good idea, it has been declared as illegal trademark infringement. Today, many companies have computer programs scanning the Internet for improper use of their trademarks.

Once you have made sure that your site is passively listed in all the search engines, you may want to actively promote your site. However, self-promotion is seen as a bad thing on the Internet, especially if its purpose is to make money.

Newsgroups are places on the Internet where people interested in a specific topic can exchange information. For example, expectant mothers have a group where they can trade advice and experiences. If you have a product that would be great for expectant mothers, that would be a good place for it to be discussed. However, if you log into the group and merely announce your product, suggesting people order it from your website, you will probably be *flamed* (sent a lot of hate mail).

If you join the group, however, and become a regular, and, in answer to someone's problem, mention that you "saw this product that might help," your information will be better received. It may seem unethical to plug your product without disclosing your interest, but this is a procedure used by many large companies. They hire buzz agents to plug their product all over the Internet and create positive buzz for the product. So, perhaps it has become an acceptable marketing method and consumers know to take plugs with a grain of salt. Let your conscience be your guide.

Keep in mind that Internet publicity works both ways. If you have a great product and people love it, you will get a lot of business. If you sell a shoddy product, give poor service, and do not keep your customers happy, bad publicity on the Internet can kill your business.

Besides being an equalizer between large and small companies, the Internet can be a filtering mechanism between good and bad products.

Spamming
Sending unsolicited email advertising (called *spam*) started out as a mere breach of Internet etiquette (*netiquette*) but has now become a state and federal crime. The ability to reach millions of people with advertising at virtually no cost was too good for too many businesses to pass up and this resulted in the clogging of most users' email boxes and the near shut down of some computer systems. Some people ended up with thousands of offers every day.

To prevent this, many states passed anti-spamming laws and Congress passed the *CAN-SPAM Act*. This law:

- bans misleading or false headers on email;

- bans misleading subject lines;

- requires allowing recipients to opt out of future mailings;

- requires the email be identified as advertising; and,

- requires the email include a valid physical address.

Each violation can result in up to an $11,000 fine, and the fines can be raised if advertisers violate other rules such as not harvesting names and not using permutations of existing names. More information can be found on the Federal Trade Commission's website (**www.ftc.gov**).

Advertising
Advertising on the Internet has grown in recent years. At first, small, thin rectangular ads appeared at the top of websites; these are called *banner ads*. Lately they have grown bigger, can appear anywhere on the site, and usually blink or show a moving visual.

The fees can be based on how many people view an ad, how many click on it, or both. Some larger companies, such as Amazon.com, have affiliate programs in which they will pay a percentage of a purchase if a customer comes from your site to theirs and makes a purchase.

For sites that have thousands of visitors, the ads have been profitable—some sites reportedly make over $100,000 a year.

Example:
One financially successful site is Manolo's Shoe Blog (**http://shoeblogs.com**). It is written by a man who loves shoes, has a great sense of humor, and writes in endearing broken English. Because he is an expert in his field, his suggestions are taken by many readers who click through to the products and purchase them.

LEGAL ISSUES
Before you set up a web page, you should consider the many legal issues associated with it.

Jurisdiction
Jurisdiction is the power of a court in a particular location to decide a particular case. Usually, you have to have been physically present in a jurisdiction or have done business there before you can be sued there. Since the Internet extends your business's ability to reach people in faraway places, there may be instances when you could be subject to legal jurisdiction far from your own state (or country). There are a number of cases that have been decided in this country regarding the Internet and jurisdiction, but very few cases have been decided on this issue outside of the United States.

In most instances, U.S. courts use the pre-Internet test—whether you have been present in another jurisdiction or have had enough contact with someone in the other jurisdiction. The fact that the Internet itself is not a "place" will not shield you from being sued in another state when you have shipped your company's product there, have entered into a contract with a resident of that state, or have defamed a foreign resident with content on your website.

According to the court, there is a spectrum of contact required between you, your website, and consumers or audiences. (*Zippo Manufacturing Co. v. Zippo Dot Com, Inc.*, 952 F. Supp. 1119 (W.D. Pa 1997).) The more interactive your site is with consumers, the more you target an audience for your goods in a particular location, and the farther you reach to send your goods out into the world, the more it becomes possible for someone to sue you outside of your own jurisdiction—so weigh these risks against the benefits when constructing and promoting your website.

The law is not even remotely final on these issues. The American Bar Association, among other groups, is studying this topic in detail. At present, no final, global solution or agreement about jurisdictional issues with websites exists.

One way to protect yourself from the possibility of being sued in a faraway jurisdiction would be to state on your website that those using the site or doing business with you agree that jurisdiction for any actions regarding your site or your company will be in your home county.

For extra protection, you can have a preliminary page that must be clicked before entering your website. However, this may be overkill for a small business with little risk of lawsuit. If you are in any business for which you could have serious liability, you should review some competitors' sites and see how they handle the liability issue. They often have a place to click for a "legal notice" or "disclaimer" on their first page.

You may want to consult with an attorney to discuss the specific disclaimer you will use on your website, where it should appear, and whether you will have users of your site actively agree to this disclaimer or just passively read it. However, these disclaimers are not enforceable everywhere in the world. Until there is global agreement on jurisdictional issues, this may remain an area of uncertainty for some time to come.

Libel   *Libel* is any publication that injures the reputation of another. This can occur in print, writing, pictures, or signs. All that is required for publication is that you transmit the material to at least one other person. When putting together your website, you must keep in mind that it is visible to millions of people all over the planet, and that if you libel a person or company you may have to pay damages. Many countries do not have the freedom of speech that we do, and a statement that is not libel in the United States may be libelous elsewhere. If you are concerned about this, alter the content of your site or check with an attorney about libel laws in the country you think might take action against you.

Copyright Infringement

It is so easy to copy and borrow information on the Internet that it is easy to infringe copyrights without even knowing it. A copyright exists for a work as soon as the creator creates it. There is no need to register the copyright or to put a copyright notice on it. Therefore, practically everything on the Internet belongs to someone.

Some people freely give their works away. For example, many people have created web artwork (gifs and animated gifs) that they freely allow people to copy. There are numerous sites that provide hundreds or thousands of free gifs that you can add to your web pages. Some require you to acknowledge the source and some do not. You should always be sure that the works are free for the taking before using them.

Linking and Framing

One way to violate copyright laws is to improperly link other sites to yours, either directly or with framing. *Linking* is when you provide a link that takes the user to the linked site. *Framing* occurs when you set up your site so that when you link to another site, your site is still viewable as a frame around the linked site.

While many sites are glad to be linked to others, some, especially providers of valuable information, object. Courts have ruled that linking and framing can be a copyright violation. One rule that has developed is that it is usually okay to link to the first page of a site, but not to link to some valuable information deeper within the site. The rationale for this is that the owner of the site wants visitors to go through the various levels of his or her site (viewing all the ads) before getting the information. By linking directly to the information, you are giving away his or her product without the ads.

The problem with linking to the first page of a site is that it may be a tedious or difficult task to find the needed page from there. Many sites are poorly designed and make it nearly impossible to find anything.

If you wish to link to another page, the best solution is to ask permission. Email the webmaster or person in charge of the site, if an email address is given, and explain what you want to do. If he or she grants permission, be sure to print out a copy of his or her email for your records.

Privacy

Since the Internet is such an easy way to share information, there are many concerns that it will cause a loss of individual privacy. The two main concerns arise when you post information that others consider private, and when you gather information from customers and use it in a way that violates their privacy.

While public actions of politicians and celebrities are fair game, details about their private lives are sometimes protected by law, and details about persons who are not public figures are often protected. The laws in each state are different, and what might be allowable in one state could be illegal in another. If your site will provide any personal information about individuals, you should discuss the possibility of liability with an attorney.

Several well-known companies have been in the news lately for violations of their customers' privacy. They either shared what the customer was buying or downloading, or looked for additional information on the customer's computer. To let customers know that you do not violate certain standards of privacy, you can subscribe to one of the privacy codes that have been created for the Internet. These allow you to put a symbol on your site guaranteeing to your customers that you follow the code.

The following are the websites of two organizations that offer this service and their fees at the time of this publication.

www.privacybot.com $100

www.bbbonline.com $200 to $7,000

Protecting Yourself

The easiest way to protect yourself personally from the various possible types of liability is to set up a corporation or limited liability company to own the website. This is not foolproof protection since, in some cases, you could be sued personally as well, but it is one level of protection.

COPPA   If your website is aimed at children under the age of 13, or if it attracts children of that age, then you are subject to the federal *Children Online Privacy Protection Act of 1998* (COPPA). This law requires such websites to:

- give notice on the site of what information is being collected;

- obtain verifiable parental consent to collect the information;

- allow the parent to review the information collected;

- allow the parent to delete the child's information or to refuse to allow the use of the information;

- limit the information collected to only that necessary to participate on the site; and,

- protect the security and confidentiality of the information.

HIRING A WEBSITE DESIGNER

If you hire someone to design your website, you should make sure of what rights you are buying. Under copyright law, when you hire someone to create a work, you do not get all rights to that work unless you clearly spell that out in a written agreement.

For example, if your designer creates an artistic design to go on your website, you may have to pay extra if you want to use the same design on your business cards or letterhead. Depending on how the agreement is worded, you may even have to pay a yearly fee for the rights.

If you spend a lot of money promoting your business and a logo or design becomes important to your image, you would not want to have to pay royalties for the life of your business to someone who spent an hour or two putting together a design. Whenever you purchase a creative work from someone, be sure to get a written statement of what rights you are buying. If you are not receiving all rights for all uses for all time, you should think twice about the purchase.

If the designer also is involved with hosting your site, you should be sure you have the right to take the design with you if you move to another host. You should get a backup of your site on a CD in case it is ever lost or you need to move it to another site.

FINANCIAL TRANSACTIONS

The existing services for sending money over the Internet, such as PayPal, usually offer more risk and higher fees than traditional credit card processing. Under their service agreements, you usually must agree that they can freeze your account at any time and can take money out of your bank account at any time. Some do not offer an appeal process. Before signing up for any of these services, you should read their service agreement carefully and check the Internet for other peoples' experiences with them. For example, for PayPal you can check **www.nopaypal.com**.

For now, the easiest way to exchange money on the Internet is through traditional credit cards. Because of concerns that email can be abducted in transit and read by others, most companies use a secure site in which customers are guaranteed that their card data is encrypted before being sent.

When setting up your website, you should ask the provider if you can be set up with a secure site for transmitting credit card data. If they cannot provide it, you will need to contract with another software provider. Use one of the major search engines listed on page 76 to look for companies that provide credit card services to businesses on the Internet.

As a practical matter, there is very little to worry about when sending credit card data by email. If you do not have a secure site, another option is to allow purchasers to fax or phone in their credit card data. However, keep in mind that this extra step will lose some business unless your products are unique and your buyers are very motivated.

The least effective option is to provide an order form on the site that can be printed out and mailed in with a check. Again, your customers must be really motivated or they will lose interest after finding out this extra work is involved.

FTC RULES

Because the Internet is an instrument of interstate commerce, it is a legitimate subject for federal regulation. The Federal Trade Commission (FTC) first said that all of its consumer protection rules applied to the Internet, but lately it has been adding specific rules and issuing publications. The following publications are available from the FTC website at **www.ftc.gov/bcp/menus/business/adv.shtm** or by mail from:

Federal Trade Commission

CRC-240

Washington, DC 20580

❂   *A Businessperson's Guide to Federal Warranty Law*

❂   *A Dealer's Guide to the Used Car Rule*

❂   *Ads for Business Opportunities: How To Detect Deception*

❂   *Advertising Consumer Leases*

❂   *Frequently Asked Advertising Questions: A Guide for Small Business*

❂   *Advertising and Marketing on the Internet: Rules of the Road*

❂   *Advertising Retail Electricity and Natural Gas*

❂   *Big Print. Little Print. What's the Deal?*

❂   *A Business Guide to the Federal Trade Commission's Mail or Telephone Order Merchandise Rule*

❂   *Complying With the Appliance Labeling Rule: Labeling Light Bulbs*

✪   *Complying with the Appliance Labeling Rule:*
     A Guide for Retailers

✪   *Complying with the Environmental Marketing Guides*

✪   *Complying With the Funeral Rule*

✪   *Complying with the Made In the USA Standard*

✪   *Dietary Supplements: An Advertising Guide for Industry*

✪   *Dot Com Disclosures*

✪   *Down...But Not Out: Advertising and Labeling of Feather and*
     Down Products

✪   *Environmental Marketing Claims*

✪   *Good Pricing Practices? SCAN DO*

✪   *How to Comply with the FTC Fuel Rating Rule*

✪   *In The Loupe: Advertising Diamonds, Gemstones and Pearls*

✪   *Making Environmental Marketing Claims on Mail*

✪   *Red Flag: Bogus Weight Loss Claims*

✪   *Offering Layaways*

✪   *Screening Advertisements: A Guide for the Media*

✪   *Writing Readable Warranties*

✪   *Voluntary Guidelines for Providers of Weight Loss Products*

FRAUD

Because the Internet is somewhat anonymous, it is a tempting place for those with fraudulent schemes to look for victims. As a business consumer, you should exercise caution when dealing with unknown or anonymous parties on the Internet.

The U.S. Department of Justice, the FBI, and the National White Collar Crime Center jointly launched the Internet Crime Complaint Center (IC3). If you suspect that you are the victim of fraud online, whether as a consumer or a business, you can report incidents to the IC3 on its website, **www.ic3.gov**. The IC3 is currently staffed by FBI agents and representatives of the National White Collar Crime Center, and will work with state and local law enforcement officials to prevent, investigate, and prosecute high-tech and economic crime online.

Health and Safety Laws

As a reaction to the terrible work conditions prevalent in the factories and mills of the nineteenth-century industrial age, Congress and the states developed many laws intended to protect the health and safety of the nation's workers. These laws are difficult to understand and often seem to be very unfair to employers. Therefore, this is an area that you need to pay particular attention to as a new business. Failure to do so can result in terrible consequences for you.

FEDERAL LAWS

The federal government's laws regarding the health and safety of workers are far-reaching and very important to consider in running your business, especially if you are a manufacturer or in the oil and gas, food production, or agriculture industries.

OSHA   The point of the *Occupational Safety and Health Administration* (OSHA) is to place the duty on the employer to keep the workplace free from recognized hazards that are likely to cause death or serious bodily injury to workers. The regulations are not as cumbersome for small businesses as for larger enterprises. If you have ten or fewer employees or if you are in certain types of businesses, you do not have to keep a record of illnesses, injuries, and exposure to hazardous substances of employees. If you have eleven or more employees, OSHA's rules will apply. One important rule to know is that within forty-eight hours of an on-the-job death of an employee or injury of five or more employees on the job, the area director of OSHA must be contacted.

For more information, write or call an OSHA office.

OSHA Regional Office
61 Forsyth Street, SW
Atlanta, GA 30303
404-562-2300
www.osha.gov

You can obtain copies of OSHA publications, *OSHA Handbook for Small Business* (OSHA 2209) and *OSHA Publications and Audiovisual Programs Catalog* (OSHA 2019), from its website. It also has a poster that is required to be posted in the workplace by all employers. It is available on its website at **www.osha.gov/ Publications/poster.html**.

Hazard Communication Standard

The *Hazard Communication Standard* requires that employees be made aware of the hazards in the workplace. (Title 29, Code of Federal Regulations (C.F.R.), Section (Sec.) 1910.1200.) It is especially applicable to those working with chemicals, but this can even include offices that use copy machines. Businesses using hazardous chemicals must have a comprehensive program for informing employees of the hazards and for protecting them from contamination.

For more information, you can contact OSHA at the previously mentioned address, phone number, or website. It can supply a copy of the regulation and a booklet called *OSHA 3084*, which explains the law.

EPA

The *Worker Protection Standard for Agricultural Pesticides* requires safety training, decontamination sites and, of course, posters. The Environmental Protection Agency (EPA) will provide information on compliance with this law. It can be reached at 800-241-1754 or through its website at **www.epa.gov**.

FDA   The *Pure Food and Drug Act of 1906* prohibits the misbranding or adulteration of food and drugs. It also created the Food and Drug Administration (FDA), which has promulgated tons of regulations and which must give permission before a new drug can be introduced into the market. If you will be dealing with any food or drugs, keep abreast of FDA policies. Its website is **www.fda.gov**. Its small business site is **www.fda.gov/ora/fed_state/small_business** and its local small business representative can be reached at:

FDA, Northeast Region
Atlanta District Office
60 Eighth Street, NE
Atlanta, GA 30909
404-253-1161

Hazardous   There are regulations that control the shipping and packing of
Materials   hazardous materials. For more information, contact:
Transportation

U.S. Department of Transportation
Pipeline and Hazardous Materials Safety Administration
Office of Contracts and Procurement, PHA-30
1200 New Jersey Avenue, SE
East Building, 2nd Floor
202-366-8553
http://hazmat.dot.gov

Click on the "Code of Federal Regulations (CFR)" link, and follow the link to "Browse and/or search the CFR."

CPSC   The Consumer Product Safety Commission (CPSC) has a set of rules that cover the safety of products. The commission feels that because its rules cover products, rather than people or companies, they apply to everyone producing such products. However, federal laws do not apply to small businesses that do not affect interstate commerce. Whether a small business would fall under a CPSC rule would depend on the size and nature of that business.

The CPSC rules are contained in the Code of Federal Regulations, Title 16 in the following parts. These can be found at most law libraries, some public libraries, and on the Internet at

www.gpoaccess.gov/nara/index.html. The CPSC's site is
www.cpsc.gov.

Product	Part
Antennas, CB and TV	1402
Architectural Glazing Material	1201
Articles Hazardous to Children Under 3	1501
Baby Cribs—Full Size	1508
Baby Cribs—Non-Full Size	1509
Bicycle Helmets	1203
Bicycles	1512
Carpets and Rugs	1630, 1631
Cellulose Insulation	1209, 1404
Cigarette Lighters	1210
Citizens Band Base Station Antennas	1204
Coal and Wood Burning Appliances	1406
Consumer Products Containing Chlorofluorocarbons	1401
Electrically Operated Toys	1505
Emberizing Materials Containing Asbestos (banned)	1305
Extremely Flammable Contact Adhesives (banned)	1302
Fireworks Devices	1507
Garage Door Openers	1211
Hazardous Lawn Darts (banned)	1306
Hazardous Substances	1500
Human Subjects	1028
Lawn Mowers—Walk-Behind	1205
Lead-Containing Paint (banned)	1303
Matchbooks	1202
Mattresses	1632
Pacifiers	1511
Patching Compounds Containing Asbestos (banned)	1304
Poisons	1700
Rattles	1510
Self-Pressurized Consumer Products	1401
Sleepwear—Children's	1615, 1616
Swimming Pool Slides	1207
Toys—Electrical	1505
Unstable Refuse Bins (banned)	1301

Every day there are proposals for new laws and regulations. It would
be impossible to include every conceivable one in this book. To be up
to date on the laws that affect your type of business, join a trade

association for your industry and subscribe to newsletters that cover your industry. Attending industry conventions is a good way to learn more and to discover new ways to increase your profits.

GEORGIA STATE LAWS

As in all states, there are laws unique to Georgia that impose safety, health, and environmental protection requirements on particular businesses. These laws ostensibly protect employees, consumers, and the public in general. The laws cover many areas and regulate such diverse activities as amusement rides, asbestos removal, contact lenses, fireworks displays, bathhouses, bedding, blasting operations, boiler and pressure vessels, boxers, liquefied petroleum, roller skating centers, motor common carriers, motor contract carriers, pets, and tanning facilities. Additionally, there are many health, safety, and environmental laws, rules, and regulations pertaining to all the various health care providers.

In addition to the specific laws for specific businesses, there are many health, safety, and environmental laws that apply to all, or most, businesses.

Safety Rules, Regulations, and Reporting Requirements

Chapter 300-3-1 of the Georgia Rules and Regulations requires a report on forms furnished by the Department of Labor's Inspection Division (404-679-0687) for each accidental injury or occupational disease resulting from time losses that your employees suffer in connection with their employment. This is intended to assist in preventing future hazards. There are numerous safety specifications for things like tools, floors, stairs, ladders, extension cords, hazardous materials, storage space, removal of nails, drinking water, warning signs, mirrors on vehicles, traffic aisles, exits, toilet seats, etc. For the most part, it is unrealistic for small businesses to be proactive in this area unless the owners have a tremendous amount of industrial analysis time.

A good start would be to write to Georgia's Department of Labor and request the following publications:

✪   *The Employer's Handbook;*

✪   *Georgia Wage Survey;* and,

✪   *Unemployment Insurance Information for Employers.*

You can request whichever ones you need from:

Georgia Department of Labor
Economic Development and Employer Relations
Suite 265
Sussex Place
148 International Boulevard, N.E.
Atlanta, GA 30303

Or you can download them from its website:

www.dol.state.ga.us

Safe Work Place   Section 34-2-10 of the O.C.G.A. requires all employers to adopt and use methods and processes to make the employment safe, and to do anything else needed to protect the life, health, safety, and welfare of the employees. O.C.G.A., Section 34-7-20, states that a Georgia employer must provide safe machinery and warn of defects or dangers. The employer must also exercise reasonable care in employing people and must not keep those known to be incompetent.

Scaffolding   Scaffolding or staging of any type must be constructed according to the requirements of O.C.G.A., Section 34-1-1. Violation of the law is a misdemeanor.

Digging and Blasting   It is unlawful to do any blasting, grading, trenching, digging, ditching, augering, scraping, or any other operation that changes the level or grade of land with a machine unless you have notified the gas companies that have filed with the clerk of your county Superior Court at least three days before proceeding. You are also encouraged, for your own personal safety and your financial health, to notify other utility companies. As a practical matter, most utility companies will charge you if you cut their underground lines or cables. You should always call them ahead of time to notify them that you will be excavating or blasting and ask them to locate the lines. If they incorrectly mark the lines or indicate that they are deeper than they really are and you cut them, you do not have to pay for the repairs.

Call the *Utilities Protection Center* at 800-282-7411, before starting any digging or blasting. This statewide service will contact all utility companies with lines in your area if the companies are registered with the service. If they are not registered, you will have to contact each utility company yourself. This can be tedious, but if your company involves underground operations such as laying cable or installing sprinkler systems, it can potentially be a life-saving measure.

Secure Work Loads

Whether on or in a vehicle, any load you transport in Georgia must be adequately secured to prevent it from dumping onto the roadway or shifting pursuant to O.C.G.A., Section 40-6-254.

Transporting Hazardous Material

If your business transports any other hazardous materials, it is subject to the rules and regulations of O.C.G.A. Chapter 46-11 (*Transportation of Hazardous Materials Act*). Also, if your business includes transporting biological waste, your vehicle must be marked in accordance with O.C.G.A., Section 40-6-253.1.

O.C.G.A., Section 12-8-67, states that you must have a manifest properly issued to transport hazardous waste through Georgia. You must report any spills or releases of oil and hazardous material to the Department of Natural Resources Emergency Operations Center at 800-241-4113. O.C.G.A., Title 12-8-3(2), covers liability for the release of hazardous wastes, hazardous constituents, or hazardous substances into the environment. O.C.G.A., Section 12-8-7, concerns hazardous product packing.

If your business deals with radioactive material in any form, you should read O.C.G.A., Chapter 31-13. The penalties and cleanup costs can be substantial. You should call the Georgia Public Service Commission at 404-656-4501 and ask about the rules and regulations.

Railroad Crossings

O.C.G.A., Section 40-6-142, requires certain types of motor vehicles to stop at railroad crossings.

Site Inspections

Most often used under the auspices of restaurant inspections, O.C.G.A., Section 31-12-8, gives the Department of Human Resources and the county boards of health the power to come on to your premises for the purpose of conducting studies pertaining to *where people congregate to work.* They can issue orders and directives to stop or minimize any practice, operation, or condition that is a hazard to the health and safety of the employees or the general public. Furthermore, anyone who knows or suspects that there is a condition that is injurious to public health, safety, or comfort must notify the department.

The department has substantial powers; nonetheless, it is pretty underfunded. So it is unlikely that it will simply use the power to abuse and annoy. It can obtain an inspection warrant, bring an action for injunction to stop the public nuisance, and collect costs incurred by it in stopping the problem. Until you pay those costs, allow for there to be a lien, comparable to a tax lien on the property. (O.C.G.A., Section 31-5-10.)

Mass Gatherings
O.C.G.A., Chapter 31-27, applies if your business includes mass gatherings of people and the gathering is likely to attract 5,000 or more people and continue for fifteen or more consecutive hours. You will have to get a permit from the Department of Human Resources.

Dumping Waste
O.C.G.A., Section 12-8-2, prohibits you from dumping any sanitary sewer, kitchen, or toilet waste into a public storm or sanitary sewer pipeline through manholes or otherwise, unless you obtain permission from the owner.

Food, Drugs, and Cosmetics
O.C.G.A., Title 26, governs the hundreds of laws for foods, drugs, and cosmetics. Many of the laws pertain to safety and health issues.

Smoking
Localities may have stricter smoking ordinances with which you should be familiar. However, if your business is used by or open to the public you can designate a no-smoking policy by putting up a no-smoking sign. O.C.G.A., Section 16-12-2, prohibits smoking if the sign is posted. Violation of the law is punishable by a fine.

Employment and Labor Laws

Like they have with health and safety laws, Congress and the states have heavily regulated the actions that employers can take with regard to hiring and firing, improper employment practices, and discrimination. Because the penalties can be severe, educate yourself on the proper actions to take and consult a labor and employment lawyer, if necessary, prior to making important employee decisions.

HIRING AND FIRING LAWS

For small businesses, there are not many rules regarding who you may hire or fire. Fortunately, the ancient law that an employee can be fired at any time (or may quit at any time) still prevails for small businesses. But in certain situations, and as you grow, you will come under a number of laws that affect your hiring and firing practices.

One of the most important things to consider when hiring someone is that if you fire him or her, he or she may be entitled to unemployment compensation. If so, your unemployment compensation tax rate will go up, which can cost you a lot of money. Therefore, you should only hire people you are sure you will keep, and you should avoid situations in which your former employees can make claims against your company.

One way this can be done is by hiring only part-time workers. The drawback to this is that you may not be able to attract the best employees. When hiring dishwashers or busboys, this may not be an issue, but when hiring someone to develop a software product, you do not want him or her to leave halfway through the development.

A better solution is to screen applicants first and only hire those who you feel certain will work out. Of course, this is easier said than done. Some people interview well but then turn out to be incompetent at the job.

The best record to look for is someone who has stayed a long time at each of his or her previous jobs. Next best is someone who has not stayed as long (for good reasons) but has always been employed. The worst type of hire would be someone who is or has been collecting unemployment compensation.

The reason those who have collected compensation are a bad risk is that if they collect in the future—even if it is not your fault—your employment of them could make you chargeable for their claims.

Example:
You hire someone who has been on unemployment compensation and he or she works out well for a year, but then he or she quits to take another job and is fired after a few weeks. In this situation, you would be chargeable for most of the unemployment claim because his or her last five quarters of work are analyzed. Look for a steady job history.

The competence of an employee is often more important than his or her experience. An employee with years of typing experience may be fast, but may also be unable to figure out how to use your new computer, whereas a competent employee can learn the equipment quickly and eventually gain speed. Of course, common sense is important in all situations.

The bottom line is that you cannot know if an employee will be able to fill your needs from a résumé and an interview. Once you have found someone who you think will work out, offer him or her a job with a ninety-day probationary period. If you are not completely satisfied with him or her after the ninety days, offer to extend the probationary period for an additional ninety days rather than end the relationship immediately. Of course, all of this should be in writing.

Background Checks   Checking references is important, but beware that a former boss may be a good friend or even a relative. It has always been considered acceptable to exaggerate on résumés, but in recent years some applicants have been found to be completely fabricating sections of their education and experience.

Polygraph Tests   Under the federal *Employee Polygraph Protection Act*, you cannot require an employee or prospective employee to take a polygraph test unless you are in the armored car, security alarm system, guard, or pharmaceutical business.

Drug Tests   Under the *Americans with Disabilities Act* (ADA), drug testing can only be required of applicants who have been offered jobs conditioned upon passing the drug test. Under certain circumstances, Georgia law, O.C.G.A., Section 34-9-414, allows employers to test employees before and after they are hired. Employers can obtain discounts on drug tests if they qualify under the drug-free workplace program. (see O.C.G.A., Section 50-24-3 and Section 33-9-40.2.) Employers can also deny medical and indemnity benefits for failure to pass a test.

FIRING

In most cases, unless you have a contract with an employee for a set time period, you can fire him or her at any time. This is only fair, since the employee can quit at any time. This type of employment is called *at will*. You should make it clear when offering a job to someone that, upon acceptance, he or she will be an at-will employee. The exceptions to this are if you fired someone based on illegal discrimination, for filing some sort of health or safety complaint, or for refusing your sexual advances.

NEW HIRE REPORTING

In order to track down parents who do not pay child support, federal law requires the reporting of new hires. The *Personal Responsibility and Work Opportunity Reconciliation Act* (PRWORA) provides that such information must be reported by employers to their state government.

Within ten days of starting a business, an employer must complete a **Georgia New Hire Reporting Form**. (see form 8, p.243.) A **Georgia Employee's Withholding Allowance Certificate (G-4)** (form 12, p.255) must be filed for the state and is kept in-house until there are more than fourteen employees, after which they need to be copied and sent to the state.

Within ten days of hiring a new employee, an employer must provide the state with information about the employee including his or her name, Social Security number, and address. This information can be submitted in several ways, including by mail, by fax, or over the Internet. It may also be faxed to the toll-free number, 888-541-0521, or mailed to:

Georgia New Hire Reporting Program
P.O. Box 38480
Atlanta, GA 30334

For more information about the program, call 888-541-0469 or visit:

www.ga-newhire.com

EMPLOYMENT AGREEMENTS

To avoid misunderstandings with employees, you should use an employment agreement or an employee handbook. These can spell out in detail the policies of your company and the rights of your employees. They can protect your trade secrets and spell out clearly that employment can be terminated at any time by either party.

While it may be difficult or awkward to ask an existing employee to sign such an agreement, an applicant hoping you will hire him or her will usually sign whatever is necessary to obtain the job. However, because of the unequal bargaining position, do not use an agreement that would make you look bad if the matter ever went to court.

If having an employee sign an agreement is too awkward, you can usually obtain the same rights by putting the company policies in an employee manual. Each existing and new employee should be given a copy, along with a letter stating that the rules apply to all employees and that by accepting or continuing employment at your company, they agree to abide by the rules. Have an employee sign a receipt for the letter and manual as proof that he or she received it.

One danger of an employment agreement or handbook is that it may be interpreted to create a long-term employment contract. To avoid this, be sure that you clearly state in the agreement or handbook that the employment is *at will* and can be terminated at any time by either party.

Some other things to consider in an employment agreement or handbook include:

- what the salary and other compensation will be;

- what the hours of employment will be;

- what the probationary period will be;

- that the employee cannot sign any contracts binding the employer; and,

- that the employee agrees to arbitration rather than filing a lawsuit.

NOTE: EMPLOYMENT AGREEMENTS *are so important that I have included a draft of one for you. (see form 19, p.283.) Only use this as a guide, though—your circumstances are most likely different.*

INDEPENDENT CONTRACTORS

One way to avoid problems with employees and taxes at the same time is to have all your work done through independent contractors. This can relieve you of most of the burdens of employment laws, as well as the obligation to pay Social Security and Medicare taxes for the workers.

An independent contractor is, in effect, a separate business that you pay to do a job. You pay them just as you pay any company from which you buy products or services. At the end of the year, if the amount paid exceeds $600, you will issue a 1099 form instead of the W-2 that you issue to employees.

This may seem too good to be true, and in some situations, it is. The IRS does not like independent contractor arrangements because it is too easy for the independent contractors to cheat on their taxes. To limit the use of independent contractors, the IRS has strict regulations on who may and may not be classified as an independent contractor. Also, companies who do not appear to pay enough in wages for their field of business are audited.

Using independent contractors for jobs not traditionally done by independent contractors puts you at high risk for an IRS audit. For example, you could not get away with hiring a secretary as an independent contractor. One of the most important factors considered in determining if a worker can be an independent contractor is the amount of control the company has over his or her work. If you need someone to paint your building and you agree to pay a certain price to have it done according to the painter's own methods and schedule, you can pay the painter as an independent contractor. However, if you tell the painter when and how to do the work, and you provide the tools and materials, the painter will be classified as an employee.

If you just need some typing done and you take it to a typing service and pick it up when it is ready, you will be safe in treating those workers as independent contractors. However, if you need someone to come into your office to type on your machine at your schedule, you will probably be required to treat that person as an employee for tax purposes.

The IRS has a form you can use in determining if a person is an employee or an independent contractor, called **DETERMINATION OF WORKER STATUS (IRS FORM SS-8)**. It is included in Appendix D of this book along with instructions. (see form 10, p.247.)

Independent Contractors vs. Employees

In deciding whether to make use of independent contractors or employees, you should weigh the following advantages and disadvantages using independent contractors.

Advantages.

○ Lower taxes. You do not have to pay Social Security, Medicare, unemployment, or other employee taxes.

○ Less paperwork. You do not have to handle federal withholding deposits or the monthly employer returns to the state or federal government.

○ Less insurance. You do not have to pay workers' compensation insurance, and since the workers are not your employees, you do not have to insure against their possible liabilities.

○ More flexibility. You can use independent contractors when you need them and not pay to use them when business is slow.

Disadvantages.

○ The IRS and state tax offices are strict about when workers can qualify as independent contractors. They will audit companies whose use of independent contractors does not appear to be legitimate.

○ If your use of independent contractors is found to be improper, you may have to pay back taxes and penalties and have problems with your pension plan.

○ While employees usually cannot sue you for their injuries (if you have covered them with workers' compensation), independent contractors can sue you if their injuries were your fault.

✪   If you are paying someone to produce a creative work (writing, photography, artwork), you receive less rights to the work of an independent contractor.

✪   You have less control over the work of an independent contractor and less flexibility in terminating him or her if you are not satisfied with the job he or she is doing.

✪   You have less loyalty from an independent contractor who works sporadically for you and possibly others than from your own full-time employees.

For some businesses, the advantages outweigh the disadvantages. For others, they do not. Consider your business plans and the consequences of each type of arrangement. Keep in mind that it will be easier to start with independent contractors and switch to employees than to hire employees and fire them to hire independent contractors.

TEMPORARY WORKERS

Another way to avoid the hassles of hiring employees is to get workers from a temporary agency. In this arrangement, you may pay a higher amount per hour for the work, but the agency will take care of all the tax and insurance requirements. Since these can be expensive and time-consuming, the extra cost may be well worth it.

Whether or not temporary workers will work for you depends upon the type of business you are in and the tasks you need performed. For jobs such as sales management, you would probably want someone who will stay with you long term and develop relationships with the buyers. For order fulfillment, temporary workers might work out well.

Another advantage of temporary workers is that you can easily stop using those who do not work out well for you, but if you find one who is ideal, you may be able to hire him or her on a full-time basis.

In recent years, a new wrinkle has developed in the temporary worker area. Many large companies are using temps because it is so much cheaper than paying the benefits demanded by full-time employees.

Example:

Microsoft Corp. has had as many as 6,000 temporary workers, some of whom work for them for years. Some of the temporary workers recently won a lawsuit declaring that they are really employees and are entitled to the same benefits as other employees (such as pension plans).

The law is not yet settled in this area as to what arrangements will result in a temporary worker being declared an employee. That will take several more court cases, some of which have already been filed. The following are a few things you can do to protect yourself.

- Be sure that any of your benefit plans make it clear that they do not apply to workers obtained through temporary agencies.

- Do not keep the same temporary workers for longer than a year.

- Do not list temporary workers in any employee directories or hold them out to the public as your employees.

- Do not allow them to use your business cards or stationery.

DISCRIMINATION LAWS

Federal Law There are numerous federal laws forbidding discrimination based upon race, sex, pregnancy, color, religion, national origin, age, and disability. The laws apply to both hiring and firing, and to employment practices such as salaries, promotions, and benefits. Most of these laws only apply to an employer who has fifteen or more employees for twenty weeks of a calendar year or has federal contracts or subcontracts. Therefore, you most likely will not be required to comply with the law immediately upon opening your business. However, there are similar state laws that may apply to your business.

One exception is the *Equal Pay Act*. It applies to employers with two or more employees and requires that women be paid the same as men in the same type of job.

Employers with fifteen or more employees are required to display a poster regarding discrimination. This poster is available from the *Equal Employment Opportunity Commission* (EEOC), by calling 800-669-3362 or visiting its website at **www.eeoc.gov/posterform.html**. Employers with 100 or more employees are required to file an annual report with the EEOC.

When hiring employees, some questions are illegal or inadvisable to ask. The following subjects should not be included on your employment application or in your interviews, unless the information is somehow directly tied to the duties of the job.

- ✪ Do not ask about an applicant's citizenship or place of birth. After hiring an employee, you must ask about his or her right to work in this country.

- ✪ Do not ask a female applicant her maiden name. You can ask if she has been known by any other name in order to do a background check.

- ✪ Do not ask if applicants have children, plan to have them, or have child care. You can ask if an applicant will be able to work the required hours.

- ✪ Do not ask if the applicant has religious objections for working Saturday or Sunday. You can mention if the job requires such hours and ask whether the applicant can meet this job requirement.

- ✪ Do not ask an applicant's age. You can ask if an applicant is 18 or over, or, for a liquor-related job, if he or she is 21 or over.

- ✪ Do not ask an applicant's weight.

- ✪ Do not ask if an applicant has AIDS or is HIV positive.

- Do not ask if the applicant has filed a workers' compensation claim.

- Do not ask about the applicant's previous health problems.

- Do not ask if the applicant is married or whether his or her spouse would object to the job, hours, or duties.

- Do not ask if the applicant owns a home, furniture, or car, as it is considered racially discriminatory.

- Do not ask if the applicant has ever been arrested. You can ask if the applicant has ever been *convicted* of a crime.

The most recent applicable law is the *Americans with Disabilities Act* (ADA). Under this law, employers who do not make *reasonable accommodations for disabled employees* will face fines of up to $100,000, as well as other civil penalties and civil damage awards.

The ADA currently applies to employers with fifteen or more employees. Employers who need more than fifteen employees might want to consider independent contractors to avoid problems with this law, particularly if the number of employees is only slightly more than fifteen.

To find out how this law affects your business, review the publications available from the federal government to assist businesses with ADA compliance. The *Title III Technical Assistance Manual* and the *ADA Guide for Small Businesses* are available from the official ADA website at **www.usdoj.gov/crt/ada/publicat.htm** or by calling the ADA information line at 800-514-0301.

Tax benefits. There are three types of tax credits to help small businesses with the burden of these laws.

- Businesses can deduct up to $15,000 a year for making their premises accessible to the disabled and can depreciate the rest. (Internal Revenue Code (IRC) Section 190.)

- Small businesses (under $1,000,000 in revenue and under thirty employees) can get a tax credit each year for 50% of the cost of making their premises accessible to the disabled, but this only applies to the amount between $250 and $10,250. (IRC Section 44.)

- Small businesses can get a credit of up to 40% of the first $8,500 of wages paid to certain new employees who qualify. (see IRS Publications 334 and 954.)

Georgia Law   *Records.* To protect against potential claims of discrimination, all employers should keep detailed records showing reasons for hiring or not hiring applicants and for firing employees.

Georgia generally follows the federal rules. Employees between 40 and 70 cannot be fired for age alone, although if age is a factor in poor performance, there may be an exception. (See O.C.G.A., Section 34-1-2.) You cannot discharge anyone for complaining to the labor commissioner for sexual discrimination. (See O.C.G.A., Section 34-1-3.) You cannot refuse to hire, discharge, or discriminate against the handicapped unless the job cannot be modified to work around the handicap. (See O.C.G.A., Section 45-19-22.) You cannot discriminate on the basis of gender. (See O.C.G.A., Section 34-5-1.)

Employers cannot discriminate against an employee for going to jury duty or for going to court under a subpoena. (See O.C.G.A., Section 34-1-3.)

In the event of a discrimination claim, Georgia law gives either party the right to arbitration (as opposed to a court case), and this can save time and money for both sides. (See O.C.G.A., Section 34-5-6.)

SEXUAL HARASSMENT

In today's employment climate, any employer must pay attention to state and federal laws regarding sexual harassment in the workplace.

Federal Law   In the 1980s, the Equal Employment Opportunity Commission interpreted *Title VII* of the *Civil Rights Act of 1964* to forbid sexual harassment. After that, the courts took over and reviewed all types of conduct in the workplace. The numerous lawsuits that followed revealed a definite trend toward expanding the definition of sexual harassment and favoring employees.

The EEOC has held the following in sexual harassment cases.

- The victim and the harasser may be a woman or a man.

- The victim does not have to be of the opposite sex.

- The harasser can be the victim's supervisor, an agent of the employer, a supervisor in another area, a coworker, or a nonemployee.

- The victim does not have to be the person harassed but could be anyone affected by the offensive conduct.

- Unlawful sexual harassment may occur without economic injury to or discharge of the victim.

- The harasser's conduct must be unwelcome.

- An employer can be held liable for sexual harassment of an employee by a supervisor, even if the employer was unaware of the supervisor's conduct.

Some of the actions that have been considered harassment are:

- displaying sexually explicit posters in the workplace;

- requiring female employees to wear revealing uniforms;

- rating the sexual attractiveness of female employees as they passed male employees' desks;

- continued sexual jokes and innuendos;

- demands for sexual favors from subordinates;

- ✪ unwelcomed sexual propositions or flirtation;

- ✪ unwelcomed physical contact; and,

- ✪ whistling or leering at members of the opposite sex.

The law in the area of sexual harassment is still developing, so it is difficult to make clear rules of conduct.

Some things a business can do to protect against claims of sexual harassment include the following.

- ✪ Distribute a written policy against all kinds of sexual harassment to all employees.

- ✪ Encourage employees to report all incidents of sexual harassment.

- ✪ Ensure there is no retaliation against those who complain.

- ✪ Make clear that the policy is *zero tolerance*.

- ✪ Explain that sexual harassment includes both requests for sexual favors and a work environment that some employees may consider hostile.

- ✪ Allow employees to report harassment to someone other than their immediate supervisor in case that person is involved in the harassment.

- ✪ Promise as much confidentiality as possible to complainants.

Georgia Law   Georgia's *Civil Rights Act* enacts the federal statutes prohibiting sexual harassment. (O.C.G.A., Section 45-19-21.)

Common Law   Although both the federal and Georgia civil rights laws only apply to businesses with fifteen or more employees, it is possible for an employee of a smaller employer to sue for sexual harassment in civil court. However, this is difficult and expensive and would only be worthwhile when there were substantial damages.

WAGE AND HOUR LAWS

The *Fair Labor Standards Act* (FLSA) applies to all employers who are engaged in *interstate commerce* or in the production of goods for interstate commerce (anything that will cross the state line), and all employees of hospitals, schools, residential facilities for the disabled or aged, and public agencies. It also applies to all employees of enterprises that gross $500,000 or more per year.

While many small businesses might not think they are engaged in interstate commerce, the laws have been interpreted so broadly that nearly any use of the mail, interstate telephone service, or other interstate services, however minor, is enough to bring a business under the law.

Minimum Wage

The federal wage and hour laws are contained in the federal *Fair Labor Standards Act*. In 2007, congress passed and President Bush signed the *Fair Minimum Wage Act of 2007*, raising the minimum wage to $5.85 an hour beginning July 24, 2007. It also provides that the minimum wage will rise to $6.55 per hour on July 24, 2008, and to $7.25 per hour on July 24, 2009. In certain circumstances a wage of $4.25 may be paid to employees under 20 years of age for a ninety-day training period.

For employees who regularly receive more than $30 a month in tips, the minimum wage is $2.13 per hour. But if the employee's tips do not bring him or her up to the full $5.85 minimum wage, then the employer must make up the difference.

Overtime

The general rule is that employees who work more than forty hours a week must be paid time-and-a-half for hours worked over forty. However, there are many exemptions to this general rule based on salary and position. These exceptions were completely revised in 2004 and an explanation of the changes, including a tutorial video, are available at **www.dol.gov/esa**. For answers to questions about the law, call the Department of Labor at 866-4-USA-DOL (866-487-2365).

Exempt Employees

While nearly all businesses are covered, certain employees are exempt from the FLSA. Exempt employees include employees who are considered executives (administrative and managerial), professionals, computer professionals, and outside salespeople.

Whether or not one of these exceptions applies to a particular employee is a complicated legal question. Thousands of court cases have been decided on this issue, but they have given no clear answers. In one case a person could be determined to be exempt because of his or her duties, but in another a person with the same duties could be found not exempt.

One thing that is clear is that the determination is made on the employee's function and not just the job title. You cannot make a secretary exempt by calling him or her a manager if most of his or her duties are clerical. For more information, contact:

Atlanta District Office
U.S. Department of Labor, OLMS
61 Forsyth Street, SW
Suite 8B85
Atlanta, GA 30303
404-562-2083
or
866-4US-WAGE (866-487-9243)
www.dol.gov/esa/whd

Some employees in Georgia are not subject to these rules. Examples are college and high school students, sharecropper and farmers, domestic help, employers grossing less that $40,000, employers with less than five employees, people making tips, and land renters. Federal law, with some exceptions, requires overtime for all hours worked over forty at time and a half. Except for child labor laws, Georgia law only prohibits workers in textile plants from working more than ten hours a day without getting overtime.

PENSION AND BENEFIT LAWS

Small businesses are not required by law to provide any types of special benefits to employees. Such benefits are given to attract and keep employees. With pension plans, the main concern is if you start one, it must comply with federal tax laws.

Holidays   Employers are not required by federal or Georgia law to give employees time off for holidays. You can require them to work Thanksgiving

Day and Christmas, and dock their pay or fire them for failing to show. Of course, you will not have much luck keeping employees with such a policy.

Most companies give full-time employees a certain number of paid holidays, such as New Year's Day (January 1), Memorial Day (last Monday in May), Independence Day (July 4), Labor Day (first Monday in September), Thanksgiving Day (fourth Thursday in November), and Christmas (December 25). Some employers include other holidays such as Martin Luther King Jr.'s birthday (third Monday in January), President's Day (third Monday in February), Columbus Day (second Monday in October), and Veterans' Day (November 11). If one of the holidays falls on a Saturday or Sunday, many employers give the preceding Friday or following Monday off.

Sick Days

There is no federal or Georgia law mandating that an employee be paid for time that he or she is home sick. The situation seems to be that the larger the company, the more paid sick leave is allowed. Part-time workers rarely get sick leave and small business sick leave is usually limited for the simple reason that they cannot afford to pay for time that employees do not work.

Breaks

There are no federal or Georgia laws requiring coffee breaks or lunch breaks. However, it is common sense that employees will be more productive if they have reasonable breaks for nourishment or to use the toilet facilities.

Pension Plans and Retirement Accounts

Few small new businesses can afford to provide pension plans for their employees. The first concern of a small business is usually how the owner can shelter income in a pension plan without having to set up a pension plan for an employee. Under most pension plans, this is not allowed.

IRA. Anyone with $3,000 of earnings can put up to that amount in an *individual retirement account*. Unless the person or that person's spouse is covered by a company pension plan and has income over a certain amount, the amount put into the account is fully tax deductible.

ROTH IRA. Contributions to a *Roth IRA* are not tax deductible. However, when the money is taken out, it is not taxable. People who expect to still have taxable income when they withdraw from their IRA can benefit from these.

SEP IRA, SAR-SEP IRA, SIMPLE IRA. Using these types of IRA accounts, a person can put a much greater amount into a retirement plan and deduct it from his or her taxable income. In most cases employees must also be covered by such plans. The best source for more information is a mutual fund company (such as Vanguard, Fidelity, Dreyfus, etc.), or a local bank, which can set up the plan and provide all the rules. These have an advantage over qualified plans since they do not have high annual fees. One Internet site that contains some useful information on these accounts is:

www.retirement-information.com/iraaccts.htm

Qualified Retirement Plans. Qualified retirement plans are 401(k) plans, Keough plans, and corporate retirement plans. These are covered by the *Employee Retirement Income Security Act* (ERISA), which is a complicated law meant to protect employee pension plans. Congress did not want employees who contributed to pension plans all their lives ending up with nothing when the plan went bankrupt. Check with a bank or mutual fund for details.

FAMILY AND MEDICAL LEAVE ACT

Congress passed the *Family and Medical Leave Act of 1993* (FMLA), which requires an employee to be given up to twelve weeks of unpaid leave when:

- ✪ the employee or employee's spouse has a child;

- ✪ the employee adopts a child or takes in a foster child;

- ✪ the employee needs to care for an ill spouse, child, or parent; or,

- ✪ the employee becomes seriously ill.

The law only applies to employers with fifty or more employees. Also, the most highly paid 10% of an employer's salaried employees can be denied this leave because of the disruption to business their loss could cause.

CHILD LABOR LAWS

The federal *Fair Labor Standards Act* also contains rules regarding the hiring of children. The basic rules state that children under 16 years old may not be hired, except in a few jobs (such as acting and newspaper delivery). Also, those under 18 may not be hired for dangerous jobs. Children may not work more than three hours a day (eighteen hours a week) in a school week or more than eight hours a day (forty hours a week) in a nonschool week. If you plan to hire children, you should check the federal *Fair Labor Standards Act*, which is in Chapter 8, Title 29, United States Code (29 USC Chapter 8), as well as the related regulations that are in Title 29 of the Code of Federal Regulations (29 C.F.R.).

Georgia Law   Children 12 and under can work in homes or on farms. Children under 16 cannot work in hazardous jobs and can only work between 6 a.m. and 9 p.m. when school is out. The rules regarding hazardous occupations are detailed. (See Georgia Labor Code Section 300-7-2.01.) Children cannot work more than four hours per day when school is in session and forty hours per week total (eight hours per day) when school is out. Children must provide proof of age to their employer and this proof can come from the child's principal. There are special rules for children delivering messages, selling newspapers, and working in entertainment. You may wish to speak directly with an attorney regarding these rules.

IMMIGRATION LAWS

There are strict penalties for any business that hires aliens who are not eligible to work. You must verify both the identity and the employment eligibility of anyone you hire by using the **EMPLOYMENT ELIGIBILITY VERIFICATION (FORM I-9)**. (see form 5, p.237.) Both you and the employee must fill out the form, and you must check an employee's identification cards or papers. Fines for hiring illegal aliens range from $250 to $2,000 for the first offense and up to $10,000 for the third offense. Failure to maintain the proper paperwork may result in a fine of up to $1,000. The law does not apply to independent contractors with whom you may contract, and it does not penalize you if the employee used fake identification.

There are also penalties that apply to employers of four or more persons for discriminating against eligible applicants because they appear foreign or because of their national origin or citizenship status.

Appendix D has a list of acceptable documentation and a blank form. (see form 5, p.237.) The blank form can also be downloaded at **www.uscis.gov/files/form/i-9.pdf**.

For more information, call 800-357-2099. For the *Handbook for Employers: Instructions for Completing Form I-9*, check the United States Citizenship and Immigration Services (USCIS) website at **www.uscis.gov**.

Foreign Employees

If you wish to hire employees who are foreign citizens and are not able to provide the proper documentation, they must first obtain a work visa from USCIS.

Work visas for foreigners are not easy to get. Millions of people around the globe would like to come to the United States to work, but the laws are designed to keep most of them out to protect the jobs of American citizens.

Whether or not a person can get a work visa depends on whether there is a shortage of U.S. workers available to fill the job. For jobs requiring few or no skills, it is practically impossible to get a visa. For highly skilled jobs, such as nurses and physical therapists, and for people of exceptional ability, such as Nobel Prize winners and Olympic medalists, obtaining a visa is fairly easy.

There are several types of visas, and different rules for different countries. For example, the North American Free Trade Agreement (NAFTA) has made it easier for some types of workers to enter the

United States from Canada and Mexico. For some positions, the shortage of workers is assumed by the USCIS. For others, a business must first advertise a position available in the United States. Only after no qualified persons apply can it hire someone from another country.

The visa system is complicated and subject to regular change. If you wish to hire a foreign worker, you should consult with an immigration specialist or a book on the subject.

HIRING OFF THE BOOKS

Because of the taxes, insurance, and red tape involved with hiring employees, some new businesses hire people *off the books*. The employers pay them in cash and never admit they are employees. While the cash paid in wages would not be deductible, they consider this a smaller cost than compliance. Some even use off the books receipts to cover it.

Except when your spouse or child is giving you some temporary help, this is a terrible idea. Hiring people off the books can result in civil fines, loss of insurance coverage, and even criminal penalties. When engaged in dangerous work like roofing or using power tools, you are risking millions of dollars in potential damages if a worker is seriously injured or killed.

It may be more costly and time-consuming to comply with the employment laws, but if you are focused on long-term growth with less risk, it is the wiser way to go.

FEDERAL CONTRACTS

Companies that do work for the federal government are subject to several laws. The *Davis-Bacon Act* requires contractors engaged in U.S. government construction projects to pay wages and benefits that are equal to or better than the prevailing wages in the area.

The *McNamara-O'Hara Service Contract Act* sets wages and other labor standards for contractors furnishing services to agencies of the U.S. government.

The *Walsh-Healey Public Contracts Act* requires the Department of Labor to settle disputes regarding manufacturers supplying products to the U.S. government.

MISCELLANEOUS LAWS

In addition to the broad categories of laws affecting businesses, there are several other federal and state laws that you should be familiar with.

Federal Law   Federal law regulates affirmative action, layoffs, unions, and informational posters.

Affirmative action. In most cases, the federal government does not yet tell employers who they must hire, especially new small businesses. The only situation in which a small business would need to comply with affirmative action requirements would be if it accepted federal contracts or subcontracts. These requirements could include the hiring of minorities or of Vietnam veterans.

Layoffs. Companies with one hundred or more full-time employees at one location are subject to the *Worker Adjustment and Retraining Notification Act (29 USC Chapter 23)*. This law requires a sixty-day notification prior to certain layoffs, and has other strict provisions.

Unions. The *National Labor Relations Act of 1935 (29 USC Section 151 et seq.)* gives employees the right to organize or join a union. There are things employers can do to protect themselves, but you should consult a labor attorney or a book on the subject before taking action that might be illegal and could result in fines.

Poster laws. There are laws regarding what posters you may or may not display in the workplace. A federal judge in 1991 ruled that Playboy posters in a workplace were sexual harassment. This ruling is being appealed by the American Civil Liberties Union (ACLU). In addition, there are other poster laws that require certain posters to be displayed to inform employees of their rights. Not all businesses are required to display all posters. The following list provides guidance in determining the poster requirements for your business.

✪ All employers subject to minimum wage provisions must display the wage and hour poster, which is available from:

U.S. Department of Labor
200 Constitution Avenue, NW
Washington, DC 20210
866-4-USWAGE
www.dol.gov/esa/regs/compliance/posters/flsa.htm

✪ Employers with fifteen or more employees for twenty weeks of the year and employers with federal contracts or subcontracts of $10,000 or more must display the sex, race, religion, ethnic, age, equal pay, and disability discrimination poster, which is available from:

EEOC
1801 L Street, NW
Suite 100
Washington, DC 20507
202-693-0300

✪ The poster also specifically prohibits discrimination against Vietnam veterans in the case of employers with federal contracts or subcontracts of $10,000 or more.

✪ Employers with government contracts subject to the *Service Contract Act* or the *Public Contracts Act* must display a notice to employees working on government contracts, which is available from:

Employment Standards Administration
U.S. Department of Labor
200 Constitution Avenue, NW
Washington, DC 20210
202-693-0023

- ✪ Employers who employ fifty or more employees in twenty or more work weeks and who are engaged in commerce or in any industry or activity affecting commerce are required to post a notice explaining employees' rights under the federal *Family and Medical Leave Act*. The poster is available from the Employment Standards Administration, or online at **www.dol.gov/esa/regs/compliance/posters/fmla.htm**.

Employment at will. Georgia is an *employment at will* state, which means that if you hire someone for an indefinite period of time, you can discharge him or her, and he or she can quit, for no particular reason, as long as the discharge does not violate other laws like the discrimination laws. (See O.C.G.A., Section 34-7-1.) This law is being adjusted constantly as the market forces act on Georgia's industry.

You should always be sure to document any adverse action taken against an employee. Keep complete records on each employee and document his or her conduct and performance. Have a policy and procedures manual or employee handbook, and be sure to follow your own rules when disciplining employees.

Under employment at will, you cannot contract with a labor organization to require that an employee must be a member of the organization or pay the organization any money. Similarly, you cannot require as a condition of employment that anyone be, or refrain from being, a member or pay money to a labor organization. Also, one or more people cannot try to make anyone join a labor organization or influence a person's decision regarding a strike. You can only deduct labor organization fees from the employee's paycheck at the employee's request. (See O.C.G.A., Chapter 34-6.)

You also cannot use force, intimidation, violence, or threats to try to keep someone from leaving or continuing employment with a business. (See O.C.G.A., Section 34-6-2.)

Tortious interference with employment relations. The rules are different for contracted employees and noncontracted employees. If a competitor whisks away one of your noncontractual employees, you may be able to sue provided the competitor used improper means to solicit your employee. *Improper means* includes actions such as telling your employee that your business is insolvent, or using confidential information not obtained properly to solicit your employee. (See O.C.G.A., Section 51-9-1.)

If you have a binding contract of employment with an employee for a specific time period and someone induces your employee to break the contract, you may be able to recover damages from the person that interfered. You will have to show that the contractual relationship existed, that the other person intentionally interfered with that relationship, and that your relationship with your employee was damaged because of the other person's actions.

Common day of rest. A wonderfully well-intentioned law with no penalties involves a common day of rest. Any employer that operates on either Saturday or Sunday, and who employs anyone whose habitual day of worship falls on a workday, is supposed to make all reasonable accommodations to the religious, social, and physical needs of the employee so the employee may enjoy the same benefits as employees in other occupations. However, agricultural operations, employers with any charitable or religious purposes, medical staff, and the government are exempt from this law. (See O.C.G.A., Section 10-1-20.)

Payment of wages. Unless you are in the farming, sawmill, or turpentine industries, you must pay your skilled or unskilled wage workers in manual, mechanical, or clerical labor by the week by U.S. currency (cash), by check, or by credit to their bank. There must be at least two pay periods each month of equal length, and you must pay the full amount due for the particular pay period. You also must cash your employee's check if requested. This does not include officials, superintendents, or other heads or subheads of departments who may be employed by the month or year on specific salaries. (See O.C.G.A., Chapter 34-7.)

Military employees. If any employee leaves your employment, other than a temporary position, in order to perform military service (including the reserves), and seeks re-employment with you within ninety days after being relieved from the service, you must rehire that person to the same position or another position with the same seniority, status, and pay. If your circumstances have changed so much that this is impossible or unreasonable, or if the person is no longer qualified to perform the duties of the position, you do not have to rehire him or her. (See O.C.G.A., Section 38-2-279.)

Child support garnishment and wage assignments. If you receive an order from a court to withhold and deliver to the human resources department disposable earnings that are due for child support by one of your employees, you must respond to that order within twenty days and keep in your possession any disposable earnings of the responsible parent, which may be subject to the order. If you fail to do so, you will be liable to the department in an amount equal to 100% of the value of the debt, which is the basis of the order, plus costs, interest, and reasonable attorney's fees.

Similarly, your employee can make an assignment of his or her wages to the department. You must recognize the written wage assignment and cannot terminate the employee because of the assignment. You are entitled to $25 against the employee's income for the administrative costs of setting up the assignment in the first income deduction. You can deduct $3 from the paycheck for your administrative costs thereafter so long as the assignment is in effect.

You cannot fire an employee just because his or her wages have been garnished. (O.C.G.A., Section 18-4-7.)

Advertising and Promotion Laws

Because of the unscrupulous and deceptive advertising techniques and multitude of con artists trying to steal from innocent consumers, numerous federal and state statutes have been enacted that make it unlawful to use improper advertising and promotional techniques in soliciting business.

ADVERTISING LAWS AND RULES

This section discusses various federal and Georgia laws and regulations relating to advertising.

Federal Law   The federal government regulates advertising through the *Federal Trade Commission* (FTC). The rules are contained in the *Code of Federal Regulations* (C.F.R.). You can find these rules in most law libraries and many public libraries. If you plan any advertising that you think may be questionable, you might want to check the rules. As you read the rules discussed, you will probably think of many violations you see every day.

Federal rules do not apply to every business. Small businesses that operate only within the state and do not use the postal service may be exempt.

Therefore, a violation could be prosecuted by the state rather than the federal government. Some of the important rules are summarized as follows. You can also obtain copies of the rules from your library.

Deceptive pricing. When prices are being compared, it is required that actual and not inflated prices are used.

Example:
If an object would usually be sold for $7, you should not first offer it for $10 and then start offering it at 30% off.

It is considered misleading to suggest that a discount from list price is a bargain if the item is seldomly sold at list price. If most surrounding stores sell an item for $7, it is considered misleading to say it has a *retail value* of $10, even if there are some stores elsewhere selling it at that price. (16 C.F.R. Ch. I, Part 233.)

Bait advertising. *Bait advertising* is placing an ad when you do not really want the respondents to buy the product offered but to switch to another item. (16 C.F.R. Ch. I, Part 238.)

Use of free, half-off, and similar words. Use of words such as *free*, *1¢ sale*, and the like must not be misleading. This means that the *regular price* must not include a markup to cover the *free* item. The seller must expect to sell the product without the free item at some time in the future. (16 C.F.R. Ch. I, Part 251.)

Substantiation of claims. The FTC requires that advertisers be able to substantiate their claims. (16 C.F.R. Sec 3.40; 48 F.R. Page 10471.) Some information on this policy is found on the Internet at:

www.ftc.gov/bcp/guides/ad3subst.htm

Endorsements. Rules forbid endorsements that are misleading. An example is a quote from a film review that is used in such a way as to change the substance of the review. It is not necessary to use the exact words of the person endorsing the product as long as the opinion is not distorted. If a product is changed, an endorsement that does not apply to the new version cannot be used. For some items, such as drugs, claims cannot be used without scientific proof. Endorsements by organizations cannot be used unless one is sure that the membership holds the same opinion. (16 C.F.R. Ch. I, Part 255.)

Unfairness. Any advertising practices that can be deemed as *unfair* are forbidden by the FTC. (15 USC Sec. 45.) An explanation of this policy is located on the Internet at:

www.ftc.gov/bcp/policystmt/ad-unfair.htm

Negative option plans. When a seller uses a sales system in which the buyer must notify the seller if he or she does not want the goods, the seller must provide the buyer with a form to decline the sale and at least ten days in which to decline. Bonus merchandise must be shipped promptly and the seller must promptly terminate any who so request after completion of the contract. (16 C.F.R. Ch. I, Part 425.)

Laser Eye Surgery. (15 U.S.C. Sections 45, 52–57.) Under the laws governing deceptive advertising, the FTC and the FDA are regulating the advertising of laser eye surgery. Anyone involved in this area should obtain a copy of these rules. They are located on the Internet at **www.ftc.gov/bcp/guides/eyecare2.shtm**.

Food and dietary supplements. Under the *Nutrition Labeling Education Act of 1990*, the FTC and the FDA regulate the packaging and advertising of food and dietary products. Anyone involved in this area should obtain a copy of these rules. (21 USC Sec. 343.) They are located on the Internet at:

www.ftc.gov/bcp/menus/resources/guidance/adv.shtm

Jewelry and precious metals. The FTC has numerous rules governing the sale and advertising of jewelry and precious metals. Anyone in this business should obtain a copy of these rules. (61 F.R. Page 27212.) They are located on the Internet at:

www.ftc.gov/bcp/guides/jewel-gd.shtm

Georgia Law   ***Deceptive trade practices.*** The Georgia *Deceptive Trade Practices Act* tries to protect consumers and businesses from other businesses that use practices misrepresenting the source, quality, quantity, or reason for price reduction of goods or services. If a practice creates a likelihood of confusion or misunderstanding, you may be stopped from that practice and required to pay costs and attorney's fees. The person who complains about your practice does not have to show that you are competitors or that your practice actually caused misunderstanding. (See O.C.G.A., Sections 10-1-370 thru 375.)

A person engages in a deceptive trade practice when he or she, in the course of his or her business:

- passes off goods or services as those of another;

- causes a likelihood of confusion or of misunderstanding as to the source, sponsorship, approval, or certification of goods or services;

- causes a likelihood of confusion or of misunderstanding as to affiliation, connection, or association with or certification by another;

- uses deceptive representations or designations of geographic origin in connection with goods or services;

- represents that goods or services have sponsorship, approval, characteristics, ingredients, uses, benefits, or quantities that they do not have or that a person has a sponsorship, approval, status, affiliation, or connection that he or she does not have;

- represents that goods are original or new if they are deteriorated, altered, reconditioned, reclaimed, used, or secondhand;

- represents that goods or services are of a particular standard, quality, or grade or that goods are of a particular style or model when they are of another;

- disparages the goods, services, or business of another by false or misleading representation of fact;

- advertises goods or services with intent to sell them as advertised;

- advertises goods or services with intent not to apply reasonably expectable public demand, unless the advertisement discloses a limitation of quantity;

✪   makes false or misleading statements of fact concerning the reasons for, existence of, or amounts of price reductions; or,

✪   engages in any other conduct that similarly creates a likelihood of confusion or misunderstanding.

Fair business practices. The purpose of this Georgia law is to protect consumers and legitimate business enterprises from unfair or deceptive practices in the conduct of any trade or commerce in Georgia. It is very similar to the *Deceptive Trade Practices Act*, with some variations. (See O.C.G.A., Sections 10-1-390 thru 407.)

O.C.G.A., Section 10-1-393, lists examples (not exclusive) of unfair or deceptive practices in consumer transactions. The section is fourteen pages long. By way of illustration, some illegal practices include:

✪   passing off goods or services as those of another;

✪   causing actual confusion or actual misunderstanding as to the source, sponsorship, approval, or certification of goods or services (note that it must be actual confusion);

✪   causing actual confusion or actual misunderstanding as to affiliation, connection, or association with or certification by another (note that it must be actual confusion);

✪   using deceptive representations or designations of geographic origin in connection with goods or services. For instance, if you advertise in the Yellow Pages and you are a nonlocal business for that telephone service area, you must state the nonlocal location of the business if you list a local number; and,

✪   conducting a going-out-of-business sale for more than ninety days.

There are also provisions for health spas, career consulting firms, hospitals and long-term care facilities, campground and marine membership organizations, holiday or vacation giveaways, real estate financiers, personal care providers, DUI or drug use risk reduction program participants, and home health services providers.

Office supply transactions and telephone classified advertising directory solicitations are specifically addressed in O.C.G.A., Section 10-1-393.1. The prohibitions are very similar to those found in the deceptive trade practices laws previously mentioned.

O.C.G.A., Section 10-1-393.4, deems it an unfair and deceptive business practice to sell goods or services in an area in which a state of emergency has been declared at a price higher than such goods or services sold for prior to such declaration. Exceptions are detailed in the code.

Sales of business opportunities. If you plan to engage in multilevel marketing, laws surrounding the selling of business opportunities to others, or be involved at any level in a multilevel distribution company, you need to be very familiar with the sale of business opportunities found in O.C.G.A., Sections 10-1-410 through 417.

The provisions pertaining to these structures are designed to avoid illegal pyramid schemes. The law is complex, but basically it requires bonding or a trust account and specific, written disclosures and contracts. You cannot represent income or earning potential unless you have documented dates to substantiate the claims. If you violate these provisions, use any untrue or misleading statements, fail to deliver the goods or equipment necessary to begin operation within forty-five days of the date specified in the contract, or fail to comply with the bonding, notification, and contractual requirements, you may be found guilty of a misdemeanor of a high and aggravated nature. Plus, the individual officers and directors of a violating corporation, partner, or sole proprietor may be subject to a penalty. You may be sued in civil court for an injunction to stop your activities, and you can be sued for damages, including three times the actual damage for intentional violations, attorney's fees, and expenses of litigation. Such behavior is also a violation of the *Fair Business Practices Act*.

These laws do not include a landlord, property manager, or owner who licenses or leases pushcarts or kiosks within or adjacent to a retail center containing divided retail floor space and common areas to sell goods or services not supplied by the landlord, property manager, or owner.

Warranties. Georgia has various laws regarding warranties.

- The *Motor Vehicle Warranty Rights Act* (*Lemon Law*). (See O.C.G.A., Sections 10-1-780 through 794.)

- The *Farm Tractor Warranty Act*. (See O.C.G.A., Sections 10-1-810 through 819.)

- The *Assistive Technology Warranty Act*. (See O.C.G.A., Sections 10-1-870 through 875.)

- The *Motorized Wheelchair Warranty Act*. (See O.C.G.A., Sections 10-1-890 through 894.)

- Art dealer warranties. (See O.C.G.A., Section 10-1-433.)

- Boats and other watercraft capacities. (See O.C.G.A., Section 52-7-45.)

- Farm equipment manufacturers, distributors, and dealers. (See O.C.G.A., Section 13-8-17.)

- The *Uniform Commercial Code Implied Warranty* and other warranty provisions and exclusions. (See the discussion in Chapter 14 about the UCC.)

INTERNET SALES LAWS

There are not yet specific laws governing Internet transactions that are different from laws governing other transactions. The FTC feels that its current rules regarding deceptive advertising, substantiation, disclaimers, refunds, and related matters must be followed by Internet businesses and that consumers are adequately protected by them. For some specific guidelines on Internet advertising, see the FTC's site at:

http://ftc.gov/bcp/conline/pubs/buspubs/ruleroad.htm

EMAIL ADVERTISING

The *Controlling the Assault of Non-Solicited Pornography and Marketing Act of 2003* (CANSPAM) has put numerous controls on how you can use email to solicit business for your company. It requires unsolicited commercial email messages to be labeled, and the message must include opt-out instructions and the sender's physical address. Some of the prohibited activities under the act are:

- false or misleading information in an email;

- deceptive subject heading;

- failure to include a functioning return address;

- mailing to someone who has asked not to receive solicitations;

- failure to include a valid postal address;

- omitting an opt-out procedure;

- failure to clearly mark the email as advertising; and,

- including sexual material without adequate warnings.

Some of the provisions contain criminal penalties as well as civil fines. For more information on the CANSPAM Act, visit **www.ftc.gov/bcp/conline/pubs/ buspubs/canspam.shtm**. For text of the act plus other spam laws around the world, see **www.spamlaws.com**.

HOME SOLICITATION LAWS

The Federal Trade Commission has rules governing door-to-door sales. In any such sale it is a deceptive trade practice to fail to furnish a receipt explaining the sale (in the language of the presentation) and giving notice that there is a right to back out of the contract within three days, known as a right of *rescission*. The notice must be supplied in duplicate, must be in at least 10-point type, and must be captioned either *Notice of Right to Cancel* or *Notice of Cancellation*. The notice must be worded as follows on the next page.

NOTICE OF CANCELLATION

_____
Date

YOU MAY CANCEL THIS TRANSACTION, WITHOUT ANY PENALTY OR OBLIGATION, WITHIN THREE BUSINESS DAYS FROM THE ABOVE DATE.

IF YOU CANCEL, ANY PROPERTY TRADED IN, ANY PAYMENTS MADE BY YOU UNDER THE CONTRACT OR SALE, AND ANY NEGOTIABLE INSTRUMENT EXECUTED BY YOU WILL BE RETURNED TO YOU WITHIN 10 BUSINESS DAYS FOLLOWING RECEIPT BY THE SELLER OF YOUR CANCELLATION NOTICE, AND ANY SECURITY INTEREST ARISING OUT OF THE TRANSACTION WILL BE CANCELLED.

IF YOU CANCEL, YOU MUST MAKE AVAILABLE TO THE SELLER AT YOUR RESIDENCE, IN SUBSTANTIALLY AS GOOD CONDITION AS WHEN RECEIVED, ANY GOODS DELIVERED TO YOU UNDER THIS CONTRACT OR SALE; OR YOU MAY, IF YOU WISH, COMPLY WITH THE INSTRUCTIONS OF THE SELLER REGARDING THE RETURN SHIPMENT OF THE GOODS AT THE SELLER'S EXPENSE AND RISK.

IF YOU DO MAKE THE GOODS AVAILABLE TO THE SELLER AND THE SELLER DOES NOT PICK THEM UP WITHIN 20 DAYS OF THE DATE OF YOUR NOTICE OF CANCELLATION, YOU MAY RETAIN OR DISPOSE OF THE GOODS WITHOUT ANY FURTHER OBLIGATION. IF YOU FAIL TO MAKE THE GOODS AVAILABLE TO THE SELLER, OR IF YOU AGREE TO RETURN THE GOODS AND FAIL TO DO SO, THEN YOU REMAIN LIABLE FOR PERFORMANCE OF ALL OBLIGATIONS UNDER THE CONTRACT.

TO CANCEL THIS TRANSACTION, MAIL OR DELIVER A SIGNED AND DATED COPY OF THIS CANCELLATION NOTICE OR ANY OTHER WRITTEN NOTICE, OR SEND A TELEGRAM, TO _____, AT _____ NOT LATER THAN MIDNIGHT OF _____ (date).

I HEREBY CANCEL THIS TRANSACTION.

_____   _____
(Buyer's signature)   (Date)

The seller must complete the notice and orally inform the buyer of the right to cancel. He or she cannot misrepresent the right to cancel, assign the contract until the fifth business day, or include a confession of judgment in the contract. (For more specific details, see the rules contained at 16 C.F.R. Ch. I, Part 429.)

Georgia Law   People call lawyers' offices weekly to inquire about their right to rescind a home solicitation. O.C.G.A., Section 10-1-2 through 16, entitled *The Retail Installment and Home Solicitation Act*, covers these sales. *Retail installment sales* are transactions to sell or furnish goods or services using a contract providing for installment payments or a revolving account. You may have three days to change your mind about such contracts; however, you are restricted.

These rights only apply when you have:

- ✪   retail sales of goods or services;

- ✪   solicited in person;

- ✪   the buyer's agreement or offer to purchase made at a home other than that of the person soliciting the sale;

- ✪   the contract signed at the time of the solicitation; and,

- ✪   the purchase price payable in installments.

A retail installment contract must be in writing and be completed to all essential provisions prior to signing by the buyer. If delivery of the goods or services is not made at the time the buyer signs the contract, the seller can insert the identification of the goods or services and the due date of the first installment on his or her copy of the contract. The contract must contain other information specified in O.C.G.A., Section 10-1-3.

The contract must be in at least 6-point type and contain a clear and conspicuous notice that says:

> ## NOTICE TO THE BUYER
> Do not sign this before you read it, or if it contains any blank spaces. You are entitled to an exact copy of the paper you sign. You have the right to pay in advance the full amount due and, under certain conditions, to obtain a partial refund of the time price differential.

The rules for revolving accounts are in O.C.G.A., Section 10-1-4. Other requirements for this type of sale are similar to those for retail installment contracts. However, you cannot use clothing, software, or other nondurable items as security for retail installment contracts or revolving accounts.

You must send the buyer a copy of the revolving account agreement prior to the date the first payment is due and the notice on that contract must state:

> ## NOTICE TO THE BUYER
> Do not sign this before you read it, or if it contains any blank spaces. You are entitled to an exact copy of the paper your sign. You have the right to pay in advance the full amount due.

A buyer can cancel a home solicitation sale agreement until 12:00 midnight of the third business day after the day he or she signed it. It must be sent by certified mail, return receipt requested, and postmarked by the deadline. If the buyer cancels, you must refund the transaction within ten days after cancellation of all deposits, down payments, and other goods exchanged. You can charge the buyer 5% of the gross sales price of the merchandise purchased or $25, whichever is less. You can also receive the actual cost of picking up any merchandise from the sales location or $5, whichever is less.

You can charge for late payments beyond ten days of the due date. The charge cannot exceed 5% of the installment or $5, whichever is less. You can provide in the agreement that reasonable attorney's fees be paid if referred for collection to an attorney who is not a salaried employee of the seller. You can also provide for the collection of court costs. You can also charge $20 or 5% of the face amount for any check that bounces that was written to pay on an installment contract or revolving account.

You must apply any payments first to unpaid interest or finance charges, then to the goods. As to goods purchased on different dates, the first purchased must be deemed first paid for; and as to goods purchased on the same date, the lowest priced must be deemed first paid.

You can sell the contracts to others. However, if you do not notify the retail buyer that he or she needs to send payment to someone else, any payment to the last known owner of the contract is binding on all subsequent owners. Furthermore, if you violated any of the provisions of this law, even if you sell the contract the retail buyer can still come after you.

Repossession. Repossession can be scary stuff for both the merchant and the consumer. O.C.G.A., Section 10-1-10, governs repossession rights and remedies if the retail buyer does not pay according to the agreement signed.

Mail order and telephone sales. It is all right to enter into a retail installment contract by mail or telephone without personal solicitation if there is a printed solicitation of business (such as a catalog). The printed solicitation must be readily available to the public and clearly set forth the cash price and other terms of sales. All the provisions relating to the contracts apply, except that you do not have to deliver a copy of the contract (as you would with an in-home solicitation). And, you can insert the set amounts of money and other required terms in the printed solicitation in the appropriate blank spaces. You must send the buyer a written statement of any items inserted in the blank spaces. There are civil and criminal penalties for violation of this law.

TELEPHONE SOLICITATION LAWS

Telephone solicitations are governed by the *Telephone Consumer Protection Act (47 USC Sec. 227)* and the *Federal Communications Commission* (FCC) rules implementing the act (47 C.F.R. Sec. 64.1200). Violators of the act can be sued for $500 in damages by consumers and can be fined $10,000 by the FCC. Some of the requirements under the law are:

✪ calls can only be made between 8 a.m. and 9 p.m.;

✪ solicitors must keep a *do not call* list and honor requests to not call;

✪ there must be a written policy stating that the parties called are told the name of the caller, the caller's business name, and the caller's buiness phone number or address. They must also be informed that the call is a sales call and the nature of the goods or services;

✪ personnel must be trained in the policies; and,

✪ recorded messages cannot be used to call residences.

In 2003, the FCC introduced the national *Do Not Call Registry*, with which individuals could register their telephone numbers and prohibit certain telephone solicitors from calling the registered numbers. Once a person registers a telephone number, it remains on the registry for five years. Telemarketing firms can receive heavy fines for violating the registry statute, with fines ranging up to $11,000 per violation. Not all telephone solicitations are barred, however. The following solicitations are still allowed to be made to a person whose telephone number has been entered in the registry:

✪ calls from companies with which the registered person has a prior business relationship;

✪ calls for which the recipient has given written consent;

✪ calls that do not include advertisements; and,

✪ calls from charitable organizations.

It is illegal under the act to send advertising faxes to anyone who has not consented to receiving such faxes or is an existing customer.

Georgia Law   ***Automatic dialing and recorded message equipment.*** You cannot use or contract to use *automatic dialing and disseminated prerecorded statement* (ADAD) equipment to advertise, sell, lease, rent, or give goods or services for personal, family, or household use; or, to conduct polls or solicit information without meeting certain criteria. The requirements are strict unless you have written consent. (See O.C.G.A., Sections 46-5-23 and 24.)

ADAD cannot call unlisted numbers, hospitals, nursing homes, fire protection agencies, or law enforcement agencies. A permit must be obtained to use ADAD equipment from the *Public Service Commission*. You can make ADAD calls:

- ✪ for nonprofit organizations or for other than commercial profit-making purposes and for calls that do not involve the advertisement or offering for sale, lease, or rental of goods, services, or property;

- ✪ for payment of, service of, or warranty coverage of previously ordered or purchased goods or services; and,

- ✪ for collection of lawful debts. It is a misdemeanor to violate these rules. You cannot use this equipment or the United States mail to solicit people to use a "976" number and other numbers requiring per-call fees.

Harassing and obscene use. It is also a misdemeanor for you to use or allow anyone to use your telephone for the purpose of harassing or threatening anyone. It is a misdemeanor for you, by means of telephone communication for commercial purposes, to make directly or with an electronic recording device, any suggestion or proposal that is obscene or indecent.

Fax machines. You cannot use your facsimile machine, or contract to use someone else's, to transmit an unsolicited fax message for the commercial purpose of advertising or offering the sale, lease, rental, or gift of any goods, services, or real or personal property unless the recipient has consented or you have a prior contractual or business relationship between you and the recipient.

Unsolicited merchandise. If you send anyone merchandise that was not ordered or requested, you may have sent them a gift for which they do not have to pay. Do not send them bills for the merchandise since they can seek an injunction against you and recover attorney's fees and costs from you. Similarly, if you engage in a membership organization that makes retail sales of merchandise to its members, and a member notifies you by certified mail, return receipt requested, that he or she terminates his or her membership, do not send any more merchandise or it will likewise be considered an unconditional gift. (See O.C.G.A., Sections 10-1-50 and 51.)

Do not call list. Georgia law allows consumers to be put on a *do not call list* and businesses who call persons on the list can be fined. For more information, call 800-282-5813 or visit the following website.

www.ganocall.com

WEIGHTS AND LABELING

Beginning in 1994, all food products are required to have labels with information on the nutritional values, such as calories, fat, and protein. For most products, the label must be in the required format so that consumers can easily compare products. However, if such a format will not fit on the product label, the information may be presented in another form that is easily readable.

In 1994, federal rules requiring metric measurement of products took effect. Metric measures do not have to be the first measurement on the container, but they must be included. Food items that are packaged as they are sold, such as delicatessen items, do not have to contain metric labels.

Georgia Law   ***Bulk sales.*** Whenever the quantity is determined by the seller, or is in excess of $20, and in all cases of bulk deliveries of heating fuel, there must be a delivery ticket containing the name and address of the vendor and purchaser; the date delivered; the quantity delivered; and, the quantity upon which the price is based. The ticket cannot differ from the delivered quantity; must identify the goods or commodities in the most descriptive terms commercially practical, including any quantity representation made in connection with the sale; and, must include the count of individually wrapped packages, if more than one.

Information required on packages. Generally, any package kept, offered, or exposed for sale must have on the outside a plain conspicuous declaration of the commodity in the package (unless it can be identified through the wrapper or container), the quantity of contents, the name and place of business of the manufacturer, and the packer (unless it is sold where it is packed). Also, when dealing with packages of different weights, you must state the price per single unit of weight.

The commissioner of agriculture has promulgated rules and regulations about weights and measures, which are found in Georgia Rules and Regulations, Chapter 40-15.

Payment and Collection Laws

Depending on the business you are in, you may be paid by cash, checks, credit cards, or some sort of financing arrangement, such as a promissory note or mortgage. Both state and federal laws affect the type of payments you collect. Failure to follow the laws can cost you considerably.

CASH

Cash is probably the easiest form of payment, and it is subject to few restrictions. The most important one is that you keep an accurate account of your cash transactions and that you report all of your cash income on your tax return. Recent efforts to stop the drug trade have resulted in some serious penalties for failing to report cash transactions and for money laundering. The laws are so sweeping that even if you deal in cash in an ordinary business you may violate the law and face huge fines and imprisonment.

The most important law to be concerned with is the one requiring the filing of the **REPORT OF CASH PAYMENTS OVER $10,000 RECEIVED IN A TRADE OR BUSINESS (IRS FORM 8300)**. (see form 18, p.277.) A transaction does not have to happen in one day. If a person brings you smaller amounts of cash that add up to $10,000 and the government can construe them as one transaction, then the form must be filed. Under this law, *cash* also includes travelers' checks and money orders but not cashier's checks or bank checks.

CHECKS

It is important to accept checks in your business. While a small percentage will be bad, most checks will be good, and you will be able to accommodate more customers. To avoid having problems with checks, abide by the following rules.

Bad Checks   It is a crime to issue a bad check, money order, or debit card draft in Georgia. (See O.C.G.A., Section 16-9-20.) If someone presents you an instrument (check, money order, or debit card draft) for present consideration (a current purchase), labor, or rent and it bounces, you must use the following procedure to enable the magistrate's court in the county where the check was issued to proceed.

- ✪   Record on the instrument or see that it is recorded on the instrument, the full name, residence address, and phone number of the person issuing the instrument.

- ✪   Witness the signing or endorsement of the instrument and initial the check, money order, or debit card draft.

- ✪   Cash or deposit the instrument within thirty days of when it was given to you.

- ✪   After receiving the dishonored instrument back from your bank, send a **FORMAL NOTICE PRIOR TO CRIMINAL ACTION ON A BAD CHECK** (see form 6, p.239) demanding payment within ten days (after receipt of the notice) of the check amount plus a service charge (which cannot exceed $25 or 5% of the face amount of the check, whichever is greater). Send the notice by certified mail with return receipt requested. You can use one notice for all bad instruments delivered by the same person or business within a ten-day period.

✪   If the ten days expire and you do not receive payment, you can take a copy of the notice letter, and your return receipt showing the date of delivery of the notice, to the magistrate court and fill out an application for a warrant.

Once you file the application, the court will issue a warrant. When the person is arrested, he or she may pay the sheriff. The court then sends you the instrument amount, the service charge you claimed, and costs (presumed to be $20). If the person does not pay, he or she will have to go to court and stand trial for a misdemeanor or felony, depending upon the amounts involved. If the case does go to trial, he or she may be liable to you for the amount of the check, damages in double the amount of the check (but no more than $500), and court costs you incurred. (See O.C.G.A., Section 13-6-15.)

A few hints. If you get the check back from your bank, look at all the stamps and see how many times it was presented for payment to your customer's bank. If you cannot tell, call your bank and ask them their normal procedure and whether they usually present the check for payment twice. If it has not been presented twice, you may want to run it through again—if you have reason to believe the funds should be available. If at all possible, take the check to the bank of the offending account and try to cash it. You will need identification, including something proving you are a corporate officer or owner of the business to which the check is written. You may want to try this one or two times. Sometimes you can catch funds going through the account before others do.

If you receive a bounced check and you are surprised that this particular person or business had insufficient funds, call and ask if they are aware that the check bounced. Sometimes there has been an error at the bank or in someone's bookkeeping. You can avoid unpleasant repercussions with an otherwise good customer if you straighten the problem out amicably.

Obviously, there are judgment calls to be made, and you learn quickly the usual stories. If you hear "the check's in the mail," you might choose to believe it for a day or two. But do not be fooled.

Stopped Payment   Georgia also has a policy on *stop payment* checks. If someone writes you a stop payment check for a good or services on merchandise, you try to cash the check within thirty days without any luck, and you send a certified letter with a **Stopped Payment Check Notice** (see form 7, p.241), you are allowed to put a lien on the merchandise and, probably with the help of a lawyer, take the property back or have it sold to recover part of the money and your costs. (See O.C.G.A., Section 44-14-516.) You can also recover up to $500 for your time and trouble. (See O.C.G.A., Section 13-6-15.)

Refunds after Cashing Check

A popular scam is for a person to purchase something by using a check and return the next day to demand a refund. After making the refund, the business discovers the initial payment check bounced. Do not make refunds until checks clear.

CREDIT CARDS

In our buy-now, pay-later society, credit cards can add greatly to your sales potential, especially with large, discretionary purchases. For *MasterCard*, *Visa*, and *Discover*, the fees you pay are about 2%, and this amount is easily paid for by the extra purchases that the cards allow. (*American Express*, however, charges 4%–5%.)

A business that has an account with a financial institution that allows the business to accept credit card transactions is said to have obtained *merchant status*. For businesses that have a *retail outlet*, there is usually no problem getting merchant status. Most commercial banks can handle it. *Discover* can also set you up to accept its card as well as *MasterCard* and *Visa*, and it will wire the money into your bank account daily. However, for mail order businesses, especially those operating out of the home, it is much harder to get merchant status. (*American Express* will accept mail order companies operating out of the home. However, not as many people have its cards.)

Some companies open a small storefront (or share one) to get merchant status and then process mostly mail orders. The processors usually do not want to accept you if you will do more than 50% mail order. This is because credit card companies fear mail order fraud. However, if you have not had many complaints from your customers, you may be allowed to process mostly mail orders.

You might be tempted to try to run your charges through another business. This may be okay if you actually sell your products through it; however, if you run your business charges through its account, the other business may lose its merchant status. Someone who bought a book by mail from you and then has a charge on his or her statement from a florist shop will probably call the credit card company saying that he or she bought anything from the florist shop. Too many of these complaints, and the account will be closed.

Georgia Law O.C.G.A., Section 10-1-393.3, forbids a merchant from requiring a customer to provide his or her personal or business telephone number when paying by credit card. It also prohibits imprinting a credit card number on a check or recording the number of the purchaser's credit card as a condition of accepting a check for payment. A merchant can record a credit card number as a condition to cashing or accepting a check if there is an agreement with the credit card issuer to cash or accept checks as a service to its customers and the issuer has guaranteed payment.

Also, a merchant can ask for a credit card as a means of identification or to show credit worthiness or financial responsibility (although he or she does not have to accept a check if a card is presented). He or she can record the type of card and its expiration date on the check or elsewhere. And, he or she can record the customer's address or telephone number if it is necessary for shipping, delivery, or installation of goods or for special orders.

FINANCING LAWS

Some businesses can make sales more easily if they finance the purchases themselves. If the business has enough capital to do this, it can earn extra profits on the financing terms. However, because of abuses, many consumer protection laws have been passed by both the federal and state governments.

Federal Law Two important federal laws regarding financing are called the *Truth in Lending Act* and the *Fair Credit Billing Act*. These are implemented by what is called *Regulation Z* (commonly known as *Reg. Z*), issued by the Board of Governors of the Federal Reserve System. It is contained in Volume 12 of the *Code of Federal Regulations*, page 226.

The regulation covers all transactions in which the following four conditions are met:

1. credit is offered;

2. the offering of credit is regularly done;

3. there is a finance charge for the credit or there is a written agreement with more than four payments; and,

4. the credit is for personal, family, or household purposes.

It also covers credit card transactions in which only the first two conditions are met. It applies to leases if the consumer ends up paying the full value and keeping the item leased. It does not apply to the following transactions:

*   transactions with businesses or agricultural purposes;

*   transactions with organizations such as corporations or the government;

*   transactions of over $25,000, which are not secured by the consumer's dwelling;

*   credit involving public utilities;

*   credit involving securities or commodities;

*   home fuel budget plans; and,

*   student loan programs.

The way for a small business to avoid Reg. Z violations is to avoid transactions that meet the conditions or to make sure all transactions fall under the exceptions. This is easy for many businesses. Instead of extending credit to customers, accept credit cards and let the credit card company extend the credit. However, if your customers usually do not have credit cards, or if you are in a business that often extends credit (such as used car sales), consult a lawyer who is knowledgeable about Reg. Z.

Georgia Law   The state of Georgia regulates financing arrangements. If you discriminate based upon race, sex, religion, national origin, or marital status you can be fined up to $1,000. (See O.C.G.A., Sections 7-6-1 and 2.)

If you offer any kind of retail financing, you should check O.C.G.A., Sections 10-1-1 through 10, which cover retail installment sales and revolving accounts. Motor vehicle sales are covered by the *Motor Vehicle Finance Act*. (See O.C.G.A., Sections 10-1-30 through 41.)

USURY

The maximum amount of interest on a loan of $3,000 or less is 16% simple interest. If the rate is not in writing, all that can be enforced is 7%. For loans over $3,000, the rate is 5% per month, simple interest; therefore, interest charges over 60% per year would be illegal and void. Some federal laws override Georgia's laws. For example, credit card loans and service charges on open accounts often exceed these amounts in Georgia without being usurious.

SECURITIES LAWS

Both the state and federal governments have long and complicated laws dealing with the sales of *securities*. There are also hundreds of court cases attempting to explain what these laws mean. A thorough explanation of this area of law is beyond the scope of this book.

Basically, securities have been held to exist in any case in which a person provides money with the expectation that he or she will profit through the efforts of another person. This can apply to any situation where someone buys stock in or makes a loan to your business. The laws require a disclosure of the risks involved and in some cases registration of the securities with the government. There are some exemptions, such as for small amounts of money and for limited numbers of investors.

Penalties for violation of securities laws are severe, including triple damages and prison terms. Consult a specialist in securities laws before letting anyone invest in your business. You can often get an introductory consultation at a reasonable rate to explain your options.

COLLECTIONS

The *Fair Debt Collection Practices Act of 1977* bans the use of deception, harassment, and other unreasonable acts in the collection of debts. It has strict requirements whenever someone is collecting a debt for someone else. If you are in the collection business, you must obtain a copy of this law.

The Federal Trade Commission has issued some rules that prohibit deceptive representations, such as:

- ✪ pretending to be in the motion picture industry, the government, or a credit bureau;

- ✪ using questionnaires that do not say their purpose is collecting a debt; or,

- ✪ any combination of these.

Georgia Law   Georgia's laws on collection do not add much to what the federal laws provide. Under Georgia law, you may be guilty of a misdemeanor if you repeatedly call a customer and harass him or her or his or her family, threaten bodily harm, or intentionally fail to hang up. (See O.C.G.A., Section 16-11-39.1.)

REFUND AND EXCHANGE POLICIES

Georgia has a business-friendly policy on returns. A business is not required to offer refunds or exchanges. However, if a retail establishment has a policy of no refunds or exchanges, a notice of such policy should be posted at the point of sale.

Many businesses do offer refunds or exchanges if customers return an item, in its original condition, promptly after purchase. This is done to build good customer relations and hope that the customer will come back. But under the law, a business may insist that all sales are final.

Business Relations Laws

At both the federal and state levels, there exist many laws regarding how businesses relate to one another. Some of the more important ones are discussed in this chapter.

THE UNIFORM COMMERCIAL CODE

The *Uniform Commercial Code* (UCC) is a set of laws regulating numerous aspects of doing business. In order to avoid having a patchwork of different laws around the fifty states, a national group drafted this set of uniform laws. Although some states have modified some sections of the laws, the code is basically the same in most states. In Georgia, the UCC is contained in Title 11 of the *Official Code of Georgia Annotated* (O.C.G.A.). Each chapter of the UCC is concerned with a different aspect of commercial relations such as sales, warranties, bank deposits, commercial paper, and bulk transfers.

Businesses that wish to know their rights in all types of transactions should obtain a copy of the UCC and become familiar with it. It is especially useful in transactions between merchants. However, its meaning is not always clear from a reading of the statutes.

COMMERCIAL DISCRIMINATION

The *Robinson-Patman Act of 1936* prohibits businesses from injuring competition by offering the same goods at different prices to different buyers. This means that the large chain stores should not be getting a better price than a small shop. It also requires that promotional allowances must be made on proportionally the same terms to all buyers.

As a small business, you may be a victim of a Robinson-Patman Act violation, but fighting a much larger company in court would probably be too expensive for you. Your best bet, if an actual violation has occurred, would be to see if you could get the government to prosecute it. For more information on what constitutes a violation, see the Federal Trade Commission and the Department of Justice's joint site at **www.ftc.gov/bc/compguide/index.htm**.

RESTRAINING TRADE

One of the earliest federal laws affecting business is the *Sherman Antitrust Act of 1890*. The purpose of this law is to protect competition in the marketplace by prohibiting monopolies.

Examples of some prohibited actions are:

- ✪ agreements between competitors to sell at the same prices;

- ✪ agreements between competitors on how much will be sold or produced;

- ✪ agreements between competitors to divide up a market;

- ✪ refusing to sell one product without a second product; and,

- ✪ exchanging information among competitors that results in similarity of prices.

As a new business, you probably will not be in a position to violate the act, but you should be aware of it in case a larger competitor tries to put you out of business.

INTELLECTUAL PROPERTY PROTECTION

As a business owner, you should know enough about *intellectual property* laws to protect your own creations and to keep from violating the rights of others. *Intellectual property* is the product of human creativity, such as writings, designs, inventions, melodies, and processes. Intellectual property is something that can be stolen without being physically taken. For example, if you write a book, someone can steal the words from your book without stealing a physical copy of it.

As the Internet grows, intellectual property is becoming more valuable. Smart business owners will take the actions necessary to protect their company's intellectual property. Additionally, business owners should know intellectual property laws to make certain they do not violate the rights of others. Even an unknowing violation of the law can result in stiff fines and penalties.

The following paragraphs explain the types of intellectual property and the ways to protect them.

Patent   A *patent* is protection given to new and useful inventions, discoveries, and designs. To be entitled to a patent, a work must be completely *new* and *unobvious*. The first inventor who files for a patent gets it. Once an invention is patented, no one else can make use of that invention, even if they discover it independently. In general, a new patent lasts for 20 years from the date of filing the patent application with the United States Patent and Trademark Office (USPTO). Patents cannot be renewed. The patent application must clearly explain how to make the invention, so when the patent expires, others will be able to freely make and use the invention. Patents are registered with the United States Patent and Trademark Office. Patentable items include mechanical devices or new drug formulas.

Copyright   A *copyright* is protection given to *original* works of authorship, such as written works, musical works, visual works, performance works, or computer software programs. A copyright exists from the moment of creation, but one cannot register a copyright until it has been fixed in tangible form. Also, titles, names, or slogans cannot be copyrighted. A copyright currently gives the author and his or her heirs exclusive right to the work for the life of the author plus 70 years. Copyrights first registered before 1978 last for 95 years. This was previously 75 years, but was extended 20 years to match the European system. Copyrights are registered with the Register of Copyrights at the Library of Congress. The fee to register a copyright is $30. Examples of works that are copyrightable include books, paintings, songs, poems, plays, drawings, and films.

Contact the U.S. Copyright Office at:

Library of Congress
101 Independence Avenue, SE
Washington, DC 20559
202-707-3000
www.copyright.gov

Trademark   A *trademark* is protection given to a name or symbol that is used to distinguish one person's goods or services from those of others. It can consist of letters, numbers, packaging, labeling, musical notes, colors, or a combination of these. If a trademark is used on services, as opposed to goods, it is called a *service mark*. A trademark lasts indefinitely if it is used continuously and renewed properly. Trademarks are registered with the United States Patent and Trademark Office and with individual states. (This is explained further in Chapter 3.) Examples of trademarks include the *Chrysler* name on automobiles, the red border on Time Magazine, and the shape of the *Coca-Cola* bottle.

Trade Secret   A *trade secret* is information or a process that provides a commercial advantage that is protected by keeping it a secret. Examples of trade secrets may be a list of successful distributors, the formula for *Coca-Cola*, or some unique source code in a computer program. Trade secrets are not registered anywhere, but they are protected by the fact that they are not disclosed. They are protected only for as long as they are kept secret. If you independently discover the formula for *Coca-Cola* tomorrow, you can freely market it. (But you cannot use the trademark *Coca-Cola* on your product to market it.)

Georgia Law   There are civil and criminal penalties for stealing or taking a *trade secret*. A trade secret means information including, but not limited to: technical or nontechnical data, a formula, a pattern, a compilation, a program, a device, a method, a technique, a drawing, a process, financial data, financial plans, product plans, or a list of actual or potential customers or suppliers that derives economic value or potential from not being generally known. (See O.C.G.A., Section 16-8-13.) In addition to the imposition of an injunction, the civil penalties may include damages up to twice the amount of the actual damages incurred and attorney's fees. However, it works the other way, too—if you claim in bad faith that someone misappropriated your trade secret, you may be hit with attorney's fees. (See O.C.G.A., Sections 10-1-760 through 767, for the civil provisions on trade secrets.)

There are special rules for computer software. If you deal with the creation or manufacture of computer software, you should be especially mindful of these provisions.

Nonprotectable Creations

Some things are just not protectable, such as ideas, systems, and discoveries that are not allowed any protection under law. If you have a great idea, such as selling packets of hangover medicine in bars, you cannot stop others from doing the same thing. If you invent a new medicine, you can patent it; if you pick a distinctive name for it, you can register the name as a trademark; or, if you create a unique picture or instructions for the package, you can copyright it. However, you cannot stop others from using your basic business idea of marketing hangover medicine in bars.

Notice the subtle differences between the protective systems available. If you invent something two days after someone else does and that person has patented it, you cannot even use it for yourself. But if you write the same poem as someone else and neither of you copied the other, both of you can copyright the poem. If you patent something, you can have the exclusive rights to it for the term of the patent, but you must disclose how others can recreate it after the patent expires. However, if you keep it a trade secret, you have exclusive rights as long as no one learns the secret.

We are in a time of transition of the law of intellectual property. Every year new changes are made in the laws and new forms of creativity win protection. For more information, consult a new edition of a book on these types of property.

Endless Laws

The state of Georgia and the federal government have numerous laws and rules that apply to every aspect of every type of business. There are laws governing such things as fence posts, hosiery, rabbit raising, refund policies, frozen desserts, and advertising. Every business is affected by one or another of these laws.

Some activities are covered by both state and federal laws. In such cases, you must obey the stricter of the rules. In addition, more than one agency of the state or federal government may have rules governing your business. Each of these may have the power to investigate violations and impose fines or other penalties.

Penalties for violations of these laws can range from a warning to a criminal fine and even jail time. In some cases, employees can sue for damages. Since ignorance of the law is no excuse, it is your duty to learn what laws apply to your business.

Very few people in business know the laws that apply to their businesses. If you take the time to learn them, you can become an expert in your field and avoid problems with regulators. You can also fight back if one of your competitors uses an illegal method to compete with you.

The laws and rules that affect most businesses are explained in this section. Following the explanation is a list of more specialized laws. You should read through this list and see which ones may apply to your business. Then go to your public library or law library and read them. Some may not apply to your phase of the business. If any of them do apply, you should make copies to keep on hand.

FEDERAL LAWS

The federal laws that are most likely to affect small businesses are rules of the Federal Trade Commission (FTC). The FTC has some rules that affect many businesses, such as labeling, warranties, and mail order sales. Other rules affect only certain industries.

If you sell goods by mail, you should send for the FTC's booklet, *A Business Guide to the Federal Trade Commission's Mail or Telephone Order Merchandise Rule*. It is also available online at **www.ftc.gov/bcp/conline/pubs/buspubs/mailorder.htm**. You should ask for the latest information on the subject if you are going to be involved in an industry such as those listed as follows, or using warranties or your own labeling. The address is:

Federal Trade Commission
Consumer Response Center
600 Pennsylvania Avenue, NW
Washington, DC 20580
202-326-2222

The rules of the FTC are contained in the *Code of Federal Regulations* (C.F.R.) in Title 16. Some of the industries covered are:

Industry	Part
Adhesive Compositions	235
Aerosol Products Used for Frosting Cocktail Glasses	417
Automobiles (New car fuel economy advertising)	259
Business Opportunities and Franchises	436
Cigarettes	408
Decorative Wall Paneling	243
Dog and Cat Food	241

Dry Cell Batteries	403
Extension Ladders	418
Fiber Glass Curtains	413
Food (Games of Chance)	419
Funerals	453
Gasoline (Octane posting)	306
Gasoline	419
Home Entertainment Amplifiers	432
Home Insulation	460
Household Furniture	250
Jewelry	23
Law Books	256
Luggage and Related Products	24
Mail Order Merchandise	435
Nursery	18
Ophthalmic Practices	456
Photographic Film and Film Processing	242
Private Vocational and Home Study Schools	254
Retail Food Stores (Advertising)	424
Sleeping Bags	400
Television Sets	410
Textile Wearing Apparel	423
Textiles	236
Tires	228
Used Automobile Parts	20
Used Lubricating Oil	406
Used Motor Vehicles	455
Watches	245
Wigs and Hairpieces	252

Some other federal laws that affect businesses are as follows:

✪ *Alcohol Administration Act*

✪ *Child Protection and Toy Safety Act* (1969)

✪ *Clean Water Act*

✪ *Comprehensive Smokeless Tobacco Health Education Act* (1986)

- *Consumer Credit Protection Act* (1968)

- *Consumer Product Safety Act* (1972)

- *Energy Policy and Conservation Act*

- *Environmental Pesticide Control Act of 1972*

- *Fair Credit Reporting Act* (1970)

- *Fair Packaging and Labeling Act* (1966)

- *Flammable Fabrics Act* (1953)

- *Food, Drug, and Cosmetic Act*

- *Food Safety Enforcement Enhancement Act of 1997*

- *Fur Products Labeling Act* (1951)

- *Hazardous Substances Act* (1960)

- *Hobby Protection Act*

- *Insecticide, Fungicide, and Rodenticide Act*

- *Magnuson-Moss Warranty Act*

- *Nutrition Labeling and Education Act of 1990*

- *Poison Prevention Packaging Act of 1970*

- *Solid Waste Disposal Act*

- *Textile Fiber Products Identification Act*

- *Toxic Substance Control Act*

- *Wool Products Labeling Act* (1939)

Homeland Security Concerns

The recent formation of the U.S. Department of Homeland Security (DHS) has caused a variety of new issues to arise that affect business. New laws designed to protect national interests have been and will continue to be enacted that will directly impact how businesses are operated. The DHS also has a need for products and services that will ensure national security. This, in turn, will provide for many opportunities for companies engaged in businesses that can deliver those goods and services. For more information about DHS opportunities, contact the department at:

U.S. Department of Homeland Security
Washington, DC 20528
www.dhs.gov/dhspublic

Sarbanes-Oxley Act

In the wake of crises at Enron and other publicly traded companies several years ago, Congress enacted the *Sarbanes-Oxley Act* in 2002. The purpose of this legislation is to, as Congress stated, *protect investors by improving the accuracy and reliability of corporate disclosures made pursuant to the securities law*. The act applies to all publicly traded companies, no matter how small. Among other things, the act requires that:

✪ corporate officers certify that they have reviewed the company's financial reports and that no false or misleading information is contained therein;

✪ changes in the financial standing or operations of the company be disclosed;

✪ the company makes no loans to insiders; and,

✪ compliance with the act is achieved by certain set deadlines.

The text of the *Sarbanes-Oxley Act* can be found online at **www.law.uc.edu/CCL/SOact/toc.html**.

Punishment for violations of the act includes multimillion dollar fines and prison time, so it is extremely important that the Sarbanes-Oxley requirements are followed. Firms offering assistance with compliance to companies is becoming big business in and of itself. It may pay off for you to consider hiring an expert to guide your business through the compliance process.

GEORGIA STATE LAWS

Like all states, Georgia has thousands of laws covering all aspects of business. Here are some of the most common. You should occasionally check the index of the Georgia code to see if any new laws apply to any aspects of your business.

(All citations are referred from the Official Code of Georgia Annotated (O.C.G.A.).)

BUSINESS	TITLE-CHAPTER-SECTION
Accountants	43-3-1 through 38
Adjusters	33-23-1 through 44
Adult bookstores & movies	36-60-3
Agricultural products dealers	2-9-1 through 16
Air conditioning contractors	43-14-1 through 18
Alcoholic beverages	Title 3
Alligator farms	27-1-2
Amusement rides	34-12-1 to 20
Animals	Title 4
Animal technicians	43-50-50 through 57
Antennae	46-6-11
Antifreeze	10-1-200 through 211
Appliances	44-13-100
Aquaculture	27-4-251 through 263
Architects	43-4-1 through 37
Artificial flavors	26-2-62 through 28
Artificial gas, retail sales	48-8-2
Asbestos	12-12-1 through 25
Athlete agents	43-4A-1 through 19
Athletic trainers	43-5-1 through 15
Attorneys	15-19-1 through 58
Auctioneers	43-6-1 through 26
Audiologists	43-44-1 through 18
Auditors	9-7-1 through 23
Bail bondsmen	17-6-50 through 55
Bait	27-1-2
Bakeries	26-2-21
Banking and finance	Title 7
Barbers	43-7-1 through 27
Barley	2-9-30 through 45

Basketball machines	48-17-1 through 14
Bathhouses	31-12-11
Beauty pageants	10-1-830 through 836
Bedding products	31-25-1 through 13
Billiard rooms	43-8-1 through 3
Biohazardous material	40-6-253.1
Biological permits	4-9-1 through 9
Bird dealers licensing	4-10-1 through 12
Blasting	25-8-1 through 12
Blood & blood products	31-24-1 through 8
Boats & other watercraft	52-7-1 through 77
Boiler & pressure vessels	34-11-1 through 22
Boxing match licenses	31-31-1 through 7
Brake fluid	10-1-180 through 189
Bread & flour	26-2-290 through 297
Brokers & mortgage lenders	7-1-1000 through 1020
Building & housing	Title 8
Bus & rail passengers	16-12-121 through 125
Buying clubs or services	10-1-590 through 605
Campgrounds	10-1-392
Career consulting firms	10-1-392 through 3
Catalog sales	10-1-5
Caterers	3-11-1 through 5
Cemeteries	44-3-130 through 152
Charitable solicitations	43-17-1 through 23
Child care institutions	49-5-1 through 21
Chiropractors	43-9-1 through 20
Chop shops	16-8-80 through 86
Cigars & cigarettes	48-11-1 through 29
Circuses	48-13-9 through 10
Clinical laboratories	31-22-1 through 13
Coin dealers	43-37-1 through 7
Coin op'd amusement mach.	48-17-1 through 14
Computer-related offenses	16-9-90 through 94
Construction industry	43-14-1 through 18
Cosmetologists	43-10-1 through 20
Counselors, professional	43-10A-1 through 24
Court reporters	15-14-20 through 36
Creameries	26-2-230 through 250
Dairy products, coop	2-10-80 through 111

Day care centers	49-5-1 through 21
Dental hygienists	43-11-1 through 82
Dietic counselors	43-11A-1 through 19
Dentists	43-11-1 through 82
Dietitians	43-11A-1 through 19
Dog racing	10-1-550
Drinking water	12-5-170 through 193
Driver education	43-13-1 through 11
Drugs & cosmetics	26-3-1 through 24
Dry cleaners' lien	44-14-450 through 456
Dynamite	25-8-1 through 12
Eggs	26-2-260 through 274
Embalmers	43-18-1 through 108
Emergency medical services	31-11-1 through 61
Engineers, professional	43-15-1 through 31
Farm equipment	13-8-11 through 45
Feeds	2-13-1 through 23
Fertilizers	2-12-1 through 21
Financial institutions	7-1-1 through 958
Fine arts	10-1-510
Fire sprinkler contractors	25-11-1 through 11
Firearms & weapons	16-11-120 through 125
Firearms dealers	43-16-1 through 12
Fireworks	25-10-1 through 8
Fish	26-2-310 through 320
Food service establishments	26-2-370 through 378
Foresters	12-6-40 through 63
Frozen desserts	26-2-239 through 240
Fruit	2-9-1 through 16
Fundraisers & solicitors	43-17-1 through 23
Funeral directors	43-18-1 through 108
Gambling	16-12-20 through 38
Garden equipment	44-14-460 through 466
Gem dealers	43-2-1 through 43-2-5
Geologists	43-19-1 through 28
Ginseng	12-6-150 through 157
Glass installations	8-2-90 through 95
Grain dealers	2-9-30 through 45
Ground water use	12-5-90 through 107
Hatchery operators & dealers	4-7-1 through 8

Health spas	10-1-393.2
Hearing aids	43-20-1 through 21
Horticultural growing media	2-12-100 through 110
Innkeepers	43-21-1 through 15
Insurance	Title 33
Interior decorators	43-4-30 through 37
Itinerant traders	43-32-1 through 7
Junk dealers	43-22-1 through 5
Junkyards	32-6-240 through 248
Kennels	4-11-1 through 16
Kosher foods	26-2-330 through 335
Land surveyors	43-15-1 through 31
Landscape architects	43-23-1 through 20
Librarians	43-24-1 through 7
Liming materials	2-12-40 through 54
Limited edition art reproduction	10-1-430 through 437
Livery stable keepers	44-12-71 through 74
Livestock dealers	4-6-1 through 11
Loan brokers	7-7-1 through 6
Low-voltage contractors	43-14-1 through 18
Marriage & family therapists	43-10A-1 through 24
Mental health	Title 37
Metal dealers	10-1-350 through 357
Milk and milk products	26-2-230 through 250
Model glue	16-13-90 through 96
Money orders, licensure	7-1-681 through 692
Motion pictures, bidding	10-1-290 through 294
Motor vehicle dismantlers	43-48-1 through 21
Motor vehicle franchises	10-1-620 through 627
Motor vehicle racetracks	43-25-1 through 10
Motor vehicle rebuilders	43-48-1 through 21
Nurseries	2-7-1 through 31
Nurses	43-26-1 through 39
Nursing home administrators	43-27-1 through 12
Occupational therapists	43-28-1 through 17
Oil & gas deep drilling	12-4-40 through 53
Opticians	43-29-1 through 22
Optometrists	43-30-1 through 15
Outdoor advertising	32-6-70 through 97
Paint	10-1-120 through 127

Pawnbrokers	44-12-130 through 138
Peddlers	43-32-1 through 7
Pest control, structural	43-45-1 through 26
Pesticide use & application	2-7-90 through 114
Pets	4-8-1 through 4-14-1
Pharmacists	26-4-1 through 163
Physical therapists	43-33-1 through 21
Physician assistants	43-34-1 through 151
Physicians	43-34-1 through 151
Pine straw	12-6-200 through 207
Plant diseases	2-7-1 through 31
Plumbers	43-14-1 through 18
Podiatrists	43-35-1 through 14
Polygraph examiners	43-36-1 through 22
Poultry dealers, brokers	4-4-80 through 84
Precious metal & gem dealers	43-37-1 through 7
Printers, advertising	10-1-421 & 426
Private detective, ops. of	43-38-1 through 17
Product packaging	12-8-160 through 166
Psychologists	43-39-1 through 20
Quarries	44-9-70 through 76
Real estate appraisers	43-39A-1 through 27
Real estate brokers & sales	43-40-1 through 32
Respiratory care	43-34-1 through 151
Roadhouses & dance halls	43-21-50 through 62
Roadside markets	2-10-130 through 140
Roller skates	51-1-43
Salvage dealers	43-48-1 through 21
Scrap metal processors	43-43-1 through 5
Security agencies, ops. of	43-38-1 through 17
Seeds	2-11-20 through 34
Self-service storage facility	10-4-210 through 215
Shooting preserves	27-3-110 through 114
Social workers	43-10A -1 through 24
Soft drinks	26-2-350 through 357
Speech pathologists	43-44-1 through 18
Stables	4-11-1 through 16
Stenographic reporters	15-14-1 through 36
Surface mining	12-4-70 through 84
Tailors	44-14-450 through 456

Tanning facilities	31-38-1 through 12
Tobacco warehousing	10-1-140 through 155
Transient merchants	43-46-1 through 7
Treated timber products	2-14-100 through 113
Underground storage tanks	12-13-1 through 22
Used-car dealers	43-47-1 through 16
Utility contractors	43-14-1 through 18
Veterinarians	43-50-1 through 59
Veterinarian technicians	43-50-1 through 59
Warehouses	10-4-1 through 33
Watches, used	43-49-3 through 4
Water treatment plants	43-51-1 through 15
Water wells	12-5-120 through 137
Weighers, public	10-2-40 through 54
Wheelchairs	10-1-390 through 394
Wildlife	27-1-1 through 5-11
Wineries	3-6-21.1 through .2

Bookkeeping and Accounting

It is beyond the scope of this book to explain all the intricacies of setting up a business's bookkeeping and accounting systems. However, if you do not set up an understandable bookkeeping system, your business will undoubtedly fail.

Without accurate records of where your income is coming from and where it is going, you will be unable to increase your profits, lower your expenses, obtain needed financing, or make the right decisions in all areas of your business. The time to decide how you will handle your bookkeeping is when you open your business, not a year later when it is tax time.

INITIAL BOOKKEEPING

If you do not understand business taxation, you should pick up a good book on the subject as well as the IRS tax guide for your type of business (proprietorship, partnership, or corporation). The IRS tax book for small businesses is Publication 334, *Tax Guide for Small Businesses*. There are also instruction booklets for each type of business's form: Schedule C for proprietorships, Form 1120 or 1120S for C corporations and S corporations, and 1165 for partnerships and businesses that are taxed like partnerships (LLCs and LLPs).

Keep in mind that the IRS does not give you the best advice for saving on taxes and does not give you the other side of contested issues. For that, you need a private tax guide or advisor.

The most important thing to do is to set up your bookkeeping so that you can easily fill out your monthly, quarterly, and annual tax returns. The best way to do this is to get copies of the returns, note the totals that you will need to supply, and set up your bookkeeping system to group those totals.

For example, for a sole proprietorship you will use *Schedule C* to report business income and expenses to the IRS at the end of the year. Use the categories on that form to sort your expenses. To make your job especially easy, every time you pay a bill, put the category number on the check.

ACCOUNTANTS

Most likely your new business will not be able to afford hiring an accountant to handle your books, but that is good. Doing them yourself will force you to learn about business accounting and taxation. The worst way to run a business is to know nothing about the tax laws and turn everything over to an accountant at the end of the year to find out what is due.

You should know the basics of tax law before making basic decisions such as whether to buy or rent equipment or premises. You should understand accounting so you can time your financial affairs appropriately. If you were a boxer who only needed to win fights, you could turn everything over to an accountant. If your business needs to buy supplies, inventory, or equipment and provides goods or services throughout the year, you need to at least have a basic understanding of the system within which you are working.

Once you can afford an accountant, weigh the cost against your time and the risk that you will make an error. Even if you think you know enough to do your own corporate tax return, you might take it to an accountant one year to see if you have been missing any deductions that you did not know about. You might decide that the money saved is worth the cost of the accountant's services.

COMPUTER PROGRAMS

Today, every business should keep its books by computer. There are inexpensive programs, such as Quicken, that can instantly provide you with reports of your income and expenses and the right figures to plug into your tax returns. Most programs offer a tax program each year that will take all of your information and print it out on the current year's tax forms.

TAX TIPS

Here are a few tax tips that may help businesses save money.

- ✪ Usually when you buy equipment for a business you must *amortize* the cost over several years. That is, you do not deduct the entire cost when you buy it, but take, say, 25% of the cost off your taxes each year for four years. (The time is determined by the theoretical usefulness of the item.) However, small businesses are allowed to write off the entire cost of a limited amount of items under *Internal Revenue Code, Section 179*. If you have income to shelter, use it.

- ✪ Owners of S corporations do not have to pay Social Security or Medicare taxes on the part of their profits that is not considered salary. As long as you pay yourself a reasonable salary, other money you take out is not subject to these taxes.

- ✪ Do not neglect to deposit withholding taxes for your own salary or profits. Besides being a large sum to come up with at once in April, there are penalties that must be paid for failure to do so.

- ✪ Be sure to keep track of, and remit, your employees' withholdings. You will be personally liable for them even if your business is a corporation.

- ✪ If you keep track of your use of your car for business, you can deduct mileage (see IRS guidelines for the amount, as it can change each year). If you use your car for business a considerable amount of the time, you may be able to depreciate it.

❂   If your business is a corporation, if you designate the stock as *section 1244 stock*, and then if the business fails, you are able to get a much better deduction for the loss.

❂   By setting up a retirement plan, you can exempt up to 20% of your salary from income tax. But do not use money you might need later. There are penalties for taking it out of the retirement plan.

❂   When you buy things that will be resold or made into products that will be resold (i.e., you buy from a wholesaler), you do not have to pay sales tax on those purchases.

chapter 18

Paying Federal Taxes

As we all know, the federal government levies many different types of taxes on individuals and businesses. It is very important that you consult an accountant or attorney to properly comply with and take advantage of the incredibly complex federal tax code and regulations. The following sections discuss several of the most important federal taxes that will most likely affect your new business.

INCOME TAX

The following section describes the manner in which each type of business pays taxes.

Proprietorship

A proprietor reports profits and expenses on Schedule C attached to the usual Form 1040 and pays tax on all the net income of the business. Each quarter Form 1040ES (estimated tax) must be filed along with payment of one-quarter of the amount of income tax and Social Security tax estimated to be due for the year. Publication 334, *Tax Guide for Small Business*, is available online at **www.irs.gov**.

Partnership

A partnership files a return showing the income and expenses but pays no tax. Each partner is given a form showing his or her share of the profits or losses and reports these on Schedule E of Form 1040. Each quarter, Form 1040ES must be filed by each partner along with payment of one-quarter of the amount of income tax and Social Security tax estimated to be due for the year.

C Corporation

A regular corporation is a separate taxpayer and pays tax on its profits after deducting all expenses, including officers' salaries. If dividends are distributed, they are paid out of after-tax dollars and the shareholders pay tax a second time when they receive the dividends. If a corporation needs to accumulate money for investment, it may be able to do so at lower tax rates than the shareholders pay. But if all profits will be distributed to shareholders, the double-taxation may be excessive unless all income is paid as salary. A C corporation files Form 1120.

S Corporation

A small corporation has the option of being taxed like a partnership. If Form 2553 *(Election by a Small Business Corporation)* is filed by the corporation and accepted by the Internal Revenue Service, the S corporation will only file an informational return listing profits and expenses. Each shareholder will be taxed on a proportional share of the profits (or be able to deduct a proportional share of the losses). Unless a corporation will make a large profit that will not be distributed, S-status is usually best in the beginning. An S corporation files Form 1120S and distributes Form K-1 *(Shareholder's Share of Income, Credits, Deductions, etc.)* to each shareholder. If any money is taken out by a shareholder that is not listed as wages subject to withholding, the shareholder will usually have to file Form 1040ES each quarter along with payment of the estimated withholding on the withdrawals.

Limited Liability Companies

Limited liability companies and limited liability partnerships are allowed to elect to be taxed either as a partnership or a corporation by the IRS. To make this election, you file Form 8832, *Entity Classification Election* with the IRS.

Tax Workshops and Booklets

The IRS conducts workshops to inform businesses about the tax laws. (Do not expect an in-depth study of the loopholes.) For more information, call the IRS toll free at 800-829-1040 or write to the IRS at the following address:

Internal Revenue Service
401 West Peachtree Street NW
Atlanta, GA 30308
404-338-7962

WITHHOLDING, SOCIAL SECURITY, AND MEDICARE TAXES

If you need basic information on business tax returns, the IRS publishes a rather large booklet that answers most questions and is available free of charge. Call or write the IRS and ask for Publication No. 334. If you have any questions, look up its toll-free number in the phone book under United States Government/Internal Revenue Service. If you want more creative answers and tax saving information, find a good accountant. However, to get started, you will need the following.

Employer Identification Number

If you are a sole proprietor with no employees, you can use your Social Security number for your business. If you are a corporation, a partnership, or a proprietorship with employees, you must obtain an *employer identification number* (EIN). This is done by filing the **APPLICATION FOR EMPLOYER IDENTIFICATION NUMBER (IRS FORM SS-4)**. (see form 9, p.245.) It usually takes a week or two to receive it. You will need this number to open bank accounts for the business, so you should file this form as soon as you decide to go into business. A sample, filled-in form is included in Appendix C. You can also get your EIN immediately online at the following IRS website: **https://sa1.www4.irs.gov/modiein/individual/index.jsp**. Be sure to have all the information asked for on the SS-4 available.

Employee's Withholding Allowance

You must have each employee fill out a W-4 form to calculate the amount of federal taxes to be deducted and to obtain his or her Social Security number. The number of allowances on this form is used with IRS Publication 15, *Circular E, Employer's Tax Guide*, to figure out the exact deductions.

Federal Tax Deposit Coupons

After taking withholdings from employees' wages, you must deposit them at a bank that is authorized to accept such funds. Your required schedule for making deposits is explained in Publication 15 and depends upon the amount of taxes withheld from employees' wages. The deposit is made using the coupons in the Form 8109 booklet, which the IRS will provide.

Estimated Tax Payment Voucher

Sole proprietors and partners usually take draws from their businesses without the formality of withholding. However, they are still required to make deposits of income and FICA taxes each quarter. If more than $500 is due in April on a person's 1040 form, not enough money was withheld each quarter. In this situation, a penalty is assessed, unless the person falls under an exception. The quarterly withholding is submitted on Form 1040ES on April 15th, June 15th, September 15th, and January 15th each year. If these days fall on a weekend, the due date is the following Monday. The worksheet with Form 1040ES can be used to determine the amount to pay. All 1099s from your company together need to be reported to the Social Security Administration on a Form W3 summary.

> **NOTE:** *One exception to the rule is that if your income is below $150,000 and if you withhold the same amount as last year's tax bill, you do not have to pay a penalty. This is usually much easier than filling out the 1040ES worksheet. The only caveats are that if you make more than $150,000 (married filing jointly), then you have to pay at least 110% of what is owed in taxes for a "get out of tax jail free (for a while) card." Also, if the difference between your withholding and your ultimate tax is $1,000 or less, then there is no penalty.*

Employer's Quarterly Tax Return
Each quarter you must file Form 941 to report your federal withholding and FICA taxes. If you owe more than $2,500 at the end of a quarter, you are required to make a deposit to an authorized financial institution. Most banks are authorized to accept deposits. Consult the instructions for Form 941. In some cases, electronic deposit of taxes may be required.

Wage and Tax Statement
At the end of each year, you are required to issue a W-2 Form to each employee. This form shows the amount of wages paid to the employee during the year, as well as the amounts withheld for taxes, Social Security, Medicare, and other purposes.

Miscellaneous
If you pay at least $600 to a person (not a corporation) who is not an employee (such as independent contractors), you are required to file a Form 1099 for that person. Along with the 1099s, you must file a form 1096, which is a summary sheet.

Many people are not aware of this law and fail to file these forms, but the forms are required for such things as services, royalties, rents, awards, and prizes that you pay to individuals (but not corporations). The rules for this are quite complicated, so you should either obtain

Instruction 1099 from the IRS or consult your accountant. Under the new guidelines of the IRS, it is YOUR job to know if you are dealing with a corporation in good standing (you can check by going to the secretary of state's website at **www.georgiacorporations.org**). If the corporation is NOT in good standing, or if it is an individual, use the 1099.

Earned Income Credit

People who are not liable to pay income tax may have the right to a check from the government because of the *earned income credit*. You are required to notify your employees of this in one of the following ways:

○   a W-2 Form with the notice on the back;

○   a substitute for the W-2 Form with the notice on it;

○   a copy of Notice 797; or,

○   a written statement with the wording from Notice 797.

A Notice 797 can be obtained by calling 800-829-3676, or via the Internet at **www.irs.gov/pub/irs-pdf/n797.pdf**.

EXCISE TAX

Excise taxes are taxes on certain activities or items. A few remain, but most federal excise taxes have been eliminated since World War II.

Some of the things that are subject to federal excise taxes are tobacco and alcohol, gasoline, tires and inner tubes, some trucks and trailers, firearms, ammunition, bows, arrows, fishing equipment, the use of highway vehicles of over 55,000 pounds, aircraft, wagering, telephone and teletype services, coal, hazardous wastes, and vaccines. If you are involved with any of these, obtain IRS publication No. 510, *Information on Excise Taxes*.

UNEMPLOYMENT COMPENSATION TAXES

You must pay federal unemployment taxes (FUTA) if you paid wages of $1,500 in any quarter or if you had at least one employee for twenty calendar weeks. Temporary and part-time employees are included for purposes of FUTA. The federal tax amount is 0.8% of the first $7,000 of wages paid to each employee.

If the FUTA tax is more than $100 at the end of a quarter, then the tax must be deposited quarterly; otherwise, it may be paid yearly with Form 940 or Form 940EZ. This is your annual report of federal unemployment taxes. You will receive an original form from the IRS.

The Internal Revenue Service has initiated a program, called the *Electronic Federal Tax Payment System* (EFTPS), by which business owners can pay taxes online. For many businesses, this will be a more convenient and cost effective way of making deposits than using the Federal Tax Deposit coupons. Businesses that have deposited a total of more than $200,000 in taxes in a calendar year are *required* to use EFTPS starting the second year following the year the $200,000 threshold is reached. Enrollment in EFTPS is free of charge, and can be done by contacting EFTPS at 800-555-4477 or online at **www.eftps.gov**.

Paying Georgia State Taxes

In addition to the federal taxes a Georgia business must pay, the state of Georgia imposes several of its own.

SALES AND USE TAX

Have you ever wondered how the state collects taxes? If you are starting a Georgia business, you will soon be a tax collector. When you start a business that sells goods (rather than services such as doctors, lawyers, or advertising), you have to charge tax. Leases and rentals under ninety days also incur a tax. The tax in Georgia is four cents on the dollar, and some counties and municipalities charge more. Metropolitan Atlanta businesses may also contribute to the Metropolitan Atlanta Rapid Transit Authority (MARTA) transportation system for an additional penny, but businesses get to keep back 3% of the taxes as handling charges.

Fractional charges (like $1.05) require fractional payments, and for the first ten cents there is no additional charge. From fifteen to twenty-five cents the fractional payment is one cent; from twenty-six to fifty cents it is two cents, from fifty-one to seventy-five cents it is three cents, and from seventy-six cents to one dollar it is all four cents.

Your application for a tax number is **Form CRF-002**, the **Georgia State Tax Registration Application**. (see form 13, p.257.) It must be filed upon your starting the business. A sample, filled-in form is included in Appendix C. The state will send you back a form ST-2 giving you a tax number. They will expect you to send a **Sales and Use Tax Report (ST-3)** by the twentieth of each month. (see form 16, p.267.) If your liability is less than $100 per month, you may apply to pay quarterly. All books and records must be kept for three years.

If you have any sales before you get your monthly tax return forms, you should calculate the tax and submit it anyway. Otherwise, you will be charged a penalty (even if it was not your fault) for not having the forms. In some cases, new businesses are required to post a bond to insure taxes are paid. If your business generates more than $5,000 per month in sales taxes, then Georgia requires you to file electronically. You can apply for electronic filing at the Georgia Department of Revenue website.

Exempt Purchases

One reason to get a tax number early is to exempt your purchases from tax. When you buy a product that you will resell, or will use as part of a product that you will sell, you are exempt from paying tax on that product. Although these purchases are not subject to sales tax, the burden of proof is on the seller to prove a resale purchase, unless he or she has a written statement from a purchaser stating the purchase is for resale. For this, **Form ST-5 Sales and Use Tax Certificate of Exemption** is usually used. A sample, filled-in **ST-5** is in Appendix C (see form 8, p.218.)

Even if you will be selling items wholesale or out of state, you must be registered to obtain the tax number to exempt your purchases.

Exempt Sales

There are other sales tax exemptions. State, federal, and municipal governments do not pay the tax. MARTA does not pay taxes and taxes are not collected on prescription drugs or eyeglasses. Many agricultural products are exempt, as are most sales to universities. New businesses may also avoid paying tax on new machinery placed into service for manufacturing. Also, air and water pollution control equipment may be exempt. If you are relocating a business to Georgia, you may want to investigate whether your particular circumstances apply.

If you sell to someone who claims to be exempt from sales and use taxes (for example, if he or she plans to resell merchandise he or she has purchased from you), you must have him or her complete the **CERTIFICATE OF EXEMPTION**.

You are required to collect sales and use taxes for all sales you make, unless you have documentation on file proving that a purchase was exempt from the tax. For this, you would use the same **FORM ST-5** previously mentioned. A person can fill out a form for a particular sale, or he or she can fill out one form to be used for all of his or her dealings with you.

INCOME TAX

Withholding Georgia has a state income tax that applies to individuals and to corporations that are not S corporations. This means that as a business owner, you will need to withhold income from your employees and, in some cases, from your own wages.

Withholding of Georgia income tax is similar to the federal withholding system. **GEORGIA EMPLOYEE'S WITHHOLDING ALLOWANCE CERTIFICATE (FORM G-4)** (similar to the W-4) is filled out by each employee. (see form 12, p.255.) Tax payments are made monthly with voucher GA-V. Each quarter the employer files G-7. This form must be filed, even if no taxes are due or there is a $25 penalty. When withholding exceeds $10,000 per month, it must be remitted electronically.

For a copy of the *Employer's Tax Guide,* contact:

Georgia Department of Revenue
Taxpayer Services Division
1800 Century Boulevard, NE
Atlanta, GA 30345
877-602-8477
www.georgia.gov

Corporate Income Tax   Corporations that are not S corporations must pay an income tax to the state of Georgia based upon their net income. If any of that income is later paid to the owners as dividends, it is taxed a second time (as is done under federal tax law). For this reason, most small C corporations pay out all of their profits to the owners as salaries. Though they are taxable to the recipients, they are deductible to the corporation. For more information and forms, contact the Department of Revenue.

CORPORATE NET TAX WORTH

A *net worth tax* is a tax on the value of the assets used in a business. To comply with this law, a business must report its assets as of January 1 and pay the tax due with the annual income tax return.

AD VALOREM TAXES

The noncorporate equivalent of the corporate net worth tax is the *ad valorem tax*. This tax is based on the fair market value of the tangible property held by a business on January 1 of each year. Every business licensed in the county will receive a notice in early January. The fair market value is multiplied by 40%, and then a tax rate is applied to that amount (each county has its own rate). There are exemptions for agricultural and historic properties.

Payment of this tax is very important because if you do not pay your ad valorem taxes, it is possible that you cannot sue for debts that are owed to you.

UNEMPLOYMENT TAXES

Business owners are liable for paying an unemployment tax to the state based on a rate provided by your *history*. If your purchase is a going concern, the Georgia Department of Labor account held by the seller is now yours, including all amounts of unemployment taxes paid by the seller and all liabilities for such taxes. It is certainly important to inquire if the seller has properly paid all employment taxes up to the date of sale because you will be responsible for any of his or her unpaid unemployment taxes. These taxes are put aside for employees who lose their jobs and qualify to receive unemployment compensation while they are looking for work. Your history is based on your unemployment claims and your employee's taxable wages. For example, the more former employees who claim benefits, the higher your history rating. If you are a new employer, you will be assigned a standard rate by the state. This rate may increase or decrease over the course of time, depending in large part on your unemployment experience history.

Within ten days of acquiring the business, you must request a determination of status, and the seller must give notice to the Employment Security Agency of the business sale through the Change of Status section on the back of the quarterly report. Sometimes even the purchase of a clearly identifiable part of an existing business may bring complications for the tax deposits. If you purchase part of a business, within two calendar quarters from the date of acquisition you must complete and return an application for a partial transfer of the account on Form ESA-641 and Form 641A. The application must also be accompanied by an agreement to the transfer by the seller, which is often included in the sales agreements. This transfer account will affect your history rating as well, unless you are already subject to the regulation of the Georgia Department of Labor at the time of sale.

On a partial sale, your current rate will remain in effect until the next quarter, when the Department of Labor will pick a new number. If you are not already in the pool, you will be taxed based upon the rate that is already established for the seller. The standard rate is 2.64% on the first $8,500, but this number can go way up and down.

There is an interesting tug of war going on between Georgia businesses, the State of Georgia, and the federal labor department regarding independent contractors. Under federal rules, industry standards govern many of the relationships. For example, a framing crew would clearly be an independent contractor. However, Georgia law is a little murky. Under the current Georgia rules, the framing crew *could* be employees for unemployment insurance law purposes. In the spirit of total CYA (*covering your assets*), it is a pretty good idea if you use contract labor, to pay unemployment insurance for them at the state level, but still treat them as 1099 independent contractors for federal and state tax purposes. Check with your accountant if you are unsure.

For more information on unemployment experience ratings, taxes, and contributions, you should obtain a copy of the booklet, *Unemployment Insurance: The Employers' Handbook* (DOL-224). You can get it from the Georgia Department of Labor by calling 404-232-3001 or online at:

www.dol.state.ga.us/pdf/forms/dol4e.pdf

REAL PROPERTY TAXES

Toward the end of each year, real estate is assessed and taxed. If you are a homeowner, this tax bill is probably paid through your mortgage company, and you may not even know it. You do need to know that individuals and businesses have a right to challenge the valuations of their properties and many times, these challenges are successful. A property owner has at least ten days to challenge an assessment, and it may be worth your while to consider it. Property tax exemptions of at least $2,000 and as much as $32,500 are available to property owners.

INTANGIBLE TAXES

Some items are very tangible, like a typewriter or a pizza oven. Those items are subject to ad valorem taxes. Other things are less tangible, like promissory notes and securities. If the business holds more than $20,000 in securities or $200,000 in cash, then an *intangible tax* is due. In general, the tax is ten cents per thousand. This tax is enforced, but it is unusual, and you have to request the form PL 159 and file it with the Georgia tax return.

REAL ESTATE TRANSFER TAXES

When real estate is transferred in Georgia, the seller must pay a tax of $1.00 per thousand on the sale value. If there is an exchange, both exchangers must pay the tax.

EXCISE TAXES

Additional taxes are levied on certain products. These taxes are often called *sin taxes*. They are placed on sales of tobacco and alcohol. There are also motor fuel taxes and road use taxes for big trucks and buses.

Out-of-State Taxes

As a Georgia business, if you operate your business outside the borders of the state of Georgia, you not only have to comply with Georgia and federal tax laws, but also with the laws of the states and other countries in which you do business. This can prove to be very complicated.

STATE SALES TAXES

In 1992, the United States Supreme Court struck a blow for the rights of small businesses by ruling that state tax authorities cannot force them to collect sales taxes on interstate mail orders (*Quill Corporation v. North Dakota*). Unfortunately, the court left open the possibility that Congress could allow interstate taxation of mail order sales, and since then several bills have been introduced that would do so.

At present, companies are only required to collect sales taxes for states in which they *do business*. Exactly what business is enough to trigger taxation is a legal question, and some states try to define it as broadly as possible.

If you have an office in a state, clearly you are doing business there, and any goods shipped to consumers in the state are subject to sales taxes. If you have a full-time employee working in the state much of the year, many states will consider you to be doing business there. In some states, attending a two-day trade show is enough business to trigger taxation for the entire year for every order shipped to the state. One loophole that often works is to be represented at shows by persons who are not your employees.

Because the laws are different in each state, you will have to do some research on a state-by-state basis to find out how much business you can do in a state without being subject to its taxation. You can request a state's rules from its department of revenue, but keep in mind that what a department of revenue wants the law to be is not always what the courts will rule that it is.

BUSINESS TAXES

Even worse than being subject to a state's sales taxes is being subject to its income or other business taxes. For example, California charges every company doing business in the state a minimum $800 a year fee and charges income tax on a portion of the company's worldwide income. Doing a small amount of business in the state is clearly not worth getting mired in California taxation.

For this reason, some trade shows have been moved from the state, and this has resulted in a review of the tax policies and some *safe-harbor* guidelines to advise companies on what they can do without becoming subject to taxation.

Write to the department of revenue of any state with which you have business contacts to see what might trigger your taxation.

INTERNET TAXES

State revenue departments are drooling at the prospect of taxing commerce on the Internet. Theories have already been proposed that websites available to state residents mean a company is doing business in a state. Fortunately, Congress has passed a moratorium on taxation of the Internet.

CANADIAN TAXES

The Canadian government expects American companies that sell goods by mail order to Canadians to collect taxes for them and file returns with Revenue Canada, its tax department. Those who receive an occasional unsolicited order are not expected to register, and Canadian customers who order things from the United States pay the tax plus a $5 fee upon receipt of the goods. But companies that solicit Canadian orders are expected to be registered if their worldwide income is $30,000 or more per year. In some cases a company may be required to post a bond and to pay for the cost of Canadian auditors visiting its premises and auditing its books. For these reasons, you may notice that some companies decline to accept orders from Canada.

The End...and the Beginning

If you have read through this whole book, then you know more about the rules and laws for operating a Georgia business than most people in business today. However, after learning about all the governmental regulations, you may become discouraged. You are probably wondering how you can keep track of all the laws, and how you will have any time left to make money after complying with the laws. It is not that bad—people are starting businesses every day, and they are making money.

Congratulations on deciding to start a business in Georgia! I hope you are successful in record time. If you have any unusual experiences along the way, drop me a line at the following address. The information may be useful for a future book.

Hon. Charles T. Robertson, II
P.O. Box 94
Woodstock, GA 30188
Email: crobertson@superlaw.com

Glossary

A

acceptance. Agreeing to the terms of an offer and creating a contract.

affirmative action. Hiring an employee to achieve a balance in the workplace, and to avoid existing or continuing discrimination based on minority status.

alien. A person who is not a citizen of the country.

articles of incorporation. The document that sets forth the organization of a corporation.

B

bait advertising. Offering a product for sale with the intention of selling another product.

bulk sales. Selling substantially all of a company's inventory.

C

C corporation. A corporation that pays taxes on its profits.

collections. The collection of money owed to a business.

common law. Laws that are determined in court cases rather than statutes.

consideration. The exchange of value or promises in a contract.

contract. An agreement between two or more parties.

copyright. Legal protection given to "original works of authorship."

corporation. An artificial "person" that is set up to conduct a business owned by shareholders and run by officers and directors.

D

deceptive pricing. Pricing goods or services in a manner intended to deceive the customers.

discrimination. The choosing among various options based on their characteristics.

domain name. The address of a website.

E

employee. Person who works for another under that person's control and direction.

endorsements. Positive statements about goods or services.

excise tax. A tax paid on the sale or consumption of goods or services.

express warranty. A specific guarantee of a product or service.

F

fictitious name. A name used by a business that is not its personal or legal name.

G

general partnership. A business that is owned by two or more persons.

goods. Items of personal property.

guarantee. A promise of quality of a good or service.

I

implied warranty. A guarantee of a product or service that is not specifically made, but can be implied from the circumstances of the sale.

independent contractor. Person who works for another as a separate business, not as an employee.

intangible property. Personal property that does not have a physical presence, such as the ownership interest in a corporation.

intellectual property. Legal rights to the products of the mind, such as writings, musical compositions, formulas, and designs.

L

liability. The legal responsibility to pay for an injury.

limited liability company. An entity recognized as a legal "person" that is set up to conduct a business owned and run by members.

limited liability partnership. An entity recognized as a legal "person" that is set up to conduct a business owned and run by members and that is set up for professionals such as attorneys or doctors.

limited partnership. A business that is owned by two or more persons of which one or more is liable for the debts of the business and one or more has no liability for the debts.

limited warranty. A guarantee covering certain aspects of a good or service.

M

merchant. A person who is in business.

merchant's firm offer. An offer by a business made under specific terms.

N

nonprofit corporation. An entity recognized as a legal "person" that is set up to run an operation in which none of the profits are distributed to controlling members.

O

occupational license. A government-issued permit to transact business.

offer. A proposal to enter into a contract.

overtime. Hours worked in excess of forty hours in one week, or eight hours in one day.

P

partnership. A business formed by two or more persons.

patent. Protection given to inventions, discoveries, and designs.

personal property. Any type of property other than land and the structures attached to it.

pierce the corporate veil. When a court ignores the structure of a corporation and holds its owners responsible for its debts or liabilities.

professional association. An entity recognized as a legal "person" that is set up to conduct a business of professionals such as attorneys or doctors.

proprietorship. A business that is owned by one person.

R

real property. Land and the structures attached to it.

resident alien. A person who is not a citizen of the country but who may legally reside and work there.

S

S corporation. A corporation in which the profits are taxed to the shareholders.

sale on approval. Selling an item with the agreement that it may be brought back and the sale canceled.

sale or return. An agreement whereby goods are to be purchased or returned to the vendor.

securities. Interests in a business such as stocks or bonds.

sexual harassment. Activity that causes an employee to feel or be sexually threatened.

shares. Units of stock in a corporation.

statute of frauds. Law that requires certain contracts to be in writing.

stock. Ownership interests in a corporation.

sublease. An agreement to rent premises from an existing tenant.

T

tangible property. Physical personal property such as desks and tables.

trade secret. Commercially valuable information or process that is protected by being kept a secret.

trademark. A name or symbol used to identify the source of goods or services.

U

unemployment compensation. Payments to a former employee who was terminated from a job for a reason not based on his or her fault.

usury. Charging an interest rate higher than that allowed by law.

W

withholding. Money taken out of an employee's salary and remitted to the government.

workers' compensation. Insurance program to cover injuries or deaths of employees.

Appendix A: Superior Court Clerks

Appling County
F. Floyd Hunter
P.O. Box 269
Baxley, GA 31513
912-367-8126

Atkinson County
Wilson Paulk
P.O. Box 6
Pearson, GA 31642
912-422-3343

Bacon County
Sherry Tillman
P.O. Box 376
Alma, GA 31510
912-632-4915

Baker County
Betty Bush
P.O. Box 10
Newton, GA 31770
229-734-3004

Baldwin County
Rosemary Fordham
Phillips
P.O. Box 987
Milledgeville, GA 31059
912-445-6324

Banks County
Tim Harper
P.O. Box 337
Homer, GA 30547
706-677-6240

Barrow County
Gloria M. Wall
P.O. Box 1280
Winder, GA 30680
770-307-3035

Bartow County
Gary Bell
135 West Cherokee
Avenue
Suite 233
Cartersville, GA 30120
770-387-5025

Ben Hill County
Laverne D. Wheeler
P.O. Box 1104
Fitzgerald, GA 31750
229-426-5135

Berrien County
Carol Ross
101 East Marion Avenue
Suite 3
Nashville, GA 31639
912-686-5506

Bibb County
Dianne Brannen
P.O. Box 1015
Macon, GA 31202
478-621-6527

Bleckley County
Dianne C. Brown
306 SE Second Street
Cochran, GA 31014
478-934-3210

Brantley County
Tony Ham
P.O. Box 1067
Nahunta, GA 31553
912-462-6280

Brooks County
Ginger Shiver
P.O. Box 630
Quitman, GA 31643
229-263-4747

Bryan County
Rebecca G. Crowe
P.O. Box 670
Pembroke, GA 31321
912-653-3872

Bulloch County
Sherri A. Atkins
20 Siebald Street
Statesboro, GA 30458
912-764-9009

Burke County
Sherrie J. Cochran
P.O. Box 803
Waynesboro, GA 30830
706-554-2279

Butts County
Rhonda T. Waits
P.O. Box 320
Jackson, GA 30233
770-775-8215

Calhoun County
James C. Shippey
P.O. Box 69
Morgan, GA 31766
229-849-2715

Camden County
Susan Waldron
P.O. Box 550
Woodbine, GA 31569
912-576-5622

Candler County
Linda F. Sewell
P.O. Drawer 830
Metter, GA 30439
912-685-5257

Carroll County
Kenneth Skinner
P.O. Box 1620
Carrollton, GA 30112
770-830-5830

Catoosa County
Norman L. Stone
875 Lafayette Street
Ringgold, GA 30736
706-935-4202

Charlton County
Kay Carter
P.O. Box 760
Folkston, GA 31537
912-496-2354

Chatham County
Daniel Massey
P.O. Box 10227
Savannah, GA 31412
912-652-7200

Chattahoochee County
Laura Marion
P.O. Box 120
Cusseta, GA 31805
706-989-3424

Chattooga County
Sam L. Cordle Jr.
P.O. Box 159
Summerville, GA 30747
706-857-0706

Cherokee County
Patricia Baker
90 North Street
Suite G-170
Canton, GA 30114
678-493-6511

Clarke County
Beverly Logan
P.O. Box 1805
Athens, GA 30603
706-613-3190

Clay County
Deanna Bertrand
P.O. Box 550
Fort Gaines, GA 39851
229-768-2631

Clayton County
Linda T. Miller
9151 Tara Boulevard
Jonesboro, GA 30236
770-477-3401

Clinch County
Daniel V. Leccese
P.O. Box 433
Homerville, GA 31634
912-487-5854

Cobb County
Jay C. Stephenson
P.O. Box 3490
Marietta, GA 30061
770-528-1300

Coffee County
Angela Spell
P.O. Box 10
Douglas, GA 31534
912-384-2865

Colquitt County
Carolyn Brazel
P.O. Box 2827
Moultrie, GA 31776
229-616-7420

Columbia County
Cindy Mason
P.O. Box 2930
Appling, GA 30809
706-312-7139

Cook County
Chlois Lollis
212 North Hutchinson
Avenue
Adel, GA 31620
229-896-7717

Coweta County
Cindy G. Brown
P.O. Box 943
Newman, GA 30264
770-254-2690

Crawford County
John D. Castleberry
P.O. Box 1037
Roberta, GA 31078
478-836-3328

Crisp County
Jean H. Rogers
P.O. Box 747
Cordele, GA 31010
229-276-2616

Dade County
Kathy D. Page
P.O. Box 417
Trenton, GA 30752
706-657-4778

Dawson County
Becky V. McCord
25 Tucker Avenue
Suite 106
Dawsonville, GA 30534
706-344-3510

Decatur County
Rebecca McCook
P.O. Box 336
Bainbridge, GA 39818
229-248-3026

Dekalb County
Linda Carter
556 North McDonough
Street
Suite 207
Decatur, GA 30030
404-371-2836

Dodge County
Rhett Walker
P.O. Drawer 4276
Eastman, GA 31023
478-374-2817

Dooly County
Betty Colter
P.O. Box 326
Vienna, GA 31092
229-268-4234

Dougherty County
Evonne Mull
P.O. Box 1827
Albany, GA 31702
229-431-2198

Douglas County
Cindy Chaffin
8700 Hospital Drive
Douglasville, GA 30134
770-920-7252

Early County
India E. Thompson
P.O. Box 849
Blakely, GA 31723
229-723-3033

Echols County
Paula Goss
P.O. Box 213
Statenville, GA 31648
229-559-5642

Effingham County
Elizabeth Z. Hursey
P.O. Box 387
Springfield, GA 31329
912-754-2118

Elbert County
Pat V. Anderson
P.O. Box 619
Elberton, GA 30635
706-283-2005

Emanuel County
J. Carlton Lawson
P.O. Box 627
Swainsboro, GA 30401
478-237-8911

Evans County
Gail B. McCooey
P.O. Box 845
Claxton, GA 30417
912-739-3868

Fannin County
Dana Chastain
P.O. Box 1300
Blue Ridge, GA 30513
706-632-2039

Fayette County
Sheila Studdard
P.O. Box 130
Fayetteville, GA 30214
770-716-4290

Floyd County
Joe E. Johnston
P.O. Box 1110
Rome, GA 30162
706-291-5190

Forsyth County
Douglas Sorrells
100 Courthouse Square
Room 010
Cumming, GA 30040
770-781-2120

Franklin County
Melissa Blakely
Holbrooke
P.O. Box 70
Carnesville, GA 30521
706-384-2514

Fulton County
Cathlene Robinson
136 Pryor Street, SW
Room 106
Atlanta, GA 30303
404-730-5313

Gilmer County
Glenda Sue Johnson
1 Westside Square
Ellijay, GA 30540
706-635-4462

Glascock County
Carla Stevens
P.O. Box 231
Gibson, GA 30810
706-598-2084

Glynn County
Lola Jamsky
P.O. Box 1355
Brunswick, GA 31521
912-554-7272

Gordon County
Brian Brannon
100 Wall Street,
Suite 102
Calhoun, GA 30701
706-629-9533

Grady County
Annette H. Alred
250 North Broad Street
Box 8
Cairo, GA 39828
229-377-2912

Greene County
Deborah D. Jackson
113 East North Main
Street
Suite 109
Greensboro, GA 30642
706-453-3340

Gwinnett County
Tom Lawler
P.O. Box 880
Lawrenceville, GA 30046
770-822-8100

Habersham County
David Wall
555 Monroe Street
Unit 35
Clarkesville, GA 30523
706-754-2923

Hall County
Dwight S. Wood
P.O. Box 336
Gainesville, GA 30503
770-531-7025

Hancock County
Leroy S. Wiley
P.O. Box 451
Sparta, GA 31087
706-444-6644

Haralson County
Dorthy Parker
P.O. Drawer 849
Buchanan, GA 30113
770-646-2005

Harris County
Staci K. Haralson
P.O. Box 528
Hamilton, GA 31811
706-628-4944

Hart County
William E. Holland, III
P.O. Box 386
Hartwell, GA 30643
706-376-7189

Heard County
Bryan Owensby
P.O. Box 249
Franklin, GA 30217
706-675-3301

Henry County
Judy Lewis
One Courthouse Square
McDonough, GA 30253
770-954-2121

Houston County
Carolyn V. Sullivan
201 Perry Parkway
Perry, GA 31069
478-218-4720

Irwin County
Nancy Ross
113 North Irwin Avenue
Ocilla, GA 31774
229-468-5356

Jackson County
Camie W. Thomas
P.O. Box 7
Jefferson, GA 30549
706-387-6255

Jasper County
Dan Jordan
126 West Green Street
Suite 110
Monticello, GA 31064
706-468-4901

Jeff Davis County
Myra Murphy
P.O. Box 429
Hazelhurst, GA 31539
912-375-6615

Jefferson County
Michael R. Jones
P.O. Box 151
Louisville, GA 30434
478-625-7922

Jenkins County
Elizabeth T. Landing
P.O. Box 659
Millen, GA 30442
478-982-4683

Johnson County
Patricia Glover
P.O. Box 321
Wrightsville, GA 31096
478-864-3484

Jones County
Bart W. Jackson
P.O. Box 39
Gray, GA 31032
478-986-6671

Lamar County
Robert F. Abbott
326 Thomaston Street
Box 7
Barnesville, GA 30204
770-358-5145

Lanier County
Martha B. Neugent
100 Main Street
Lakeland, GA 31635
229-482-3594

Laurens County
Allen Thomas
P.O. Box 2028
Dublin, GA 31040
478-272-3210

Lee County
Sondra Cook
P.O. Box 49
Leesburg, GA 31763
229-759-6018

Liberty County
F. Barry Wilkes
100 Main Street
Courthouse Square
Hinesville, GA 31313
912-876-3625

Lincoln County
Bruce C. Beggs
P.O. Box 340
Lincolnton, GA 30817
706-359-5505

Long County
Frank S. Middleton
P.O. Box 458
Ludowici, GA 31316
912-545-2123

Lowndes County
Sara L. Crow
P.O. Box 1349
Valdosta, GA 31603
229-333-5126

Lumpkin County
Edward E. Tucker
99 Courthouse Hill
Suite D
Dahlonega, GA 30533
706-864-3736

Macon County
Juanita Laidler
P.O. Box 337
Ogelthorpe, GA 31068
478-472-7661

Madison County
Michelle H. Strickland
P.O. Box 247
Danielsville, GA 30633
706-795-6310

Marion County
Joy Smith
P.O. Box 41
Buena Vista, GA 31803
229-649-7321

McDuffie County
Connie H. Cheatham
P.O. Box 158
Thomson, GA 30824
706-595-2134

McIntosh County
Bootie W. Goodrich
P.O. Box 1661
Darien, GA 31305
912-437-6641

Meriwether County
Louise T. Garrett
P.O. Box 160
Greenville, GA 30222
706-672-4416

Miller County
Annie L. Middleton
P.O. Box 66
Colquitt, GA 31737
229-758-4102

Mitchell County
Adayna B. Broome
P.O. Box 427
Camilla, GA 31730
229-336-2022

Monroe County
Lynn W. Ham
P.O. Box 450
Forsyth, GA 31029
478-994-7022

Montgomery County
Keith Hamilton
P.O. Box 311
Mount Vernon, GA
30445
912-583-4401

Morgan County
Jody M. Moss
P.O. Drawer 551
Madison, GA 30650
706-342-3605

Murray County
Loreine P. Mathews
P.O. Box 1000
Chatsworth, GA 30705
706-695-2932

Muscogee County
Linda Pierce
P.O. Box 2145
Columbus, GA 31902
706-653-4353

Newton County
Linda Dalton Hays
1132 Usher Street
Room 338
Covington, GA 30014
770-784-2035

Oconee County
Angie Watson
P.O. 1099
Watkinsville, GA 30677
706-769-3940

Oglethorpe County
Geneva G. Stamey
P.O. Box 68
Lexington, GA 30648
706-743-5731

Paulding County
Treva Shelton
11 Courthouse Square
Room G-3
Dallas, GA 30132
770-443-7527

Peach County
Joe Wilder
P.O. Box 389
Fort Valley, GA 31030
478-825-5331

Pickens County
Gail Brown
P.O. Box 130
Jasper, GA 30143
706-253-8763

Pierce County
Thomas W. Sauls
P.O. Box 588
Blackshear, GA 31516
912-449-2020

Pike County
Carolyn Williams
P.O. Box 10
Zebulon, GA 30295
770-567-2000

Polk County
Sheila Wells
P.O. Box 948
Cedartown, GA 30125
770-749-2114

Pulaski County
Peggy G. Fauscett
P.O. Box 60
Hawkinsville, GA 31036
478-783-1911

Putnam County
Sheila H. Layson
100 South Jefferson
Avenue
Suite 236
Eatonton, GA 31024
706-485-4501

Quitman County
Rebecca S. Fendley
P.O. Box 307
Georgetown, GA 39854
229-334-2578

Rabun County
Holly Henry-Perry
25 Courthouse Square
Suite 105
Clayton, GA 30525
706-782-3615

Randolph County
Kay Arnold
P.O. Box 98
Cuthbert, GA 38840
229-732-2216

Richmond County
Elaine C. Johnson
P.O. Box 2046
Augusta, GA 30903
706-821-2460

Rockdale County
Joanne P. Caldwell
P.O. Box 937
Conyers, GA 30012
770-929-4021

Schley County
Kathy S. Royal
P.O. Box 7
Ellaville, GA 31806
229-937-5581

Screven County
Janis Reddick
P.O. Box 156
Sylvannia, GA 30467
912-564-2614

Seminole County
Earlene Bramlett
P.O. Box 672
Donalsonville, GA
39845
229-524-2525

Spalding County
Marcia L. Norris
P.O. Box 1046
Griffin, GA 30224
770-467-4356

Stephens County
Aubre Grafton
205 North Alexander
Street
Room 202
Toccoa, GA 30577
706-886-9496

Stewart County
Patti Smith
P.O. Box 910
Lumpkin, GA 31815
912-838-6220

Sumter County
Nancy Smith
P.O. Box 333
Americus, GA 31709
229-928-4537

Talbot County
Penny Dillingham-
Mahone
P.O. Box 325
Talbotton, GA 31827
706-665-3239

Taliaferro County
Sandra S. Greene
P.O. Box 182
Crawfordville, GA 30631
706-456-2123

Tatnall County
Debbie Crews
P.O. Box 39
Reidsville, GA 30453
912-557-6716

Taylor County
Robert Taunton, Jr.
P.O. Box 248
Butler, GA 31006
478-862-5594

Telfair County
Gene Johnson
128 East Oak Street
Suite 2
McRae, GA 31055
229-868-6525

Terrell County
Louise B. Darley
513 South Main Street
Dawson, GA 31742
229-995-2631

Thomas County
David Hutchings Jr.
P.O. Box 1995
Thomasville, GA 31799
229-225-4108

Tift County
Gwen C. Pate
P.O. Box 354
Tifton, GA 31793
229-386-7816

Toombs County
Chess Fountain
P.O. Box 530
Lyons, GA 30436
912-526-3501

Towns County
Cecil Ray Dye
48 River Street
Suite E
Hiawassee, GA 30546
706-896-2130

Treutlen County
Curtis Rogers Jr.
203 Second Street
South
Suite 307
Sooperton, GA 30457
912-529-4515

Troup County
Jackie Taylor
P.O. Box 866
LaGrange, GA 30241
706-883-1740

Turner County
Linda House
P.O. Box 106
Ashburn, GA 31714
229-567-2011

Twiggs County
Pattie H. Grimsley
P.O. Box 234
Jeffersonville, GA 31044
478-945-3350

Union County
Allen Conley
114 Courthouse Street
Suite 5
Blairsville, GA 30512
706-439-6022

Upson County
Nancy B. Adams
P.O. Box 469
Thomaston, GA 30286
706-647-7835

Walker County
Bill McDaniel
P.O. Box 448
LaFayette, GA 30728
706-638-1742

Walton County
Kathy K. Trost
303 South Hammond
Drive
Suite 335
Monroe, GA 30655
770-267-1307

Ware County
Melba H. Fiveash
P.O. Box 776
Waycross, GA 31502
912-287-4340

Warren County
Shirley Cheeley
P.O. Box 227
Warrenton, GA 30828
706-465-2262

Washington County
Joy H. Conner
P.O. Box 231
Sandersville, GA 31082
478-522-3186

Wayne County
Stetson Bennett Jr.
P.O. Box 918
Jessup, GA 31598
912-427-5930

Webster County
Tina Blankenship
P.O. Box 117
Preston, GA 31824
229-828-3525

Wheeler County
Michael Morrison
P.O. Box 38
Alamo, GA 30411
912-568-7137

White County
Dena M. Adams
59 South Main Street
Suite B
Cleveland, GA 30528
706-865-2613

Whitfield County
Melica Kendrick
205 North Selvidge
Street
Dalton, GA 30720
706-275-7450

Wilcox County
Wanda F. Hawkins
103 North Broad Street
Abbeville, GA 31001
229-467-2442

Wilkes County
Mildred Peeler
23 East Court Street
Room 205
Washington, GA 30673
706-678-2423

Wilkinson County
Cinda S. Bright
P.O. Box 250
Irwinton, GA 31042
229-946-2221

Worth County
Joann Powell
201 North Main Street
Room 13
Sylvester, GA 31791
229-776-8205

Appendix B: Tax Timetable

The information in this appendix is a handy tax timetable that you can use for a quick reference of when common federal and Georgia tax obligations must be met. The table is based on your business tax year being the same as a calendar year. If your tax year starts and ends other than on January 1st and December 31st, respectively, you will need to adjust the dates given.

TAX TIMETABLE

Georgia   Federal

	Sales	Unem-ployment	G-7 Withholding	Income Tax	Est. Payment	Annual Return	Form 941	Misc.
JAN.	20th				15th		31st	31st 940 W-2 508 1099
FEB.	20th		28th	W-2s & 1099s				28th W-3
MAR.	20th					15th Corp. & Partnership		
APR.	20th	30th	30th	1st	15th	15th Personal	30th	31st 508
MAY	20th							
JUN.	20th							
JUL.	20th	31st	31st				31st	31st 508
AUG.	20th							
SEP.	20th				15th			
OCT.	20th	31st	31st				31st	31st 508
NOV.	20th							
DEC.	20th							

Appendix C: Sample, Filled-In Forms

This appendix contains forms that have been completed. These samples can give you assistance as you begin to complete specific forms to start your own business. Not all of the blank forms from Appendix D are included here as a sample.

STATE OF GEORGIA
COUNTY OF_____Cherokee_____

AFFIDAVIT TO REGISTER TRADE NAME
(Individual)

Personally, before the undersigned attesting officer authorized by law to administer oaths, appeared_____Henrietta DePeony_____ (name of applicant), who, after being first duly sworn, deposes an oath and says that he or she operates an enterprise that is located at _____5678 Forsythe Rd., Woodstock, GA 30188_____ (legal business address), and is trading under the name "_____Nature's Gardens Plus_____" (tradename), at the same address, and the nature of the enterprise is _____nursery & florist_____ (general nature of business), and any related activities to the foregoing, all under the laws of the State of Georgia.

This affidavit is made in compliance with OCGA § 10-1-490, *et seq.* this _____02-04-2007_____ (date).

_____*Henrietta DePeony*_____

_____Henrietta DePeony_____ (Name)

Sworn to and subscribed
before me this _4th day of February, 2007_____
_*John Z. Public*_____
Notary Public

STATE OF GEORGIA
COUNTY OF __Cherokee_____

AFFIDAVIT TO REGISTER TRADE NAME
(Business)

Personally, before the undersigned attesting officer authorized by law to administer oaths, appeared_____Henrietta DePeony_____ (name of applicant), who is _____co-owner_____ (title) of __Peony & Setti, Inc._____ (legal business name) who, after being first duly sworn, deposes an oath and says that _____Peony & Setti, Inc._____ (legal business name), which is located at __5678 Forsythe Rd., Woodstock, GA 30188_____ (legal business address), and is trading under the name "_____Nature's Garden Plus_____" (tradename), at the same address, and the nature of same is _____nursery & florist_____ (general nature of business), and any related activities to the foregoing, all under the laws of the State of Georgia.

This affidavit is made in compliance with OCGA § 10-1-490, *et seq.* this __02/04/2007____ _____(date).

Henrietta DePeony
Henrietta DePeony_____ (Name)

Sworn to and subscribed
before me this __4th day of February, 2007_____

*John Z. Public*_____
Notary Public

CATHY COX
Secretary of State

OFFICE OF SECRETARY OF STATE
CORPORATIONS DIVISION
Suite 315, West Tower, 2 Martin Luther King Jr., Drive
Atlanta, Georgia 30334-1530
(404) 656-2861
Trademark Search and Status Information on the Internet
http://www.sos.state.ga.us/corporations/marksearch.htm

WARREN H. RARY
Director

CURTIS A. WISE
Trademark Administrator

APPLICATION FOR REGISTRATION
TRADEMARK OR SERVICE MARK

DO NOT WRITE IN SHADED AREA - SOS USE ONLY

DOCKET # _____	REGISTRATION # _____	MARK VERIFICATION _____
DOCKET CODE _____	DATE FILED _____	AMOUNT RECEIVED _____	CHECK/ RECEIPT # _____

NOTICE TO APPLICANT: PRINT PLAINLY OR TYPE REMAINDER OF THIS FORM.

In compliance with the requirements of O.C.G.A. §10-1-442, the undersigned, having adopted and used a Trademark or Service Mark in this state for the purposes provided in the Code Chapter and desiring to file the same for public record in the Office of the Secretary of State of Georgia, does hereby certify the following:

1. Henrietta DePeony
    Name of Applicant

2. 5678 Forsythe Road   Woodstock   Georgia   30188
    Principal Business Address   City   State   Zip Code

3. If applicant is a corporation, please indicate the state of incorporation: Georgia

4. Describe the mark. The description you provide is the way the mark will be registered. (See General instructions) *(Attach additional sheet if necessary)*
    Hand-drawn peonies, poinsettias, and hyacinth surrounded by hand-drawn ivy, philodendron, and covered by a banner reading "Nature's Gardens Plus."

5. (A) If a trademark, what goods are offered or sold under the mark? OR (B) If a service mark, what services are provided under the mark?
    plants & flowers

6. Class No: 50   (A separate application must be filed for each class in which a registration of the mark is sought.)

7. Date of first use of the mark by applicant, predecessor, or licensee. (Give Month, Day and Year)
    (A) anywhere: January 12, 2007   (B) In Georgia: January 12, 2007

8. The applicant is the owner of the mark described herein and, to the best of his/her knowledge, no other person except the applicant has the right to use such mark in this State either in its identical form or in such near resemblance thereto as to be likely to cause confusion or mistake, or to deceive.
    Signature of Applicant *Henrietta DePeony*   Print Name   Henrietta DePeony
    Official Title (If signing for a corporation) president   Phone Number _____

Mail or deliver to the Secretary of State, at the above address, the following:
1) This COMPLETED application.
2) Three (3) specimens of the mark as currently used. (May be 3 samples of the same specimen. If Trademark, should be actual label or packaging used on product. If Service mark, should be advertising such as newspaper ad, brochure, etc. depicting the service rendered.)
3) A filing fee of $15.00 payable to Secretary of State. Filing fees are NON-refundable.

STATE OF Georgia
COUNTY OF Cherokee

Sworn to and subscribed before me this _____ Day of _____ 20, _____

_____   My Commission Expires _____
NOTARY PUBLIC

FORM TMAPPL

INSTRUCTIONS FOR COMPLETING TRADEMARK/SERVICE MARK APPLICATION

A **non-refundable** filing fee of $15.00 must accompany each application for registration of a trademark or service mark. This is an examination fee. Even if the mark is not registrable, fees are not refundable. Make checks or money orders payable to Secretary of State. The application must be accompanied by three (3) specimens of the mark as currently used. Three samples of the same specimen are acceptable. We strongly encourage you to submit specimens that are suitable for being placed in a legal-size file folder. If specimens are bulky or of value, i.e. jewelry, t-shirts, caps, etc., we ask that you take and submit photographs of the actual specimens. The photos should clearly and legibly depict the mark along with all material pertinent to the registration. Also, if color is a feature of the mark, then specimens reflecting the **actual** color(s) must be submitted.

Acceptable "Trademark" Specimens—For a trademark, the specimen should be the actual label or packaging used on the product.

Acceptable "Service mark" Specimens—For a service mark, the specimen should be in the form of advertising, such as a newspaper ad, leaflet, brochure, pamphlet, or any material which shows or depicts the mark and denotes the services rendered to the public. To determine whether a service mark specimen is appropriate, consider whether or not a consumer would clearly understand what services are being offered.

The mark MUST ALREADY BE IN USE IN GEORGIA for registration. Goods must already be offered for sale or in distribution in this State in order to register a trademark. Services must already be sold or otherwise rendered in this State in order to register a service mark. (O.C.G.A. 10-1-442) If a name, logo, device, etc. is not already in use, it does not meet the definition of trademark or service mark, and cannot be registered. This office does not search records of Federal registrations and cannot guarantee availability of marks. Registration of your mark provides public notice of YOUR claim to the mark. All questions on the application must be answered, specimens submitted, and the fee attached. PLEASE READ THE FOLLOWING INSTRUCTIONS.

I. Name of Applicant:
List the name of the owner/registrant of the mark. The applicant may be an individual, corporation, or other business entity.

II. Principal Business Address:
List the principal business address of the applicant. The certificate of registration will be mailed to this address unless a cover sheet included with the filing requests otherwise.

III. If Applicant is a Corporation, the State of Incorporation:
This only applies if the applicant is a corporation. List the state of incorporation.

IV. Describe the Mark:
Provide a "literal" description of the mark; simply writing "see attached" is not acceptable. For example, if your mark is 'ABC Shops', then the description should read "the words 'ABC Shops.'" If your mark is "ABC Shops" but includes a logo or design, then the description should read "the words 'ABC Shops'" accompanied by a detailed verbal description of the logo or design. If mark is only a logo or design, then a detailed verbal description of the logo or design must be written. The description must be consistent with how the mark appears in the actual specimens submitted with the application. Again, DO NOT simply attach a copy of the mark and enter "see attached." Also, the description should only include language which is relevant to how the mark is to be registered.

V. a. If a trademark, what goods are offered or sold under the mark?
List the specific goods on which the mark is used. All goods listed in Item 5 must fall within the "class" requested in Item 6. A separate application must be filed to register the goods in an additional class when appropriate. (O.C.G.A. 10-1-443 (a))
b. If a service mark, what services are provided under the mark?
List the specific services provided under the mark. All services listed in Item 5 must fall within the "class" provided in Item 6. A separate application must be filed to register the services in an additional class when appropriate. (O.C.G.A. 10-1-443 (b))
**It is important that you be VERY SPECIFIC when listing the goods or services offered under the mark in Item 5 of the application. The language that the Trademark statute assigns to each class should only be used if it specifically matches the goods or services used in connection with the mark.

VI. Class Number:
List the "class number." This number MUST correspond with the specific goods or services listed in Item 5. List only ONE class per application. If a mark is used in more than one class, it may be registered in more than one class. However, a separate application must be filed for registration in each eligible class. (O.C.G.A. 10-1-443)

VII. Date of First Use of the Mark by Applicant, Predecessor, Licensee:
(a) Anywhere and (b) In Georgia - (give month, day & year)
List the date of first use of the mark "anywhere" and the date of first use of the mark "in Georgia." If the mark has only been used in Georgia, the "date of first use" would be the same both for "anywhere" and "in Georgia". The mark must already be in use in Georgia.

VIII. The Application must be Signed and Notarized:
If applicant is an individual, then the individual must sign. If applicant is a partnership, a general partner must sign. If applicant is a corporation, an officer of the corporation must sign and designate his or her title. An attorney may sign for the applicant by including the statement "Attorney for _____." In any event, the application must be notarized.

The Secretary of State's office will review each application for correctness and will determine the availability of the registration in Georgia. Once an application is approved for registration, a certificate will be issued to the applicant. Registration is effective for ten years. Registration of a trademark or service mark does not prevent another person from registering the name as a trade name in the county where the business is located. It also does not prevent another person from incorporating under the same name. Information on registration of a trade name is obtained from the Clerk of Superior Court of the county in which a business operates. (O.C.G.A. 10-1-490) You may obtain information on the procedures for incorporation by calling (404) 656-2817. The Office of Secretary of State cannot provide legal advice regarding protection of your mark and/or business name. Questions regarding the application process may be answered by calling (404) 656-2861. This is a voice mail line. Calls made before 3:30 p.m. Eastern Standard Time will be returned the same business day.

Classification of Goods and Services

A. GOODS - (for trademark filings only)
1. Raw or partly prepared materials
2. Receptacles
3. Baggage, animal equipment, portfolios and pocketbooks
4. Abrasives
5. Adhesives
6. Chemicals and chemical compositions
7. Cordage
8. Smokers' articles, not including tobacco products
9. Explosives, firearms, equipment and projectiles
10. Fertilizers
11. Ink and inking materials
12. Construction materials
13. Hardware and plumbing and steam-fitting supplies
14. Metals and metal castings and forgings
15. Oils and greases
16. Paints and painters' materials
17. Tobacco products
18. Medicines and pharmaceutical preparations
19. Vehicles
20. Linoleum and oiled cloth
21. Electrical apparatus, machines and supplies
22. Games, toys and sporting goods
23. Cutlery, machinery and tools, and parts thereof
24. Laundry appliances and machines
25. Locks and safes
26. Measuring and scientific appliances
27. Horological instruments
28. Jewelry and precious-metals ware
29. Broom, brushes and dusters
30. Crockery, earthenware and porcelain
31. Filters and refrigerators
32. Furniture and upholstery
33. Glassware
34. Heating, lighting and ventilating apparatus
35. Belting, hose, machinery packing and non-metallic tires
36. Musical instruments and supplies
37. Paper and stationary
38. Prints and publications
39. Clothing
40. Fancy goods, furnishing and notions
41. Canes, parasols and umbrellas
42. Knitted, netted and textile fabrics and substitutes thereof
43. Thread and yarn
44. Dental, medical and surgical appliances
45. Soft drinks and carbonated waters
46. Foods and ingredients of foods
47. Wines
48. Malt beverages and liquors
49. Distilled alcoholic liquors
50. Merchandise not otherwise classified
51. Cosmetics and toilet preparations
52. Detergents and soaps

B. SERVICES - (for service mark filings only)
1. Miscellaneous (i.e., medical or personal type services)
2. Advertising and business (i.e., retail business services)
3. Insurance and financial
4. Construction and repair
5. Communications
6. Transportation and storage
7. Material treatment
8. Education and entertainment

OMB No. 1615-0047; Expires 06/30/08

Department of Homeland Security
U.S. Citizenship and Immigration Services

Form I-9, Employment
Eligibility Verification

Please read instructions carefully before completing this form. The instructions must be available during completion of this form.

ANTI-DISCRIMINATION NOTICE: It is illegal to discriminate against work eligible individuals. Employers CANNOT specify which document(s) they will accept from an employee. The refusal to hire an individual because the documents have a future expiration date may also constitute illegal discrimination.

Section 1. Employee Information and Verification. To be completed and signed by employee at the time employment begins.

Print Name: Last	First	Middle Initial	Maiden Name
REDDENBACHER	MARY	J.	HASSENFUSS

Address (Street Name and Number)	Apt. #	Date of Birth (month/day/year)
1234 LIBERTY LANE		1/26/69

City	State	Zip Code	Social Security #
WOODSTOCK	GA	30188	123-45-6789

I am aware that federal law provides for imprisonment and/or fines for false statements or use of false documents in connection with the completion of this form.

I attest, under penalty of perjury, that I am (check one of the following):
- [X] A citizen or national of the United States
- [ ] A lawful permanent resident (Alien #) A
- [ ] An alien authorized to work until _____
    (Alien # or Admission #)

Employee's Signature	Date (month/day/year)
Mary Reddenbacher	1/29/07

Preparer and/or Translator Certification. *(To be completed and signed if Section 1 is prepared by a person other than the employee.) I attest, under penalty of perjury, that I have assisted in the completion of this form and that to the best of my knowledge the information is true and correct.*

Preparer's/Translator's Signature	Print Name

Address (Street Name and Number, City, State, Zip Code)	Date (month/day/year)

Section 2. Employer Review and Verification. To be completed and signed by employer. Examine one document from List A OR examine one document from List B and one from List C, as listed on the reverse of this form, and record the title, number and expiration date, if any, of the document(s).

List A	OR	List B	AND	List C
Document title: PASSPORT				
Issuing authority: PASSPORT AGENCY WDSTK				
Document #: 123456789				
Expiration Date (if any):				
Document #: 10/5/10				
Expiration Date (if any):				

CERTIFICATION - I attest, under penalty of perjury, that I have examined the document(s) presented by the above-named employee, that the above-listed document(s) appear to be genuine and to relate to the employee named, that the employee began employment on *(month/day/year)* 01/29/07   and that to the best of my knowledge the employee is eligible to work in the United States. (State employment agencies may omit the date the employee began employment.)

Signature of Employer or Authorized Representative	Print Name	Title
Elmer T. Jones	Elmer T. Jones	president

Business or Organization Name and Address (Street Name and Number, City, State, Zip Code)	Date (month/day/year)
Fire Sale Auto Parts, Inc. 2345 Main St., Woodstock, GA 30188	01/01/07

Section 3. Updating and Reverification. To be completed and signed by employer.   GA 30188

A. New Name (if applicable)	B. Date of Rehire (month/day/year) (if applicable)

C. If employee's previous grant of work authorization has expired, provide the information below for the document that establishes current employment eligibility.

Document Title:	Document #:	Expiration Date (if any):

I attest, under penalty of perjury, that to the best of my knowledge, this employee is eligible to work in the United States, and if the employee presented document(s), the document(s) I have examined appear to be genuine and to relate to the individual.

Signature of Employer or Authorized Representative	Date (month/day/year)

Form **SS-4** (Rev. July 2007) Department of the Treasury Internal Revenue Service	**Application for Employer Identification Number** (For use by employers, corporations, partnerships, trusts, estates, churches, government agencies, Indian tribal entities, certain individuals, and others.) ▶ See separate instructions for each line. ▶ Keep a copy for your records.	OMB No. 1545-0003 EIN

Type or print clearly.

1	Legal name of entity (or individual) for whom the EIN is being requested		
	John Doe and James Doe		

2	Trade name of business (if different from name on line 1)	3	Executor, administrator, trustee, "care of" name
	Doe Company		

4a	Mailing address (room, apt., suite no. and street, or P.O. box)	5a	Street address (if different) (Do not enter a P.O. box.)
	123 Main Street		

4b	City, state, and ZIP code (if foreign, see instructions)	5b	City, state, and ZIP code (if foreign, see instructions)
	Woodstock, GA 30188		

6	County and state where principal business is located
	Woodstock, GA

7a	Name of principal officer, general partner, grantor, owner, or trustor	7b	SSN, ITIN, or EIN
	John Doe		123-45-6789

8a Is this application for a limited liability company (LLC) (or a foreign equivalent)? . . . . ☐ Yes ☐ No   **8b** If 8a is "Yes," enter the number of LLC members . . . . ▶

8c If 8a is "Yes," was the LLC organized in the United States? . . . . ☐ Yes ☐ No

9a Type of entity (check only one box). **Caution.** If 8a is "Yes," see the instructions for the correct box to check.

- [X] Sole proprietor (SSN) 123 456 7890
- [ ] Partnership
- [ ] Corporation (enter form number to be filed) ▶
- [ ] Personal service corporation
- [ ] Church or church-controlled organization
- [ ] Other nonprofit organization (specify) ▶
- [ ] Other (specify) ▶

- [ ] Estate (SSN of decedent)
- [ ] Plan administrator (TIN)
- [ ] Trust (TIN of grantor)
- [ ] National Guard [ ] State/local government
- [ ] Farmers' cooperative [ ] Federal government/military
- [ ] REMIC [ ] Indian tribal governments/enterprises
- Group Exemption Number (GEN) if any ▶

9b	If a corporation, name the state or foreign country (if applicable) where incorporated	State	Foreign country

10 Reason for applying (check only one box)

- [X] Started new business (specify type) ▶ clothing manufacturing
- [ ] Hired employees (Check the box and see line 13.)
- [ ] Compliance with IRS withholding regulations
- [ ] Other (specify) ▶

- [ ] Banking purpose (specify purpose) ▶
- [ ] Changed type of organization (specify new type) ▶
- [ ] Purchased going business
- [ ] Created a trust (specify type) ▶
- [ ] Created a pension plan (specify type) ▶

11	Date business started or acquired (month, day, year). See instructions. 10-15-2007	12	Closing month of accounting year December

14 Do you expect your employment tax liability to be $1,000 or less in a full calendar year? ☐ Yes ☐ No (If you expect to pay $4,000 or less in total wages in a full calendar year, you can mark "Yes.")

13 Highest number of employees expected in the next 12 months (enter -0- if none).

Agricultural	Household	Other

15 First date wages or annuities were paid (month, day, year). **Note.** If applicant is a withholding agent, enter date income will first be paid to nonresident alien (month, day, year) . . . . ▶ 10-22-07

16 Check **one** box that best describes the principal activity of your business.

- [ ] Construction [ ] Rental & leasing [ ] Transportation & warehousing
- [ ] Real estate [ ] Manufacturing [ ] Finance & insurance
- [ ] Health care & social assistance [ ] Wholesale-agent/broker
- [ ] Accommodation & food service [ ] Wholesale-other [ ] Retail
- [ ] Other (specify)

17 Indicate principal line of merchandise sold, specific construction work done, products produced, or services provided.

clothing manufacturing

18 Has the applicant entity shown on line 1 ever applied for and received an EIN? ☐ Yes [X] No

If "Yes," write previous EIN here ▶

Third Party Designee	Complete this section **only** if you want to authorize the named individual to receive the entity's EIN and answer questions about the completion of this form.	
	Designee's name	Designee's telephone number (include area code) ( )
	Address and ZIP code	Designee's fax number (include area code) ( )

Under penalties of perjury, I declare that I have examined this application, and to the best of my knowledge and belief, it is true, correct, and complete.

		Applicant's telephone number (include area code)
Name and title (type or print clearly) ▶ John Doe, Partner		(518) 555-0000
Signature ▶ *John Doe*	Date ▶ 10/15/07	Applicant's fax number (include area code) ( )

For Privacy Act and Paperwork Reduction Act Notice, see separate instructions.   Cat. No. 16055N   Form **SS-4** (Rev. 7-2007)

GEORGIA DEPARTMENT OF LABOR
SUITE 850 - 148 ANDREW YOUNG INTERNATIONAL BLVD NE - ATLANTA, GA 30303-1751

EMPLOYER STATUS REPORT

READ INSTRUCTIONS ON REVERSE SIDE
BEFORE COMPLETION OF FORM

1. ENTER OR CORRECT BUSINESS NAME AND ADDRESS

Jones Enterprises, Inc.
d/b/a Fire Sale Auto Parts
2345 Main Street
Woodstock, GA 30188

RETURN ORIGINAL WITHIN 10 DAYS

GEORGIA DOL ACCOUNT NUMBER (If already assigned) ☐☐☐☐☐ – ☐☐

3. TRADE NAME
Fire Sale Auto Parts

2. TYPE OF ORGANIZATION
☐ Individual ☐ Partnership ☒ Corporation ☐ Nonprofit org.
☐ Limited Liability CO. (LLC)
☐ Other (specify) _____

4. PRINCIPAL BUSINESS, FARM OR HOUSEHOLD LOCATION IN GEORGIA (Do not use a P. O. Box number)

Street Address
2345 Main Street

City		Zip Code	County	Telephone Number
Woodstock	GA	30188	Cherokee	(770) 421-6677

5. DATE FIRST BEGAN EMPLOYING WORKERS WITHIN STATE OF GA. 01/01/07
DATE OF FIRST GA. PAYROLL 01/15/07

6. ARE YOU LIABLE FOR FEDERAL UNEMPLOYMENT TAX? Yes ☐ No ☒

FEDERAL I.D. NUMBER 5 8 – 1 1 7 1 1 8 8

7. HAVE YOU...

Acquired another business? Yes ☐ No ☒

Merged with another business? Yes ☐ No ☒

Formed a corporation or partnership? Yes ☒ No ☐

Made any other change in the ownership of your business? Yes ☐ No ☒   If yes, explain _____

DATE ACQUIRED OR CHANGED

PREDECESSOR'S GEORGIA DOL ACCOUNT NUMBER ☐☐☐☐☐☐ – ☐☐

DOES THE FORMER OWNER CONTINUE TO HAVE EMPLOYEES? Yes ☐ No ☐

DID YOU ACQUIRE...
☒ All of Georgia operations?
☐ Substantially all of Georgia operations (90% or more)
☐ Part of Georgia operations (less than 90%)

FROM WHOM? (Organization name, including trade name)   ADDRESS

8. IF YOU HAD PRIVATE BUSINESS EMPLOYMENT:
Did you, or do you expect to employ at least one worker in 20 different calendar weeks during a calendar year? Yes * ☒ No ☐
* If yes, show date the 20th week first occurred: 05/05/03

Did you, or do you expect to have a quarterly payroll of $1,500 or more? Yes * ☒ No ☐
* If yes, show date this first occurred: 05/05/03

11. IF YOU ARE A NONPROFIT ORGANIZATION EXEMPT FROM INCOME TAX UNDER IRS CODE 501 (C)(3): Yes * ☐ No ☐
Did you, or do you expect to employ four or more workers in 20 different calendar weeks during a calendar year? (ATTACH COPY OF 501(C)(3) EXEMPTION LETTER)
* If yes, show date the 20th week first occurred:

9. IF YOU HAD DOMESTIC EMPLOYMENT:
Did you, or do you expect to pay cash wages of $1,000 or more in any calendar quarter? Yes* ☐ No ☒
* If yes, show date this first occurred:

10. IF YOU HAD AGRICULTURAL EMPLOYMENT:
Did you, or do you expect to employ 10 or more agricultural workers in 20 different calendar weeks during a calendar year? Yes* ☐ No ☒
* If yes, show date the 20th week first occurred:

Did you, or do you expect to have a gross cash agricultural payroll of $20,000 or more in any calendar quarter? Yes* ☐ No ☐
* If yes, show date this first occurred:

12. HOW MANY EMPLOYEES do you have, (or anticipate when in full operation)? 12

INFORMATION ABOUT OWNER, ALL PARTNERS, OR PRINCIPAL OFFICER (ATTACH ADDITIONAL SHEET, OR SHEETS, IF NECESSARY)

Name
Elmer T. Jones

Social Security Number
2 5 5 – 3 3 – 1 2 3 4

Residence Address
7955 Lucy Lane

City
Woodstock

State	Zip Code
GA	30188

Telephone
(770) 421-6677

INFORMATION ABOUT PERSON OR FIRM WHO MAINTAINS FINANCIAL RECORDS OF BUSINESS

Name
Mary Reddenbacher

Address
1234 Liberty Lane

City
Woodstock

State	Zip Code	Telephone
GA	30188	(770) 421-6677

CERTIFICATION: I hereby certify under penalties of perjury, that the foregoing statement and those contained in any attached sheets signed by me are true and correct, and that I am authorized to execute this report on behalf of the employing unit. This report must be signed by owner, partner or principal officer.

Signature	Title	Date
Elmer T. Jones	president	01/01/07

PLEASE COMPLETE INDUSTRY INFORMATION ON REVERSE SIDE.

DOL-1A (R-5/05)
TA489A

(CONTINUED)

NATURE OF BUSINESS: Information is required on all items. Attach additional sheets, if necessary.

A. How many Georgia locations do you operate?
Provide the following information for each location, attaching additional sheets if necessary.

B. Check the box that best describes the industry that relates to your business activities:

☐ Agriculture
☐ Forestry
☐ Fishing
☐ Mining
☐ Construction (specify):
___General Contractors Industrial_____ %
 Residential___% Commercial_____ %
___Speculative Building
___Special Trade Contractor (specify plumbing, etc.,)_____
___Heavy Construction (specify cable, highway, etc.,)_____

☐ Manufacturing
☐ Transportation
☐ Communication
☐ Public Utilities
☐ Wholesale Trade
☐ Retail Trade
☐ Finance
☐ Insurance
☐ Real Estate
☐ Services
☐ Public Administration
☐ Private Household
☐ Employer

C. Enter in order of importance and indicate approximate % of total annual income derived from each:

Principal Service(s) Rendered* **OR** Principal Product(s) ☐ Mfg. ☐ Grown ☐ Sold

_____ _____%
_____ _____%
_____ _____%

* If Transportation - Trucking, indicate if interstate carrier

D. If this report includes establishment(s) that only perform services for other units of the company, indicate the primary type of service or support provided. Check as many as apply:

1. ☐ Central Administration   3. ☐ Storage (warehouse)
2. ☐ Research, development,   4. ☐ Other: (specify)
   and testing   _____

FOR ASSISTANCE, call the Industry Classification Unit, (800) 338-2082

IMPORTANT - This report must be filed! The law provides that all employing units shall file a report of its employment during a calendar year. For the purpose of aiding you in complying with OCGA Section 34-8-121 of the Employment Security law, this form has been prepared to assist you in furnishing the required information. Answer all questions fully and if additional space is necessary under any item, attach signed and dated sheets which bear the words Supplement to Form DOL-1."

Each false statement or willful failure to furnish this report is punishable as a crime. Each day of such failure or refusal constitutes a separate offense.

The Georgia Employer Status Report is required of all employers having individuals performing services in Georgia regardless of number or duration of time.

The filing of this form is required at the time your business first had individuals performing service in Georgia, or when you acquired another legal entity, and may also be required again upon request.

NOTE: Disclosure of your social security number is mandatory. It will be used for the purpose of identification and it is required under the authority of 42 U.S.C. Section 405(2)(c) and OCGA Section 34-8-121(a).

INSTRUCTIONS
(NUMBERS CORRESPOND TO ITEMS ON FORM)

1. Enter or correct name and address of individual owner, partners, corporation or organization. This is the address to which you authorize us to mail all reports, correspondence, etc. If you have already been assigned a Georgia Department of Labor Account Number (Ga. DOL Acct. No) by this Department, please insert the number.
2. Indicate by check mark type of organization. If a nonprofit organization, attach copy of I.R.S. letter exempting the organization from Federal Income Tax under Section 501(c)(3)of Internal Revenue Code.
3. Trade name by which business is known if different than 1.
4. Physical location of business, farm or household in Georgia if different than 1. Please include telephone number with area code.
5. Enter the first date of employment in Georgia and the first date of Georgia payroll.
6. If you are subject to the Federal Unemployment Tax Act, and are required to file Federal Form 940, answer this question "yes". Be sure to enter your Federal Employer Identification Number whether answered "yes" or "no".
7. Answer this question if you acquired this business from another employer or if after you began employing workers you have acquired other businesses; merged with other businesses; formed or dissolved partnerships, corporations, professional associations; or if any other change in the ownership of the business has occurred. Indicate the date of acquisition or change and provide all information concerning the previous owner's name, trade name, address and DOL Account Number. Indicate by checking the appropriate block the portion of the previous owner's business involved in the acquisition or change. No transfer of experience rating history can be made unless information concerning the previous owner is provided.
8. Private Business Employment - Most employment is considered private business employment. This includes all types of work except domestic service such as maids, gardeners, cooks, etc., agricultural service and service performed for governmental or nonprofit organizations.
9. Domestic employment includes all service for a person in the operation and maintenance of a private household, local college club or local chapter of a college fraternity or sorority such as chauffeurs, cooks, babysitters, gardeners, maids, butlers, private and/or social secretaries, etc. If you had such employment, consider only cash payments made to all individuals performing domestic services to determine if $1,000 or more cash wages were paid in any calendar quarter during 1977 and subsequent quarters.
10. Consider only cash payments made to all individuals performing agricultural services to determine if $20,000 or more cash wages were paid in any calendar quarter during 1977 and subsequent quarters.
11. Answer this question only if this business is a nonprofit organization exempt from Federal Income Tax under Section 501(c)(3) of the Internal Revenue Code. Attach a copy of the I.R.S. letter granting this exemption. Nonprofit organizations with tax exemptions other than under Section 501(c)(3) should answer question 8, Private Business Employment.
12. Self-explanatory.

FOR ASSISTANCE, call the Adjudication Section, (404) 232-3301.

Please RETAIN a copy for your files.

RETURN ORIGINAL WITHIN TEN (10) DAYS TO:

Georgia Department of Labor
P. O. Box 740234
Atlanta, GA 30374-0234

The enclosed envelope requires postage.

CRF-002 (Rev. 9/07)
GEORGIA DEPARTMENT OF REVENUE
REGISTRATION & LICENSING UNIT
P. O. BOX 49512
ATLANTA, GEORGIA 30359-1512
Fax: 404-417-4317 OR 404-417-4318
NEED HELP? CALL (404) 417-4490

E-MAIL: TSD-sales-tax-lic@dor.ga.gov

(PLEASE PRINT OR TYPE)

STATE TAX REGISTRATION APPLICATION
(Please Read Instructions Before Completing)

	IDENTIFICATION SECTION	
1	IF YOU HAVE A STATE TAXPAYER IDENTIFIER (STI), ENTER HERE:	
2	REASON FOR APPLICATION [X] New Business [ ] Additional Tax Registration	

2 [ ] Application for a Master Number (4 or more Locations)   [ ] Change in Ownership Structure   [ ] Change in Alcohol Licensee*
[ ] Change in Location Address (Alcohol Only)*
[ ] New Location for a Master Sales Tax Account   Master Sales Tax Number :

3 FOR WHICH OF THE FOLLOWING ARE YOU APPLYING?
[X] Sales and Use Tax   [ ] Withholding Tax   [ ] Non-Resident Distribution
[ ] Alcohol License *   [ ] Amusement License *   [ ] Tobacco License*
[ ] Motor Fuel Distributor *   [ ] e-File/e-Pay Bulk Filer

Applications with an asterisk (*) require an additional application – See instructions for details

(If your business is a Sole Proprietorship – Your Name is the Legal Business Name)

4 LEGAL BUSINESS NAME Jones Enterprises, Inc.

5 TRADE NAME / DBA NAME Fire Sale Auto Parts, Inc.

6 TYPE OF OWNERSHIP   [ ] Sole Proprietorship   [ ] County Government   [ ] State Agency
[ ] Estate   [ ] Partnership   [ ] Municipality   [ ] Federal Agency
[ ] Fiduciary   [X] Subchapter S Corp. [ ] Professional Association   [ ] LLC
[ ] Corporation   State of Inc. Georgia   Date of Incorporation 02 / 04 / 07

7 IF THE BUSINESS LISTED ABOVE HAS A "Federal Employer ID" NUMBER, ENTER HERE: 58-117118

8 IF SEASONAL BUSINESS, STATE MONTHS BUSINESS WILL BE OPEN: Begin   Thru

9 WHAT IS THE LAST MONTH AND DAY OF YOUR ACCOUNTING YEAR: Month Dec.   Day 31

10 Which ACCOUNTING METHOD WILL YOU USE?   [ ] Cash Basis   [X] Accrual Basis

11 IF THIS APPLICATION IS FOR A BUSINESS YOU PURCHASED, PROVIDE THE FOLLOWING INFORMATION REGARDING THE FORMER OWNER, IF KNOWN.
Legal Business Name   State Tax Identifier:

Georgia Sales Tax Number: Georgia Withholding Tax Number: Alcohol License:

	ADDRESS SECTION	

12 PHYSICAL LOCATION ADDRESS, NUMBER AND STREET, SUITE/APARTMENT NUMBER (**YOU CANNOT use a P.O. Box**)
USING A POST OFFICE BOX FOR THIS ADDRESS WILL DELAY PROCESSING OF THIS APPLICATION.
NUMBER AND STREET ADDRESS
2345 Main Street

CITY	STATE	ZIP CODE	COUNTY	COUNTRY
Woodstock	GA	30188	Cherokee	U.S.A.

13 PHONE 770-421-6677   FAX   E-MAIL

14 IS THE ABOVE ADDRESS LOCATED WITHIN THE CITY LIMITS?   [X] Yes   [ ] No

NOTE: To have correspondence and reporting forms sent to separate addresses, please complete Lines 15 and 16 and indicate the related tax type(s) for each. To list additional mailing addresses use Form CRF-003.

15 MAILING ADDRESS – IF DIFFERENT FROM THE LOCATION ADDRESS ON LINE 12 ABOVE.
(Please identify tax type(s) to be mailed to the address below.)

A [ ] Sales and Use   [ ] Withholding   [ ] Amusement   [ ] Alcohol [ ] Tobacco [ ] Motor Fuel Distributor

B ADDRESSEE (c/o) (If different from or in addition to the Legal Business Name)   E-MAIL ADDRESS

C NUMBER AND STREET, P. O. BOX or RFD NO.

D	CITY	STATE	ZIP CODE	COUNTY	COUNTRY

E PHONE   FAX

16 ADDITIONAL MAILING ADDRESS – (Please identify tax type(s) to be mailed to the address below.)

A [ ] Sales and Use   [ ] Withholding   [ ] Amusement   [ ] Alcohol [ ] Tobacco [ ] Motor Fuel Distributor

B ADDRESSEE (c/o) (If different from or in addition to the Legal Business Name)   E-MAIL ADDRESS

C NUMBER AND STREET, P. O. BOX or RFD NO.

D	CITY	STATE	ZIP CODE	COUNTY	COUNTRY

E PHONE   FAX

(Please Read Instructions Before Completing)

OWNERSHIP / RELATIONSHIP SECTION
(This section MUST be completed for your application to be accepted.)

17	CHECK ALL THAT APPLY		EFFECTIVE DATE ___/___/___

☐ Owner ☒ Officer ☐ Manager ☐ Tobacco Licensee
☐ Partner ☐ Managing Member ☐ Alcohol Licensee

A	BUSINESS NAME Fire Sale Auto Parts	STI or LICENSE NO. (If Applicable)
B	GA SALES TAX NO. (If Applicable)	GA WITHHOLDING TAX NO. (If Applicable)
C	LAST NAME: Jones	FIRST: Elmer M.I. T. TITLE: President
D	SOCIAL SECURITY NUMBER 255-98-7654	Application will not be processed unless the social security number of an owner, officers, managing members or both partners is included. Reg. 560-1-1.18
D	ADDRESS 2345 Main Street	
E	CITY: Woodstock STATE: GA ZIP: 30188 COUNTY: Cherokee COUNTRY: U.S.A. PHONE	

18	CHECK ALL THAT APPLY	EFFECTIVE DATE ___/___/___

☐ Owner ☐ Officer ☐ Manager ☐ Tobacco Licensee
☐ Partner ☐ Managing Member ☐ Alcohol Licensee

A	BUSINESS NAME	STI or LICENSE NO. (If Applicable)
B	GA SALES TAX NO. (If Applicable)	GA WITHHOLDING TAX NO. (If Applicable)
C	LAST NAME	FIRST M.I. TITLE
D	SOCIAL SECURITY NUMBER	Application will not be processed unless the social security number of an owner, officers, managing members or both partners is included. Reg. 560-1-1.18
D	ADDRESS	
E	CITY STATE ZIP COUNTY COUNTRY PHONE	

(TO REPORT ADDITIONAL RELATIONSHIPS, USE FORM CRF-004)
SALES AND USE TAX SECTION

19	NATURE OF BUSINESS (If combination of two or more, list approximate percentages of receipts. Must equal 100%.)

☒ Retail 50 % ☐ Manufacturing ___ % ☐ Services (Specify) ___ % _____
☒ Wholesale 50 % ☐ Construction ___ % ☐ Other (Specify) ___ % _____

20	WHAT KIND OF BUSINESS WILL YOU OPERATE? (Be specific as to the product sold or service provided.)
21	DO YOU EXPECT TO REMIT MORE THAN $200 PER MONTH? ☒ Yes ☐ No
22	WILL YOU SELL ALCOHOLIC BEVERAGES? ☐ Yes ** ☒ No ** Additional Forms Required
23	WILL YOU SELL RETAIL TOBACCO PRODUCTS? ☐ Yes ** ☒ No ** Additional Forms Required
24	WILL YOU SELL GASOLINE AND/OR MOTOR FUEL? ☐ Yes ☒ No If "Yes", please specify the name of the dealer responsible for paying the tax on gasoline and/or motor fuel sales, if other than yourself. NAME SALES TAX NO.
25	WHEN DID OR WILL YOU START SELLING OR PURCHASING ITEMS SUBJECT TO SALES TAX? Date ___/___/___
26	WILL YOU SELL LOTTERY AT THIS LOCATION? ☐ Yes ☐ No If "Yes", PLEASE PROVIDE YOUR RETAILER NUMBER_____
27	WILL YOU HAVE EMPLOYEES? ☒ Yes ☐ No If "Yes", complete the following WITHHOLDING TAX SECTION. If "No", stop here and complete the SIGNATURE SECTION.

WITHHOLDING TAX SECTION

28	WHO WILL BE RESPONSIBLE FOR FILING AND REMITTING THE PAYROLL TAXES FOR YOUR EMPLOYEES? ☒ Applicant or Payroll Service Bureau ☐ Other If "Other", list the name and GA. Withholding No. of the business responsible for paying these taxes. NAME GA. WITHHOLDING TAX NO.
29	DO YOU EXPECT TO WITHHOLD MORE THAN $200 PER MONTH? ☒ Yes ☐ No
30	HOW MANY EMPLOYEES DOES THIS BUSINESS HAVE OR WILL HAVE? two
31	DATE ON WHICH WAGES WERE OR WILL FIRST BE PAID? 01/01/07

SIGNATURE SECTION

I HAVE EXAMINED THIS APPLICATION, AND TO THE BEST OF MY KNOWLEDGE IT IS TRUE AND CORRECT

Elmer T. Jones	*President*	01/01/07
Signature	Title	Date

MUST BE SIGNED BY OWNER, PARTNER, MANAGING MEMBER, OR
CORPORATE OFFICER AS LISTED IN THE RELATIONSHIP SECTION (17 OR 18) ABOVE.

ST-5 (REV. 05-00)

STATE OF GEORGIA
DEPARTMENT OF REVENUE
SALES AND USE TAX CERTIFICATE OF EXEMPTION
GEORGIA PURCHASER OR DEALER
EFFECTIVE JULY 1, 2000

To: _____George's Salvage Yard_____   _____January 12, 2007_____
              (SUPPLIER)   (DATE)

_____5774 Junior Road, Woodstock, GA 30188_____
                              (ADDRESS)

THE UNDERSIGNED HEREBY CERTIFIES that all tangible personal property purchased or leased after this date will be for the purpose indicated below, unless otherwise specified on a particular order, and that this certificate shall remain in effect until revoked in writing. Any tangible personal property obtained under this certificate of exemption is subject to the sales and use tax if it is used or consumed by the purchaser in any manner other than indicated on this certificate.
(Check proper box.)

[   ]   1.   Resale, rental or leased only, including but not limited to the purchase for resale of gasoline and other motor fuels.

[X]   2.   Materials for further processing, manufacture or conversion into articles of tangible personal property for resale which will become a component part of the property for sale, or be coated upon or impregnated into the product at any stage of its processing, manufacture or conversion and nonreturnable materials used for packaging tangible personal property for shipment or sale. Containers or other packaging materials purchased for reuse are not exempt.

[   ]   3.   Machinery used directly in the manufacture of tangible personal property for sale purchased as additional, replacement or upgrade machinery to be placed into an existing plant in this State.

[   ]   4.   Direct Pay Permit authorized under Regulation 560-12-1-.16. The holder of a Direct Pay Permit must pay the 3% Second Motor Fuel Tax to suppliers on purchases of gasoline.

[   ]   5.   For use by Federal Government, State Government, any county, municipality or public school system of this State, when supported by official purchase orders or for use by Hospital Authorities created by Article 4, Chapter 7, of Title 7, and County or City Housing Authorities created by Article 1, Chapter 3 of Title 8. The State of Georgia, counties, municipalities, public schools, Hospital and Housing Authorities of Georgia must pay the 3% Second Motor Fuel Tax to suppliers.
          A Georgia Sales and Use Tax Certificate of Registration Number is not required for this exemption.

[   ]   6.   Aircraft, watercraft, motor vehicles and other transportation equipment manufactured or assembled, sold and delivered by the manufacturer or assembler for use exclusively outside this State, or delivery of the crafts is for the sole purpose of removing same under its own power when it does not lend itself more reasonably to removal by other means.
          A Georgia Sales and Use Tax Certificate of Registration Number is not required for this exemption.

[   ]   7.   Aircraft, watercraft, railroad locomotives and rolling stock, motor vehicles and major components of each, which will be used principally to cross the borders of this State in the service of transporting passengers or cargo by common carriers and by carriers who hold common carrier and contract carrier authority in interstate or foreign commerce under authority granted by the United States government. Replacement parts installed by carriers in such craft or vehicles which become an integral part of the craft or vehicle are likewise exempt. Private and contract carriers are not exempt.

_____   _____
(TYPE OF BUSINESS ENGAGED IN BY THE PURCHASER)   (COMMODITY CODE)

I declare, under penalties of false swearing, that this certificate has been examined by me and to the best of my knowledge and belief is true and correct, made in good faith, pursuant to the sales and use tax laws of the State of Georgia.

_____Fire Sale Auto Parts_____   _____345-6987032_____
            (PURCHASER' S FIRM NAME)   (CERTIFICATE OF REGISTRATION NO.)

_____2345 Main Street, Woodstock, GA 30188_____
                                       (ADDRESS)

By _____*Elmer T. Jones*_____   Title _president_____
              (SIGNATURE)   (OWNER, PARTNER, OFFICIAL)

A supplier is required to have only one certificate of exemption form on file from each purchaser buying tax exempt. The supplier must exercise ordinary care to determine that the tangible personal property obtained under this certificate is for the purpose indicated. Suppliers failing to exercise such care will be held liable for the sales tax due on such purchases. For example, a supplier cannot accept a Certificate of Registration number bearing a "214" prefix since these are issued to a Contractor which has been deemed to be the consumer and is required to pay the tax at the time of purchase.

Form **ST-3** (Rev. 01/06)
Georgia Department of Revenue
Sales and Use Tax Division
P.O. Box 105296
Atlanta, Georgia 30348-5296

0702804013

☐ Amended Return
☐ Final Return
☐ One Time Only Sale
☐ EFT Payment

Name and Address

SALES AND USE #
COMMODITY CODE
COUNTY OF BUSINESS REGISTRATION

SALES AND USE TAX REPORT	USE THIS FORM ONLY FOR THE PRINTED PERIOD	To

Part A

		Part B	DEPARTMENT USE ONLY / TAX COLUMN
1. Total Sales	40000.00		
2. Total Use	4000.00		
3. Total Sales and Use	44000.00		**TAX COLUMN**
4. Taxable State Sales & Use	44000.00	---> Tax Rate X .04 =	1760.00
5. Taxable MARTA Sales & Use	31750.00	X .01 =	317.50
6. Taxable Local Option Sales & Use	21000.00	X .01 =	210.00
7. Taxable Other Local Option Sales & Use	0	X .01 =	0
8. Taxable Special Purpose Sales & Use	20000.00	X .01 =	200.00
9. Taxable Educational Sales & Use	0	X .01 =	0
10. Taxable Homestead Sales & Use	21000.00	X .01 =	210.00
11. Total Tax from Tax Column	2697.50	<--Total-->	2697.50
12. Excess Tax: Factor Amount +	0		
13. Total Tax Amount	2697.50		
14. Vendor's Compensation -	150.00		
15. Penalty (Use Penalty Worksheet) +	0		
16. Interest (1% per month or fraction thereof) +	26.98		
17. Previous Prepaid Amount -	2000.50		
18. Current Prepaid Amount +	573.98		
19. Credit (See instructions)	/////////		
20. **Remit This Amount**	1417.46		

SCHEDULE OF TOTAL EXEMPTIONS / DEDUCTIONS

Part C

A. Total State	0
B. Total MARTA	0
C. Total Local	0
D. Total Other Local	0
E. Total Special	0
F. Total Educational	0
G. Total Homestead	0

220

0702804023

Part D

I certify that this return, including the accompanying schedules or statements, has been examined by me and is, to the best of my knowledge and belief, a true and

complete return made in good faith for the period stated. This ___5th___ day of ___April___ , ___2007___

Return Prepared By ___Elmer T. Jones___   Signature ___Elmer T. Jones___   president   (123) 555-1122
                                                                                   Title   Phone Number

This return must be filed and paid by the 20th of the month following the period for which the tax is due to avoid loss of vendor's compensation and the payment of penalty and interest. **DEALERS AND CONTRACTORS MUST FILE A TIMELY RETURN EVEN THOUGH NO TAX IS DUE. DO NOT SEND CASH BY MAIL.**

Remittance by Electronic Funds Transfer (EFT) must be completed by 3:00 p.m. on the 19th. If the 20th is a Saturday, Sunday, Monday or a Federal Holiday the EFT must be completed before 3:00 p.m. on the preceding Friday.

Part E-County Distribution Schedule
Enter the 1% tax reported for each county and tax type

S&U #

County	Code	Homestead	Marta	Other Local Option
DeKalb	044			
Fulton	060			
Rockdale	122			
Towns	139			
City of Atlanta	060			
Total				

County	Code	Local	Special	Educational
DeKalb	044			
Fulton	060			
Rockdale	122			
Towns	139			
Total				

EMPLOYMENT AGREEMENT

THIS EMPLOYMENT AGREEMENT (the "Agreement") is made this __1st__ day of __January__, 20__08__, between __Fire Sales Auto Parts__ a Georgia corporation, and its affiliates, current and future (collectively, the "Corporation") and __Harold Reiser__ (the "Employee").

WITNESSETH

The Employee is a key employee of the Corporation and possesses an intimate knowledge of the business and affairs of the Corporation. The Corporation recognizes the Employee's potential for the growth and success of the Corporation and desires to assure to the Corporation the continued benefits of the Employee's expertise and knowledge. The Employee, in turn, desires to establish and continue in full-time employment with the Corporation on the terms provided herein.

Accordingly, in consideration of the mutual covenants and representations contained herein, the parties hereto agree as follows:

1. **Full-time Employment of Employee**

1.1 **Duties and Status.**

(a) The Corporation hereby engages the Employee as a full-time Employee for the period (the "Employment Period") specified in Section 4, and the Employee accepts such employment, on the terms and conditions set forth in this Agreement. During the Employment Period, the Employee shall exercise such authority and perform such Employee duties as are commensurate with the authority being exercised and duties being performed by the Employee for the Corporation immediately prior to the effective date of this Agreement. The Employee shall hold such position as assigned, being currently the position of __salesman__, or such other titles or positions as are assigned to him by the corporation or its officers.

(b) During the Employment Period, the Employee shall (i) devote his full working time and efforts to the business of the Corporation and will not engage in consulting work or any trade or business for his own account or for or on behalf of any other person, firm or corporation which competes, conflicts or interferes with the performance of his duties hereunder in any way, and (ii) accept such additional office or offices to which he may be elected by Corporation, provided that the performance of the duties of such office or offices shall be consistent with the scope of the duties provided for in subsection (a) of this Section 1.1.

1.2 **Compensation and General Benefits.** As compensation for his services under this Agreement, the Employee shall be compensated as follows:

(a) The Corporation shall pay the Employee an annual salary of __forty thousand__ Dollars ($__40__,000).

(b) The Corporation shall pay the Employee a one-time sign up bonus of $_____, which shall be payable at the time of the first paycheck issued to Employee.

(c) The Corporation shall provide other general benefits such as training, insurance, consistent with the benefits available to similarly situated employees and outlined in the Company Employee Manual.

2. **Competition; Confidential Information.** The Employee and the Corporation recognize that Employee has had access to and has acquired, will have access to and will acquire, and has assisted and may assist in developing confidential and proprietary information relating to the business and operations of the Corporation and its affiliates, including, without limiting the generality of the foregoing,

information with respect to their present and prospective products, systems, customers, agents, processes, and sales and marketing methods. The Employee acknowledges that such information has been and will continue to be of central importance to the business of the Corporation and its affiliates and that disclosure of it to, or its use by, others could cause substantial loss to the Corporation. The Employee accordingly agrees as follows:

2.1 Non-Competition.

(a) The Employee agrees that during his employment by the Corporation and for a period of **TWENTY-FOUR (24) months** following the Employee's termination of such employment or the Corporation's termination of such employment for cause (as defined in section 4.1 below), he will not (except on behalf of or with the prior written consent of the Corporation) within the "Area" and "Industries" defined below, either directly or indirectly, on his own behalf or in the service or on behalf of others engage in any business which sells products or services that are competitive with the products or services provided by the Corporation (any business carrying on such activities being herein called a "Competing Business") in any capacity similar to the capacity or capacities in which the Employee was employed by the Corporation. For purposes of this Agreement the "Area" shall be defined as the State of Georgia, and the "Industries" shall be defined as including 1) _____ and 2) _____. **For purposes of this Agreement "Business of the Company" shall mean: the business of the Company, and the business of its affiliates, current or future. Collectively such businesses shall be referred to as the "Company".**

(b) The Employee further agrees that during his employment by the Corporation and for a period of **TWENTY-FOUR (24)** months following the Employee's termination of such employment or the Corporation's termination of such employment for cause (as defined in section 4.1 below), he will not (except on behalf of or with the prior written consent of the Corporation), either directly or indirectly, on his own behalf or in the service or on behalf of others, (i) solicit or divert or appropriate to a Competing Business, or (ii) attempt to solicit, divert or appropriate to or for any Competing Business, any person or entity whose customer account with the Company was sold or serviced or pursued by or under the supervision of Employee during the term of his employment with the Corporation.

(c) The Employee agrees that during his employment by the Corporation and for a period of **TWENTY-FOUR (24)** months following the Employee's termination of such employment or the Corporation's termination of such employment for cause (as defined in section 4.1 below), he will not, either directly or indirectly, on his own behalf or in the service or on behalf of others solicit, divert or entice, or attempt to solicit, divert or entice, to any Competing Business any person employed by the Corporation, whether or not such employee is a full-time employee or a temporary employee of the Company, and whether or not such employment is pursuant to written agreement and whether or not such employment is for a determined period or is at will. The foregoing shall not apply to solicitation of former employees that have been separated from the Corporation for 6 months or more.

2.2 Confidential Information.

(a)   "Confidential Information" shall mean any and all data and information relating to the Business of the Company which is not a Trade Secret, as hereinafter defined), (i) which is or has been disclosed to the Employee, or of which the Employee became aware as a consequence of or through his employment relationship with the Corporation; and (ii) which has value to the Corporation or the Company and is not generally known by competitors; provided (iii), that no information will be deemed confidential unless such information has been reduced to writing and marked clearly and conspicuously as confidential information, or such information is otherwise treated by the Corporation as confidential, or such information failed to be properly identified and protected as a result the Employee's omission in performing such functions. The Employee, as a key employee of the Corporation, shall have a duty to identify and protect such Confidential Information on behalf of the Corporation.

(b) The Employee agrees that during the term of his employment by the Corporation and for ten (10) years thereafter, he will not disclose or make available, directly or indirectly, any Confidential Information to any person, concern or entity, except in the proper performance of his duties and responsibilities hereunder or with the prior written consent of the Corporation. This restriction shall not apply to information generally available to the public or to any information properly obtained from a source completely independent from the Corporation. The Employee, as a key employee of the Corporation, shall have a duty to identify its Confidential Information and to keep secret and to otherwise protect such Confidential Information on behalf of the Corporation.

2.3 Trade Secrets.

(a) "Trade Secrets" shall mean and include the whole or any portion of any technical or nontechnical data, formula pattern, compilation, program, device, method, technique, drawing, process, financial data, lists of actual or potential customers, lists of actual or potential suppliers, or other information which derives economic value, actual or potential, from not being generally known to, and not being readily ascertainable by proper means by, other persons who can obtain economic value from its disclosure or use.

(b) The Employee agrees that during the term of his employment by the Corporation and for ten (10) years thereafter, he will not disclose or make available, directly or indirectly, any Trade Secrets to any person, concern, or entity, except in the proper performance of his duties and responsibilities hereunder or with the prior written consent of the Corporation. This restriction shall not apply to information generally available to the public or to any information properly obtained from a source completely independent from the Corporation or the Company. The Employee, as a key employee of the Corporation, shall have a duty to identify its Trade Secrets and to keep secret and to otherwise protect such Trade Secrets on behalf of the Corporation and the Company.

2.4 **Intellectual Property.** Promptly upon request by the Corporation, the Employee will assign permanently to the Corporation exclusive rights to any patents, design patents, copyrights, trademarks, service marks, and other intellectual property rights awarded to him on the basis of (i) ideas developed in whole or in part by the Employee during the term of his employment with the Corporation and its affiliates; and (ii) ideas developed by the Employee within **SIX (6) months** following the termination of his employment by the Corporation, which are related to or result from such employment.

3. **Corporation's Remedies for Breach.** It is recognized that damages in the event of breach of Section 2 by the Employee would be difficult, if not impossible, to ascertain, and it is, therefore, agreed that the Corporation, in addition to and without limiting any other remedy or right it may have, shall have the right to an injunction or other equitable relief in any court of competent jurisdiction, enjoining any breach, and the Employee hereby waives any and all defenses he may have on the ground of lack of jurisdiction or competence of the court to grant such an injunction or other equitable relief. The existence of this right shall not preclude any other rights and remedies at law or in equity which the Corporation may have.

4. **Employment Period, Equity Options, etc.**

4.1 **Period of Employment.** The Employment Period shall commence on the date of this Agreement and shall continue indefinitely on an at-will basis until terminated by either party via written notice to the other, **but such termination shall not be effective until 14 days after giving written notice.** The foregoing notwithstanding, the Corporation may terminate the Employee's employment hereunder for "cause" and such termination shall be effective immediately and without regard to when notice of same is given the Employee. The term "cause" means (i) fraud, misappropriation, or intentional material damage to the property or business of the Corporation; (ii) commission of a felony; (iii) continuance of failure by the Employee to perform his duties in compliance with this Agreement after written notice to the Employee by his supervisor; (iv) a violation of Section 2 of this Agreement, (v) incompetence; (vi) incapacitation for a period of 14 days or more; or (vii) Employee's bankruptcy, assignment for the benefit of creditors, becoming subject to execution on a judgment, or insolvency.

4.2 **Survival of Covenants.** Termination of the Employee's employment hereunder shall in no way diminish the Employee's duty to fully honor the covenants of Section 2 herein. Further, no purported or actual breach of this Agreement by the Corporation shall in any way diminish the Employee's duty to fully honor the covenants of Section 2 herein.

5. **Notices.** Any notices, requests, demands, or other communications provided for by this Agreement shall be sufficient if in writing and shall be deemed given when delivered personally or

when sent by registered or certified mail to the Employee at the last residence address he has filed in writing with the Corporation or, in the case of the Corporation, at its principal Employee offices.

6. **Binding Agreement.** This Agreement shall be effective as of the date hereof and shall be binding upon and inure to the benefit of the Employee, his heirs, personal and legal representatives, guardians and permitted assigns. The rights and obligations of the Corporation under this Agreement shall inure to the benefit of and shall be binding upon any successor or assignee of the Corporation.

7. **Entire Agreement.** This Agreement constitutes the entire understanding of the Employee and the Corporation with respect to the subject matter hereof and supersedes any and all prior understandings written or oral. This Agreement may not be changed, modified, or discharged orally, but only by an instrument in writing signed by the parties.

8. **Tolling.** In the event that Employee shall breach any or all of the covenants set forth in Section 2 hereof, the running of the restrictions set forth in such Section breached shall be tolled during the continuation(s) of any such breach or breaches by Employee, and the running of the period of such restrictions shall commence or commence again only upon compliance by the Employee with the terms of the applicable Section breached.

9. **Waiver.** The waiver by the Corporation of any breach of this Agreement by the Employee shall not be effective unless in writing, and no such waiver shall operate or be construed as the waiver of the same or another breach on a subsequent occasion.

10. **Governing Law.** This Agreement shall be governed by and construed and enforced in accordance with the laws of the State of Georgia.

11. **Severability.** The invalidity or unenforceability of any provisions hereof shall in no way affect the validity or enforceability of any other provision.

IN WITNESS WHEREOF, the parties have executed, sealed and delivered this Employment Agreement as of the date first above written.

CORPORATION:

By: _____(seal)_____
 _Elmer T. Jones_____, Pres.

[corporate seal]

EMPLOYEE:

 _____(seal)_____
 Harold Reiser , Individually

Appendix D:
Blank Forms

The following forms may be photocopied or removed from this book and used immediately. Some of the tax forms explained in this book are not included here because you should use original returns provided by the IRS (940, 941) or the Georgia Department of Revenue (quarterly unemployment compensation form).

This page intentionally left blank.

STATE OF GEORGIA
COUNTY OF_____

AFFIDAVIT TO REGISTER TRADE NAME
(Individual)

Personally, before the undersigned attesting officer authorized by law to administer oaths, appeared_____ (name of applicant), who, after being first duly sworn, deposes an oath and says that he or she operates an enterprise that is located at _____ (legal business address), and is trading under the name "_____" (tradename), at the same address, and the nature of the enterprise is _____ (general nature of business), and any related activities to the foregoing, all under the laws of the State of Georgia.

This affidavit is made in compliance with OCGA § 10-1-490, *et seq.* this _____ (date).

_____

_____ (Name)

Sworn to and subscribed
before me this _____

_____

Notary Public

This page intentionally left blank.

STATE OF GEORGIA
COUNTY OF_____

AFFIDAVIT TO REGISTER TRADE NAME
(Business)

Personally, before the undersigned attesting officer authorized by law to administer oaths, appeared_____ (name of applicant), who is _____ (title) of _____ (legal business name) who, after being first duly sworn, deposes an oath and says that _____ (legal business name), which is located at _____ (legal business address), and is trading under the name "_____" (tradename), at the same address, and the nature of same is _____(general nature of business), and any related activities to the foregoing, all under the laws of the State of Georgia.

This affidavit is made in compliance with OCGA § 10-1-490, *et seq.* this _____ (date).

_____

_____ (Name)

Sworn to and subscribed
before me this _____

_____

Notary Public

This page intentionally left blank.

OFFICE OF SECRETARY OF STATE
CORPORATIONS DIVISION
Suite 315, West Tower, 2 Martin Luther King Jr., Drive
Atlanta, Georgia 30334-1530
(404) 656-2861
Trademark Search and Status Information on the Internet
http://www.sos.state.ga.us/corporations/marksearch.htm

WARREN H. RARY
Director

CURTIS A. WISE
Trademark Administrator

CATHY COX
Secretary of State

APPLICATION FOR REGISTRATION
TRADEMARK OR SERVICE MARK

DO NOT WRITE IN SHADED AREA - SOS USE ONLY

DOCKET #	REGISTRATION #	MARK VERIFICATION

DOCKET CODE	DATE FILED	AMOUNT RECEIVED	CHECK/ RECEIPT #

NOTICE TO APPLICANT: PRINT PLAINLY OR TYPE REMAINDER OF THIS FORM.

In compliance with the requirements of O.C.G.A. §10-1-442, the undersigned, having adopted and used a Trademark or Service Mark in this state for the purposes provided in the Code Chapter and desiring to file the same for public record in the Office of the Secretary of State of Georgia, does hereby certify the following:

1. _____

   Name of Applicant

2. _____

   Principal Business Address   City   State   Zip Code

3. If applicant is a corporation, please indicate the state of incorporation: _____

4. Describe the mark. The description you provide is the way the mark will be registered. (See General instructions) *(Attach additional sheet if necessary)*

5. (A) If a trademark, what goods are offered or sold under the mark? OR (B) If a service mark, what services are provided under the mark?

6. Class No: _____ (A separate application must be filed for each class in which a registration of the mark is sought.)

7. Date of first use of the mark by applicant, predecessor, or licensee. (Give Month, Day and Year)
   (A) anywhere: _____   (B) In Georgia: _____

8. The applicant is the owner of the mark described herein and, to the best of his/her knowledge, no other person except the applicant has the right to use such mark in this State either in its identical form or in such near resemblance thereto as to be likely to cause confusion or mistake, or to deceive.

   Signature of Applicant _____   Print Name _____

   Official Title (If signing for a corporation) _____   Phone Number _____

Mail or deliver to the Secretary of State, at the above address, the following:

1) This COMPLETED application.
2) Three (3) specimens of the mark as currently used. (May be 3 samples of the same specimen. If Trademark, should be actual label or packaging used on product. If Service mark, should be advertising such as newspaper ad, brochure, etc. depicting the service rendered.)
3) A filing fee of $15.00 payable to Secretary of State. Filing fees are NON-refundable.

STATE OF _____

COUNTY OF _____

Sworn to and subscribed before me this _____ Day of _____ 20, _____

_____   My Commission Expires _____

NOTARY PUBLIC

FORM TMAPPL

This page intentionally left blank.

STATE OF GEORGIA
COUNTY OF _____

Articles of Incorporation
of
_____[Corporation Name]_____

Article 1.
The name of the corporation is _____.

Article 2.
The corporation is authorized to issue _____ shares. [Note: Number may not be "0".]

Article 3.
The street address of the registered office is _____

_____. The registered agent at such address is _____

_____. [Note: The registered office address must be a street address at which the agent may

be personally located.] The county of the registered office is _____.

Article 4.
The name and address of each incorporator is:

Name: _____   Name: _____   Name: _____

Address: _____   Address: _____   Address: _____

_____   _____   _____

_____   _____   _____

Article 5.
The principal mailing address of the corporation is _____

_____.

IN WITNESS WHEREOF, the undersigned has executed these Articles of Incorporation.

This _____ day of _____, 2003. _____
                                                                    (Capacity in which person is signing)

OMB No. 1615-0047; Expires 06/30/08

Form I-9, Employment Eligibility Verification

Department of Homeland Security
U.S. Citizenship and Immigration Services

Please read instructions carefully before completing this form. The instructions must be available during completion of this form.

ANTI-DISCRIMINATION NOTICE: It is illegal to discriminate against work eligible individuals. Employers CANNOT specify which document(s) they will accept from an employee. The refusal to hire an individual because the documents have a future expiration date may also constitute illegal discrimination.

Section 1. Employee Information and Verification. To be completed and signed by employee at the time employment begins.

Print Name: Last	First	Middle Initial	Maiden Name

Address (Street Name and Number)	Apt. #	Date of Birth (month/day/year)

City	State	Zip Code	Social Security #

I am aware that federal law provides for imprisonment and/or fines for false statements or use of false documents in connection with the completion of this form.

I attest, under penalty of perjury, that I am (check one of the following):

☐ A citizen or national of the United States _____
☐ A lawful permanent resident (Alien #) A_____
☐ An alien authorized to work until _____
(Alien # or Admission #) _____

Employee's Signature

Date (month/day/year)

Preparer and/or Translator Certification. *(To be completed and signed if Section 1 is prepared by a person other than the employee.) I attest, under penalty of perjury, that I have assisted in the completion of this form and that to the best of my knowledge the information is true and correct.*

Preparer's/Translator's Signature	Print Name

Address (Street Name and Number, City, State, Zip Code)	Date (month/day/year)

Section 2. Employer Review and Verification. To be completed and signed by employer. Examine one document from List A OR examine one document from List B and one from List C, as listed on the reverse of this form, and record the title, number and expiration date, if any, of the document(s).

List A	OR	List B	AND	List C
Document title: _____		_____		_____
Issuing authority: _____		_____		_____
Document #: _____		_____		_____
Expiration Date *(if any):* _____		_____		_____
Document #: _____				
Expiration Date *(if any):* _____				

CERTIFICATION - I attest, under penalty of perjury, that I have examined the document(s) presented by the above-named employee, that the above-listed document(s) appear to be genuine and to relate to the employee named, that the employee began employment on *(month/day/year)* _____ **and that to the best of my knowledge the employee is eligible to work in the United States. (State employment agencies may omit the date the employee began employment.)**

Signature of Employer or Authorized Representative	Print Name	Title

Business or Organization Name and Address (Street Name and Number, City, State, Zip Code)	Date (month/day/year)

Section 3. Updating and Reverification. To be completed and signed by employer.

A. New Name (if applicable)	B. Date of Rehire (month/day/year) (if applicable)

C. If employee's previous grant of work authorization has expired, provide the information below for the document that establishes current employment eligibility.

Document Title: _____	Document #: _____	Expiration Date (if any): _____

I attest, under penalty of perjury, that to the best of my knowledge, this employee is eligible to work in the United States, and if the employee presented document(s), the document(s) I have examined appear to be genuine and to relate to the individual.

Signature of Employer or Authorized Representative	Date (month/day/year)

Form I-9 (Rev. 06/05/07) N

LISTS OF ACCEPTABLE DOCUMENTS

LIST A	LIST B	LIST C
Documents that Establish Both Identity and Employment Eligibility OR	**Documents that Establish Identity** AND	**Documents that Establish Employment Eligibility**
1. U.S. Passport (unexpired or expired)	1. Driver's license or ID card issued by a state or outlying possession of the United States provided it contains a photograph or information such as name, date of birth, gender, height, eye color and address	1. U.S. Social Security card issued by the Social Security Administration *(other than a card stating it is not valid for employment)*
2. Permanent Resident Card or Alien Registration Receipt Card (Form I-551)	2. ID card issued by federal, state or local government agencies or entities, provided it contains a photograph or information such as name, date of birth, gender, height, eye color and address	2. Certification of Birth Abroad issued by the Department of State *(Form FS-545 or Form DS-1350)*
3. An unexpired foreign passport with a temporary I-551 stamp	3. School ID card with a photograph	3. Original or certified copy of a birth certificate issued by a state, county, municipal authority or outlying possession of the United States bearing an official seal
4. An unexpired Employment Authorization Document that contains a photograph (Form I-766, I-688, I-688A, I-688B)	4. Voter's registration card	4. Native American tribal document
4. An unexpired Employment Authorization Document that contains a photograph (Form I-766, I-688, I-688A, I-688B)	5. U.S. Military card or draft record	5. U.S. Citizen ID Card *(Form I-197)*
5. An unexpired foreign passport with an unexpired Arrival-Departure Record, Form I-94, bearing the same name as the passport and containing an endorsement of the alien's nonimmigrant status, if that status authorizes the alien to work for the employer	6. Military dependent's ID card	6. ID Card for use of Resident Citizen in the United States *(Form I-179)*
5. An unexpired foreign passport with an unexpired Arrival-Departure Record, Form I-94, bearing the same name as the passport and containing an endorsement of the alien's nonimmigrant status, if that status authorizes the alien to work for the employer	7. U.S. Coast Guard Merchant Mariner Card	6. ID Card for use of Resident Citizen in the United States *(Form I-179)*
5. An unexpired foreign passport with an unexpired Arrival-Departure Record, Form I-94, bearing the same name as the passport and containing an endorsement of the alien's nonimmigrant status, if that status authorizes the alien to work for the employer	8. Native American tribal document	7. Unexpired employment authorization document issued by DHS *(other than those listed under List A)*
5. An unexpired foreign passport with an unexpired Arrival-Departure Record, Form I-94, bearing the same name as the passport and containing an endorsement of the alien's nonimmigrant status, if that status authorizes the alien to work for the employer	9. Driver's license issued by a Canadian government authority	7. Unexpired employment authorization document issued by DHS *(other than those listed under List A)*
	For persons under age 18 who are unable to present a document listed above:	
	10. School record or report card	
	11. Clinic, doctor or hospital record	
	12. Day-care or nursery school record	

Illustrations of many of these documents appear in Part 8 of the Handbook for Employers (M-274)

_____ Date

_____

_____

_____

Re: Formal Notice Prior to Criminal Action on a Bad Check

To:

YOU ARE HEREBY NOTIFIED THAT THE FOLLOWING CHECK(S) OR INSTRUMENT(S):

CHECK NUMBER   CHECK DATE   CHECK AMOUNT   NAME OF BANK

_____   _____   _____   _____

DRAWN UPON _____ AND PAYABLE TO _____ (HAS) (HAVE) BEEN DISHONORED. PURSUANT TO GEORGIA LAW, YOU HAVE TEN DAYS FROM RECEIPT OF THIS NOTICE TO TENDER PAYMENT OF THE TOTAL AMOUNT OF THE CHECK(S) OR INSTRUMENT(S), AMOUNT DUE BEING $ _____. UNLESS THIS AMOUNT IS PAID IN FULL WITHIN THE SPECIFIED TIME ABOVE, A PRESUMPTION IN LAW ARISES THAT YOU DELIVERED THE ITEM(S) WITH THE INTENT TO DEFRAUD AND THE DISHONORED CHECK(S) OR INSTRU-MENT(S) AND ALL OTHER AVAILABLE INFORMATION RELATING TO THIS INCI-DENT MAY BE SUBMITTED TO THE MAGISTRATE FOR THE ISSUANCE OF A CRIMINAL WARRANT OR CITATION OR TO THE DISTRICT ATTORNEY OR A SOLICITOR FOR CRIMINAL PROSECUTION.

_____

Owner

This page intentionally left blank.

_____ Date

_____

_____

_____

CERTIFIED MAIL
RETURN RECEIPT REQUESTED

Thirty Day Notice Prior to Double Damages

O.C.G.A. § 13-6-5 (c)

Stopped Payment Check Notice

To:

You are hereby notified that a check or instrument numbered _____, issued by _____ on _____, _____, drawn upon _____ and payable to _____ has been dishonored. Pursuant to Georgia Law, you have 30 days from the receipt of this notice to tender payments of the full amount of the check or instrument plus a service charge of $25 or 5% of the face amount of the check or instrument, whichever is greater, the total amount due being $_____. Unless this amount is paid in full within the 30-day period, the holder of the check or instrument may file a civil suit against you for two times the amount of the check or instrument but in no case more than $500, in addition to the payment of the check or instrument plus any court costs incurred by the payee in taking the action.

_____

Owner

This page intentionally left blank.

Georgia New Hire Reporting Form

Send completed forms to:
Georgia New Hire Reporting Program
PO Box 38480
Atlanta, GA 30334-0480
Fax: (404) 525-2983 or toll-free fax 1 (888) 541-0521

To ensure the highest level of accuracy, please print neatly in capital letters and avoid contact with the edges of the boxes. The following will serve as an example:

A	B	C		1	2	3

EMPLOYER INFORMATION

Federal Employer ID Number (FEIN) *(Please use the same FEIN that appears on your quarterly wage reports you submit to the State):*

Multiple medical insurance: Y/N

Primary Insurance Company Name (if available to the employee):

If available/offered: Y/N

Employer Name:

Employer Address: *(Please indicate the address where the Wage Withholding Orders should be sent).*

Employer City:

Employer State:

Zip Code (5 digit):

Employer Phone:

Extension:

Employer Fax:

E-mail:

EMPLOYEE INFORMATION

Employee Social Security Number (SSN):

Employee Starting Salary (Monthly):*   .00

Employee First Name:

Middle Initial:*

Employee Last Name:

Employee Address:

Employee City:

Employee State:

Zip Code:

Date of Hire:

Date of Birth:

Actual First Day of Work:*

Medical Insurance Company Name:*

*optional

Reports must be submitted within 10 days of date of hire or rehire

Questions? Call us at (404) 525-2985 or toll-free 1 (888) 541-0469

This page intentionally left blank.

Form **SS-4**
(Rev. July 2007)
Department of the Treasury
Internal Revenue Service

Application for Employer Identification Number

(For use by employers, corporations, partnerships, trusts, estates, churches, government agencies, Indian tribal entities, certain individuals, and others.)

▶ See separate instructions for each line.   ▶ Keep a copy for your records.

OMB No. 1545-0003

EIN

Type or print clearly.

1	Legal name of entity (or individual) for whom the EIN is being requested

| 2 | Trade name of business (if different from name on line 1) | 3 | Executor, administrator, trustee, "care of" name |

| 4a | Mailing address (room, apt., suite no. and street, or P.O. box) | 5a | Street address (if different) (Do not enter a P.O. box.) |

| 4b | City, state, and ZIP code (if foreign, see instructions) | 5b | City, state, and ZIP code (if foreign, see instructions) |

| 6 | County and state where principal business is located |

| 7a | Name of principal officer, general partner, grantor, owner, or trustor | 7b | SSN, ITIN, or EIN |

8a Is this application for a limited liability company (LLC) (or a foreign equivalent)? . . . . ☐ Yes ☐ No   **8b** If 8a is "Yes," enter the number of LLC members . . . . . ▶

8c If 8a is "Yes," was the LLC organized in the United States? . . . . ☐ Yes ☐ No

9a **Type of entity** (check only one box). **Caution.** If 8a is "Yes," see the instructions for the correct box to check.

☐ Sole proprietor (SSN) _____
☐ Partnership
☐ Corporation (enter form number to be filed) ▶ _____
☐ Personal service corporation
☐ Church or church-controlled organization
☐ Other nonprofit organization (specify) ▶ _____
☐ Other (specify) ▶

☐ Estate (SSN of decedent) _____
☐ Plan administrator (TIN) _____
☐ Trust (TIN of grantor) _____
☐ National Guard   ☐ State/local government
☐ Farmers' cooperative   ☐ Federal government/military
☐ REMIC   ☐ Indian tribal governments/enterprises
Group Exemption Number (GEN) if any ▶

9b	If a corporation, name the state or foreign country (if applicable) where incorporated	State	Foreign country

10 **Reason for applying** (check only one box)

☐ Started new business (specify type) ▶ _____
_____
☐ Hired employees (Check the box and see line 13.)
☐ Compliance with IRS withholding regulations
☐ Other (specify) ▶

☐ Banking purpose (specify purpose) ▶ _____
☐ Changed type of organization (specify new type) ▶ _____
☐ Purchased going business
☐ Created a trust (specify type) ▶ _____
☐ Created a pension plan (specify type) ▶ _____

11	Date business started or acquired (month, day, year). See instructions.	12	Closing month of accounting year

13 Highest number of employees expected in the next 12 months (enter -0- if none).

Agricultural	Household	Other

14 Do you expect your employment tax liability to be $1,000 or less in a full calendar year? ☐ Yes ☐ No (If you expect to pay $4,000 or less in total wages in a full calendar year, you can mark "Yes.")

15 First date wages or annuities were paid (month, day, year). **Note.** If applicant is a withholding agent, enter date income will first be paid to nonresident alien (month, day, year) . . . . ▶

16 Check **one** box that best describes the principal activity of your business.

☐ Construction   ☐ Rental & leasing   ☐ Transportation & warehousing
☐ Real estate   ☐ Manufacturing   ☐ Finance & insurance
☐ Health care & social assistance   ☐ Wholesale-agent/broker
☐ Accommodation & food service   ☐ Wholesale-other   ☐ Retail
☐ Other (specify)

17 Indicate principal line of merchandise sold, specific construction work done, products produced, or services provided.

18 Has the applicant entity shown on line 1 ever applied for and received an EIN? ☐ Yes ☐ No
If "Yes," write previous EIN here ▶

Third Party Designee

Complete this section **only** if you want to authorize the named individual to receive the entity's EIN and answer questions about the completion of this form.

Designee's name	Designee's telephone number (include area code) ( )
Address and ZIP code	Designee's fax number (include area code) ( )

Under penalties of perjury, I declare that I have examined this application, and to the best of my knowledge and belief, it is true, correct, and complete.

Name and title (type or print clearly) ▶

Applicant's telephone number (include area code) ( )

Signature ▶   Date ▶

Applicant's fax number (include area code) ( )

For Privacy Act and Paperwork Reduction Act Notice, see separate instructions.   Cat. No. 16055N   Form **SS-4** (Rev. 7-2007)

This page intentionally left blank.

Form SS-8
(Rev. November 2006)
Department of the Treasury
Internal Revenue Service

Determination of Worker Status
for Purposes of Federal Employment Taxes
and Income Tax Withholding

OMB No. 1545-0004

Name of firm (or person) for whom the worker performed services	Worker's name

Firm's address (include street address, apt. or suite no., city, state, and ZIP code)

Worker's address (include street address, apt. or suite no., city, state, and ZIP code)

Trade name

Daytime telephone number ( )

Worker's social security number

Telephone number (include area code) ( )

Firm's employer identification number

Worker's employer identification number (if any)

Note. If the worker is paid by a firm other than the one listed on this form for these services, enter the name, address, and employer identification number of the payer. ▶

Disclosure of Information

The information provided on Form SS-8 may be disclosed to the firm, worker, or payer named above to assist the IRS in the determination process. For example, if you are a worker, we may disclose the information you provide on Form SS-8 to the firm or payer named above. The information can only be disclosed to assist with the determination process. If you provide incomplete information, we may not be able to process your request. See *Privacy Act and Paperwork Reduction Act Notice* on page 5 for more information. **If you do not want this information disclosed to other parties, do not file Form SS-8.**

Parts I-V. All filers of Form SS-8 must complete all questions in Parts I-IV. Part V must be completed if the worker provides a service directly to customers or is a salesperson. If you cannot answer a question, enter "Unknown" or "Does not apply." If you need more space for a question, attach another sheet with the part and question number clearly identified.

Part I	**General Information**

1 This form is being completed by: ☐ Firm ☐ Worker; for services performed _____ (beginning date) to _____ (ending date).

2 Explain your reason(s) for filing this form (for example, you received a bill from the IRS, you believe you erroneously received a Form 1099 or Form W-2, you are unable to get worker's compensation benefits, or you were audited or are being audited by the IRS). _____

3 Total number of workers who performed or are performing the same or similar services _____.

4 How did the worker obtain the job? ☐ Application ☐ Bid ☐ Employment Agency ☐ Other (specify) _____

5 Attach copies of all supporting documentation (contracts, invoices, memos, Forms W-2 or Forms 1099-MISC issued or received, IRS closing agreements, IRS rulings, etc.). In addition, please inform us of any current or past litigation concerning the worker's status. If no income reporting forms (Form 1099-MISC or W-2) were furnished to the worker, enter the amount of income earned for the year(s) at issue $ _____.

If both Form W-2 and Form 1099-MISC were issued or received, explain why. _____

6 Describe the firm's business. _____

7 Describe the work done by the worker and provide the worker's job title. _____

8 Explain why you believe the worker is an employee or an independent contractor. _____

9 Did the worker perform services for the firm in any capacity before providing the services that are the subject of this determination request?
☐ Yes ☐ No ☐ N/A
If "Yes," what were the dates of the prior service? _____
If "Yes," explain the differences, if any, between the current and prior service. _____

10 If the work is done under a written agreement between the firm and the worker, attach a copy (preferably signed by both parties). Describe the terms and conditions of the work arrangement. _____

For **Privacy Act and Paperwork Reduction Act Notice, see page 5.**   Cat. No. 16106T   Form **SS-8** (Rev. 11-2006)

Part II   Behavioral Control

1   What specific training and/or instruction is the worker given by the firm? _____

2   How does the worker receive work assignments? _____

3   Who determines the methods by which the assignments are performed? _____

4   Who is the worker required to contact if problems or complaints arise and who is responsible for their resolution? _____

5   What types of reports are required from the worker? Attach examples. _____

6   Describe the worker's daily routine such as, schedule, hours, etc. _____
_____

7   At what location(s) does the worker perform services (e.g., firm's premises, own shop or office, home, customer's location, etc.)? Indicate the appropriate percentage of time the worker spends in each location, if more than one. _____

8   Describe any meetings the worker is required to attend and any penalties for not attending (e.g., sales meetings, monthly meetings, staff meetings, etc.). _____

9   Is the worker required to provide the services personally? . . . . □ Yes   □ No

10   If substitutes or helpers are needed, who hires them? _____

11   If the worker hires the substitutes or helpers, is approval required? . . . . □ Yes   □ No
If "Yes," by whom? _____

12   Who pays the substitutes or helpers? _____

13   Is the worker reimbursed if the worker pays the substitutes or helpers? . . . . □ Yes   □ No
If "Yes," by whom?

Part III   Financial Control

1   List the supplies, equipment, materials, and property provided by each party:
The firm _____
The worker _____
Other party _____

2   Does the worker lease equipment? . . . . □ Yes   □ No
If "Yes," what are the terms of the lease? (Attach a copy or explanatory statement.) _____

3   What expenses are incurred by the worker in the performance of services for the firm? _____

4   Specify which, if any, expenses are reimbursed by:
The firm _____
Other party _____

5   Type of pay the worker receives: □ Salary   □ Commission   □ Hourly Wage   □ Piece Work
□ Lump Sum   □ Other (specify) _____
If type of pay is commission, and the firm guarantees a minimum amount of pay, specify amount $ _____ .

6   Is the worker allowed a drawing account for advances? . . . . □ Yes   □ No
If "Yes," how often? _____
Specify any restrictions. _____

7   Whom does the customer pay? . . . . □ Firm   □ Worker
If worker, does the worker pay the total amount to the firm?   □ Yes   □ No   If "No," explain. _____

8   Does the firm carry worker's compensation insurance on the worker?   . . . . □ Yes   □ No

9   What economic loss or financial risk, if any, can the worker incur beyond the normal loss of salary (e.g., loss or damage of equipment, material, etc.)? _____
_____

Part IV   Relationship of the Worker and Firm

1   List the benefits available to the worker (e.g., paid vacations, sick pay, pensions, bonuses, paid holidays, personal days, insurance benefits). _____

2   Can the relationship be terminated by either party without incurring liability or penalty? . . . . ☐ **Yes** ☐ **No**
    If "No," explain your answer. _____

3   Did the worker perform similar services for others during the same time period? . . . . ☐ **Yes** ☐ **No**
    If "Yes," is the worker required to get approval from the firm? . . . . ☐ **Yes** ☐ **No**

4   Describe any agreements prohibiting competition between the worker and the firm while the worker is performing services or during any later period. Attach any available documentation. _____
    _____

5   Is the worker a member of a union? . . . . ☐ **Yes** ☐ **No**

6   What type of advertising, if any, does the worker do (e.g., a business listing in a directory, business cards, etc.)? Provide copies, if applicable.
    _____

7   If the worker assembles or processes a product at home, who provides the materials and instructions or pattern? _____
    _____

8   What does the worker do with the finished product (e.g., return it to the firm, provide it to another party, or sell it)? _____
    _____

9   How does the firm represent the worker to its customers (e.g., employee, partner, representative, or contractor)? _____
    _____

10 If the worker no longer performs services for the firm, how did the relationship end (e.g., worker quit or was fired, job completed, contract ended, firm or worker went out of business)? _____
    _____

Part V   For Service Providers or Salespersons. Complete this part if the worker provided a service directly to customers or is a salesperson.

1   What are the worker's responsibilities in soliciting new customers? _____
    _____

2   Who provides the worker with leads to prospective customers? _____

3   Describe any reporting requirements pertaining to the leads. _____
    _____

4   What terms and conditions of sale, if any, are required by the firm? _____

5   Are orders submitted to and subject to approval by the firm? . . . . ☐ **Yes** ☐ **No**

6   Who determines the worker's territory? _____

7   Did the worker pay for the privilege of serving customers on the route or in the territory? . . . . ☐ **Yes** ☐ **No**
    If "Yes," whom did the worker pay? _____
    If "Yes," how much did the worker pay? . . . . $ _____

8   Where does the worker sell the product (e.g., in a home, retail establishment, etc.)? _____
    _____

9   List the product and/or services distributed by the worker (e.g., meat, vegetables, fruit, bakery products, beverages, or laundry or dry cleaning services). If more than one type of product and/or service is distributed, specify the principal one. _____
    _____

10 Does the worker sell life insurance full time? . . . . ☐ **Yes** ☐ **No**

11 Does the worker sell other types of insurance for the firm? . . . . ☐ **Yes** ☐ **No**
    If "Yes," enter the percentage of the worker's total working time spent in selling other types of insurance . . . . _____ %

12 If the worker solicits orders from wholesalers, retailers, contractors, or operators of hotels, restaurants, or other similar establishments, enter the percentage of the worker's time spent in the solicitation . . . . _____ %

13 Is the merchandise purchased by the customers for resale or use in their business operations? . . . . ☐ **Yes** ☐ **No**
    Describe the merchandise and state whether it is equipment installed on the customers' premises. _____
    _____

Sign Here ▶

Under penalties of perjury, I declare that I have examined this request, including accompanying documents, and to the best of my knowledge and belief, the facts presented are true, correct, and complete.

_____ Title ▶ _____ Date ▶ _____
Type or print name below signature.

General Instructions

Section references are to the Internal Revenue Code unless otherwise noted.

Purpose

Firms and workers file Form SS-8 to request a determination of the status of a worker for purposes of federal employment taxes and income tax withholding.

A Form SS-8 determination may be requested only in order to resolve federal tax matters. If Form SS-8 is submitted for a tax year for which the statute of limitations on the tax return has expired, a determination letter will not be issued. The statute of limitations expires 3 years from the due date of the tax return or the date filed, whichever is later.

The IRS does not issue a determination letter for proposed transactions or on hypothetical situations. We may, however, issue an information letter when it is considered appropriate.

Definition

Firm. For the purposes of this form, the term "firm" means any individual, business enterprise, organization, state, or other entity for which a worker has performed services. The firm may or may not have paid the worker directly for these services.

If the firm was not responsible for payment for services, be sure to enter the name, address, and employer identification number of the payer on the first page of Form SS-8, below the identifying information for the firm and the worker.

The SS-8 Determination Process

The IRS will acknowledge the receipt of your Form SS-8. Because there are usually two (or more) parties who could be affected by a determination of employment status, the IRS attempts to get information from all parties involved by sending those parties blank Forms SS-8 for completion. Some or all of the information provided on this Form SS-8 may be shared with the other parties listed on page 1. The case will be assigned to a technician who will review the facts, apply the law, and render a decision. The technician may ask for additional information from the requestor, from other involved parties, or from third parties that could help clarify the work relationship before rendering a decision. The IRS will generally issue a formal determination to the firm or payer (if that is a different entity), and will send a copy to the worker. A determination letter applies only to a worker (or a class of workers) requesting it, and the decision is binding on the IRS. In certain cases, a formal determination will not be issued. Instead, an information letter may be issued. Although an information letter is advisory only and is not binding on the IRS, it may be used to assist the worker to fulfill his or her federal tax obligations.

Neither the SS-8 determination process nor the review of any records in connection with the determination constitutes an examination (audit) of any federal tax return. If the periods under consideration have previously been examined, the SS-8 determination process will not constitute a reexamination under IRS reopening procedures. Because this is not an examination of any federal tax return, the appeal rights available in connection with an examination do not apply to an SS-8 determination. However, if you disagree with a determination and you have additional information concerning the work relationship that you believe was not previously considered, you may request that the determining office reconsider the determination.

Completing Form SS-8

Answer all questions as completely as possible. Attach additional sheets if you need more space. Provide information for all years the worker provided services for the firm. Determinations are based on the entire relationship between the firm and the worker. Also indicate if there were any significant changes in the work relationship over the service term.

Additional copies of this form may be obtained by calling 1-800-829-4933 or from the IRS website at *www.irs.gov*.

Fee

There is no fee for requesting an SS-8 determination letter.

Signature

Form SS-8 must be signed and dated by the taxpayer. A stamped signature will not be accepted.

The person who signs for a corporation must be an officer of the corporation who has personal knowledge of the facts. If the corporation is a member of an affiliated group filing a consolidated return, it must be signed by an officer of the common parent of the group.

The person signing for a trust, partnership, or limited liability company must be, respectively, a trustee, general partner, or member-manager who has personal knowledge of the facts.

Where To File

Send the completed Form SS-8 to the address listed below for the firm's location. However, only for cases involving federal agencies, send Form SS-8 to the Internal Revenue Service, Attn: CC:CORP:T:C, Ben Franklin Station, P.O. Box 7604, Washington, DC 20044.

Firm's location:	Send to:
Alaska, Arizona, Arkansas, California, Colorado, Hawaii, Idaho, Illinois, Iowa, Kansas, Minnesota, Missouri, Montana, Nebraska, Nevada, New Mexico, North Dakota, Oklahoma, Oregon, South Dakota, Texas, Utah, Washington, Wisconsin, Wyoming, American Samoa, Guam, Puerto Rico, U.S. Virgin Islands	Internal Revenue Service SS-8 Determinations P.O. Box 630 Stop 631 Holtsville, NY 11742-0630
Alabama, Connecticut, Delaware, District of Columbia, Florida, Georgia, Indiana, Kentucky, Louisiana, Maine, Maryland, Massachusetts, Michigan, Mississippi, New Hampshire, New Jersey, New York, North Carolina, Ohio, Pennsylvania, Rhode Island, South Carolina, Tennessee, Vermont, Virginia, West Virginia, all other locations not listed	Internal Revenue Service SS-8 Determinations 40 Lakemont Road Newport, VT 05855-1555

Instructions for Workers

If you are requesting a determination for more than one firm, complete a separate Form SS-8 for each firm.

Form SS-8 is not a claim for refund of social security and Medicare taxes or federal income tax withholding.

If the IRS determines that you are an employee, you are responsible for filing an amended return for any corrections related to this decision. A determination that a worker is an employee does not necessarily reduce any current or prior tax liability. For more information, call 1-800-829-1040.

Time for filing a claim for refund. Generally, you must file your claim for a credit or refund within 3 years from the date your original return was filed or within 2 years from the date the tax was paid, whichever is later.

Filing Form SS-8 does not prevent the expiration of the time in which a claim for a refund must be filed. If you are concerned about a refund, and the statute of limitations for filing a claim for refund for the year(s) at issue has not yet expired, you should file Form 1040X, Amended U.S. Individual Income Tax Return, to protect your statute of limitations. File a separate Form 1040X for each year.

On the Form 1040X you file, do not complete lines 1 through 24 on the form. Write "Protective Claim" at the top of the form, sign and date it. In addition, you should enter the following statement in Part II, Explanation of Changes: "Filed Form SS-8 with the Internal Revenue Service Office in (Holtsville, NY; Newport, VT; or Washington, DC; as appropriate). By filing this protective claim, I reserve the right to file a claim for any refund that may be due after a determination of my employment tax status has been completed."

Filing Form SS-8 does not alter the requirement to timely file an income tax return. Do not delay filing your tax return in anticipation of an answer to your SS-8 request. In addition, if applicable, do not delay in responding to a request for payment while waiting for a determination of your worker status.

Instructions for Firms

If a **worker** has requested a determination of his or her status while working for you, you will receive a request from the IRS to complete a Form SS-8. In cases of this type, the IRS usually gives each party an opportunity to present a statement of the facts because any decision will affect the employment tax status of the parties. Failure to respond to this request will not prevent the IRS from issuing a determination letter based on the information he or she has made available so that the worker may fulfill his or her federal tax obligations. However, the information that you provide is extremely valuable in determining the status of the worker.

If you are requesting a determination for a particular class of worker, complete the form for one individual who is representative of the class of workers whose status is in question. If you want a written determination for more than one class of workers, complete a separate Form SS-8 for one worker from each class whose status is typical of that class. A written determination for any worker will apply to other workers of the same class if the facts are not materially different for these workers. Please provide a list of names and addresses of all workers potentially affected by this determination.

If you have a reasonable basis for not treating a worker as an employee, you may be relieved from having to pay employment taxes for that worker under section 530 of the 1978 Revenue Act. However, this relief provision cannot be considered in conjunction with a Form SS-8 determination because the determination does not constitute an examination of any tax return. For more information regarding section 530 of the 1978 Revenue Act and to determine if you qualify for relief under this section, you may visit the IRS website at *www.irs.gov.*

Privacy Act and Paperwork Reduction Act Notice. We ask for the information on this form to carry out the Internal Revenue laws of the United States. This information will be used to determine the employment status of the worker(s) described on the form. Subtitle C, Employment Taxes, of the Internal Revenue Code imposes employment taxes on wages. Sections 3121(d), 3306(a), and 3401(c) and (d) and the related regulations define employee and employer for purposes of employment taxes imposed under Subtitle C. Section 6001 authorizes the IRS to request information needed to determine if a worker(s) or firm is subject to these taxes. Section 6109 requires you to provide your taxpayer identification number. Neither workers nor firms are required to request a status determination, but if you choose to do so, you must provide the information requested on this form. Failure to provide the requested information may prevent us from making a status determination. If any worker or the firm has requested a status determination and you are being asked to provide information for use in that determination, you are not required to provide the requested information. However, failure to provide such information will prevent the IRS from considering it in making the status determination. Providing false or fraudulent information may subject you to penalties. Routine uses of this information include providing it to the Department of Justice for use in civil and criminal litigation, to the Social Security Administration for the administration of social security programs, and to cities, states, and the District of Columbia for the administration of their tax laws. We may also disclose this information to other countries under a tax treaty, to federal and state agencies to enforce federal nontax criminal laws, or to federal law enforcement and intelligence agencies to combat terrorism. We may provide this information to the affected worker(s), the firm, or payer as part of the status determination process.

You are not required to provide the information requested on a form that is subject to the Paperwork Reduction Act unless the form displays a valid OMB control number. Books or records relating to a form or its instructions must be retained as long as their contents may become material in the administration of any Internal Revenue law. Generally, tax returns and return information are confidential, as required by section 6103.

The time needed to complete and file this form will vary depending on individual circumstances. The estimated average time is: Recordkeeping, 22 hrs.; Learning about the law or the form, 47 min.; and Preparing and sending the form to the IRS, 1 hr., 11 min. If you have comments concerning the accuracy of these time estimates or suggestions for making this form simpler, we would be happy to hear from you. You can write to the Internal Revenue Service, Tax Products Coordinating Committee, SE:W:CAR:MP:T:T:SP, 1111 Constitution Ave. NW, IR-6406, Washington, DC 20224. Do not send the tax form to this address. Instead, see *Where To File* on page 4.

This page intentionally left blank.

GEORGIA DEPARTMENT OF LABOR
SUITE 850 - 148 ANDREW YOUNG INTERNATIONAL BLVD NE - ATLANTA, GA 30303-1751

EMPLOYER STATUS REPORT

READ INSTRUCTIONS ON REVERSE SIDE
BEFORE COMPLETION OF FORM

1. ENTER OR CORRECT BUSINESS NAME AND ADDRESS

RETURN ORIGINAL WITHIN 10 DAYS

GEORGIA DOL
ACCOUNT NUMBER
(If already assigned) □□□□□□ — □□

3. TRADE NAME

2. TYPE OF ORGANIZATION

□ Individual   □ Partnership   □ Corporation   □ Nonprofit org.

□ Limited Liability CO. (LLC)

□ Other (specify) _____

4. PRINCIPAL BUSINESS, FARM OR HOUSEHOLD LOCATION IN GEORGIA (Do not use a P. O. Box number)

Street Address

City   GA   Zip Code   County   Telephone Number ( )

5. DATE FIRST BEGAN EMPLOYING WORKERS WITHIN STATE OF GA.

DATE OF FIRST GA. PAYROLL

6. ARE YOU LIABLE FOR FEDERAL UNEMPLOYMENT TAX?   Yes □   No □

FEDERAL I.D. NUMBER □□ — □□□□□□□

7. HAVE YOU...

Acquired another business?   Yes □   No □

Merged with another business?   Yes □   No □

Formed a corporation or partnership?   Yes □   No □

Made any other change in the ownership of your business?   Yes □   No □   If yes, explain _____

DATE ACQUIRED OR CHANGED

PREDECESSOR'S GEORGIA DOL ACCOUNT NUMBER □□□□□□ — □□

DOES THE FORMER OWNER CONTINUE TO HAVE EMPLOYEES?   Yes □   No □

DID YOU ACQUIRE...

□ All of Georgia operations?

□ Substantially all of Georgia operations (90% or more)

□ Part of Georgia operations (less than 90%)

FROM WHOM? (Organization name, including trade name)   ADDRESS

8. IF YOU HAD PRIVATE BUSINESS EMPLOYMENT:
Did you, or do you expect to employ at least one worker in 20 different calendar weeks during a calendar year?   Yes * □   No □

* If yes, show date the 20th week first occurred:

Did you, or do you expect to have a quarterly payroll of $1,500 or more?   Yes * □   No □

* If yes, show date this first occurred:

9. IF YOU HAD DOMESTIC EMPLOYMENT:
Did you, or do you expect to pay cash wages of $1,000 or more in any calendar quarter?   Yes* □   No □

* If yes, show date this first occurred:

10. IF YOU HAD AGRICULTURAL EMPLOYMENT: Yes* □   No □
Did you, or do you expect to employ 10 or more agricultural workers in 20 different calendar weeks during a calendar year?

* If yes, show date the 20th week first occurred:

Did you, or do you expect to have a gross cash agricultural payroll of $20,000 or more in any calendar quarter?   Yes* □   No □

* If yes, show date this first occurred:

11. IF YOU ARE A NONPROFIT ORGANIZATION EXEMPT FROM INCOME TAX UNDER IRS CODE 501(C)(3):   Yes * □   No □
Did you, or do you expect to employ four or more workers in 20 different calendar weeks during a calendar year? (ATTACH COPY OF 501(C)(3) EXEMPTION LETTER)

* If yes, show date the 20th week first occurred:

12. HOW MANY EMPLOYEES do you have, (or anticipate when in full operation)?

INFORMATION ABOUT OWNER, ALL PARTNERS, OR PRINCIPAL OFFICER (ATTACH ADDITIONAL SHEET, OR SHEETS, IF NECESSARY)

Name

Social Security Number □□□ — □□ — □□□□

Residence Address

City

State   Zip Code

Telephone ( )

INFORMATION ABOUT PERSON OR FIRM WHO MAINTAINS FINANCIAL RECORDS OF BUSINESS

Name

Address

City

State   Zip Code   Telephone ( )

CERTIFICATION: I hereby certify under penalties of perjury, that the foregoing statement and those contained in any attached sheets signed by me are true and correct, and that I am authorized to execute this report on behalf of the employing unit. This report must be signed by owner, partner or principal officer.

Signature   Title   Date

PLEASE COMPLETE INDUSTRY INFORMATION ON REVERSE SIDE.

DOL-1A (R-5/05)
TA489A

(CONTINUED)

NATURE OF BUSINESS: <u>Information is required on all items. Attach additional sheets, if necessary.</u>

A. How many Georgia locations do you operate?
   Provide the following information for <u>each</u> location, attaching additional sheets if necessary.

B. Check the box that best describes the industry that relates to your business activities:

☐ Agriculture
☐ Forestry
☐ Fishing
☐ Mining
☐ Construction (specify):
  ___General Contractors Industrial ___ %
  Residential ___% Commercial ___ %
  ___Speculative Building
  ___Special Trade Contractor (specify plumbing, etc.,) _____
  ___Heavy Construction (specify cable, highway, etc.,) _____

☐ Manufacturing
☐ Transportation
☐ Communication
☐ Public Utilities
☐ Wholesale Trade
☐ Retail Trade
☐ Finance
☐ Insurance
☐ Real Estate
☐ Services
☐ Public Administration
☐ Private Household
☐ Employer

C. Enter in order of importance and indicate approximate % of total annual income derived from each:

Principal Service(s) Rendered*   **OR**   Principal Product(s)
☐ Mfg. ☐ Grown ☐ Sold

_____ _____ %
_____ _____ %
_____ _____ %

* If Transportation - Trucking, indicate if interstate carrier

D. If this report includes establishment(s) that <u>only</u> perform services for other units of the company, indicate the primary type of service or support provided. Check as many as apply:

1. ☐ Central Administration   3. ☐ Storage (warehouse)
2. ☐ Research, development,   4. ☐ Other: (specify)
   and testing   _____

FOR ASSISTANCE, call the Industry Classification Unit, (800) 338-2082

IMPORTANT - This report must be filed! The law provides that all employing units shall file a report of its employment during a calendar year. For the purpose of aiding you in complying with OCGA Section 34-8-121 of the Employment Security law, this form has been prepared to assist you in furnishing the required information. Answer all questions fully and <u>if additional space is necessary under any item, attach signed and dated sheets which bear the words Supplement to Form DOL-1."</u>

Each false statement or willful failure to furnish this report is punishable as a crime. Each day of such failure or refusal constitutes a separate offense.

The Georgia Employer Status Report is required of all employers having individuals performing services in Georgia regardless of number or duration of time.

The filing of this form is required at the time your business first had individuals performing service in Georgia, or when you acquired another legal entity, and <u>may</u> also be required again upon request.

NOTE: Disclosure of your social security number is mandatory. It will be used for the purpose of identification and it is required under the authority of 42 U.S.C. Section 405(2)(c) and OCGA Section 34-8-121(a).

INSTRUCTIONS
(NUMBERS CORRESPOND TO ITEMS ON FORM)

1. Enter or correct name and address of individual owner, partners, corporation or organization. This is the address to which you authorize us to mail all reports, correspondence, etc. If you have already been assigned a Georgia Department of Labor Account Number (Ga. DOL Acct. No) by this Department, please insert the number.
2. Indicate by check mark type of organization. If a nonprofit organization, attach copy of I.R.S. letter exempting the organization from Federal Income Tax under Section 501(c)(3)of Internal Revenue Code.
3. Trade name by which business is known if different than 1.
4. Physical location of business, farm or household in Georgia if different than 1. Please include telephone number with area code.
5. Enter the first date of employment in Georgia and the first date of Georgia payroll.
6. If you are subject to the Federal Unemployment Tax Act, and are required to file Federal Form 940, answer this question "yes". Be sure to enter your Federal Employer Identification Number whether answered "yes" or "no".
7. Answer this question if you acquired this business from another employer or if after you began employing workers you have acquired other businesses; merged with other businesses; formed or dissolved partnerships, corporations, professional associations; or if any other change in the ownership of the business has occurred. Indicate the date of acquisition or change and provide all information concerning the previous owner's name, trade name, address and DOL Account Number. Indicate by checking the appropriate block the portion of the previous owner's business involved in the acquisition or change. No transfer of experience rating history can be made unless information concerning the previous owner is provided.
8. Private Business Employment - Most employment is considered private business employment. This includes all types of work except domestic service such as maids, gardeners, cooks, etc., agricultural service and service performed for governmental or nonprofit organizations.
9. Domestic employment includes all service for a person in the operation and maintenance of a private household, local college club or local chapter of a college fraternity or sorority such as chauffeurs, cooks, babysitters, gardeners, maids, butlers, private and/or social secretaries, etc. If you had such employment, consider only cash payments made to all individuals performing domestic services to determine if $1,000 or more cash wages were paid in any calendar quarter during 1977 and subsequent quarters.
10. Consider only cash payments made to all individuals performing agricultural services to determine if $20,000 or more cash wages were paid in any calendar quarter during 1977 and subsequent quarters.
11. Answer this question only if this business is a nonprofit organization exempt from Federal Income Tax under Section 501(c)(3) of the Internal Revenue Code. Attach a copy of the I.R.S. letter granting this exemption. Nonprofit organizations with tax exemptions other than under Section 501(c)(3) should answer question 8, Private Business Employment.
12. Self-explanatory.

FOR ASSISTANCE, call the Adjudication Section, (404) 232-3301.

Please RETAIN a copy for your files.

The enclosed envelope <u>requires postage.</u>

RETURN ORIGINAL WITHIN TEN (10) DAYS TO:

Georgia Department of Labor
P. O. Box 740234
Atlanta, GA 30374-0234

Form G-4 (Rev. 10/06)

STATE OF GEORGIA

EMPLOYEE'S WITHHOLDING ALLOWANCE CERTIFICATE

1a. YOUR FULL NAME	1b. YOUR SOCIAL SECURITY NUMBER
2a. HOME ADDRESS (Number, Street, or Rural Route)	2b. CITY, STATE AND ZIP CODE

READ INSTRUCTIONS ON REVERSE SIDE BEFORE COMPLETING THIS FORM

3. **MARITAL STATUS** (If you do not wish to claim an allowance, enter "0" in the brackets beside your marital status.)

A. Single: enter 0 or 1 .... [   ]

4. **DEPENDENT ALLOWANCES**   [   ]

B. Married Filing Joint, both ....
spouses working: enter 0 or 1 or 2 .... [   ]

C. Married Filing Joint, one ....
spouse working: enter 0 or 1 or 2 .... [   ]

5. **ADDITIONAL ALLOWANCES**   [   ]
(complete worksheet below)

D. Married Filing Separate:
enter 0 or 1 or 2 .... [   ]

E. Head of Household: ....
enter 0 or 1 or 2 .... [   ]

6. **ADDITIONAL WITHHOLDING** $_____

WORKSHEET FOR CALCULATING ADDITIONAL ALLOWANCES

This worksheet must be completed if Line 5 is greater than zero.

1. COMPLETE THIS LINE ONLY IF USING STANDARD DEDUCTION:
Yourself: ☐ Age 65 or over   ☐ Blind
Spouse: ☐ Age 65 or over   ☐ Blind   Number of boxes checked _____ x 1300 = $ _____

2. ADDITIONAL ALLOWANCES FOR DEDUCTIONS:

A. Estimated Federal Itemized Deductions .... $ _____

B. Georgia Standard Deduction (enter one):   Single/Head of Household $2,300
                                            Each Spouse $1,500 $ _____

C. Subtract Line B from Line A .... $ _____

D. Allowable Deductions to Federal Adjusted Gross Income .... $ _____

E. Add the Amounts on Lines 1, 2C, and 2D .... $ _____

F. Estimate of Taxable Income not Subject to Withholding .... $ _____

G. Subtract Line F from Line E (if zero or less, stop here) .... $ _____

H. Divide the Amount on Line G by $3,000. Enter total here and on Line 5 above .... _____
This is the maximum number of additional allowances you can claim. If the remainder is over $1,500 round up.

---

7. **LETTER USED** (Marital Status A, B, C, D, or E) _____   **TOTAL ALLOWANCES** (Total of Lines 3 - 5) _____
(Employer: The letter indicates the tax tables in the Employer's Tax Guide)

---

8. **EXEMPT:** Skip this line if you entered information on Lines 3 - 7. Read the instructions for Line 8 on page 2.

I claim exemption from withholding because I incurred no Georgia income tax liability last year and I do not expect to have a Georgia income tax liability this year. **Check here** ☐

I certify under penalty of perjury that I am entitled to the number of withholding allowances or the exemption from withholding status claimed on this Form G-4. Also, I authorize my employer to deduct per pay period the additional amount listed above.

Employee's Signature _____   Date _____

Employer: Complete Line 9 and mail entire form only if the employee claims over 14 allowances or exempt from withholding. If necessary, mail form to: Georgia Department of Revenue, Withholding Tax Unit, P. O. Box 49432, Atlanta, GA 30359.

9. **EMPLOYER'S NAME AND ADDRESS:**   EMPLOYER'S FEIN: _____

EMPLOYER'S WH#: _____

Do not accept forms claiming additional allowances unless the worksheet has been completed. Do not accept forms claiming exempt if numbers are written on Lines 3 - 7.

INSTRUCTIONS FOR COMPLETING FORM G-4

Enter your full name, address and social security number in boxes 1a through 2b.

Line 3: Write the number of allowances you are claiming in the brackets beside your marital status.

    A. Single - enter 1 if you are claiming yourself

    B. Married Filing Joint, both spouses working - enter 1 if you claim yourself or 2 if you claim yourself and your spouse

    C. Married Filing Joint, one spouse working - enter 1 if you claim yourself or 2 if you claim yourself and your spouse

    D. Married Filing Separate - enter 1 if you claim yourself or 2 if you claim yourself and your spouse

    E. Head of Household - enter 1 if you claim yourself but the individual(s) for whom you maintain a home does not qualify as a dependent; or 2 if you claim yourself and a qualified dependent for whom you maintain a home

    Do not claim a deduction on Line 4 for a dependent used to qualify you as head of household

Line 4: Enter the number of dependent allowances you are entitled to claim.

Line 5: Complete the worksheet on Form G-4 if you claim additional allowances. Enter the number from Line H here.

    Failure to complete and submit the worksheet will result in automatic denial of your claim.

Line 6: Enter a specific dollar amount that you authorize your employer to withhold in addition to the tax withheld based on your marital status and number of allowances.

Line 7: Enter the letter of your marital status from Line 3. Enter total of the numbers on Lines 3 - 5.

Line 8: Check the box if you qualify to claim exempt from withholding. You can claim exempt if you filed a Georgia income tax return last year and the amount on Line 4 of Form 500EZ or Line 16 of Form 500 was zero, **and** you expect to file a Georgia tax return this year and will not have a tax liability. You can not claim exempt if you did not file a Georgia income tax return for the previous tax year. **Receiving a refund for the previous tax year does not qualify you to claim exempt.**
Do not complete Lines 3 - 7 if claiming exempt.

    EXAMPLES: Your employer withheld $500 of Georgia income tax from your wages. The amount on Line 4 of Form 500EZ or Line 16 of Form 500 was $100. Your tax liability is the amount on Line 4 or Line 16; therefore, **you do not qualify** to claim exempt.

    Your employer withheld $500 of Georgia income tax from your wages. The amount on Line 4 of Form 500EZ or Line 16 of Form 500 was $0 (zero) and you filed a prior year income tax return. Your tax liability is the amount on Line 4 or Line 16; therefore, **you qualify** to claim exempt.

NOTE: Effective January 1, 2003, the deduction allowed for the dependents increased from $2,700 to $3,000. This does not apply to the deduction allowed for you or your spouse.

O.C.G.A. § 48-7-102 requires you to complete and submit Form G-4 to your employer in order to have tax withheld from your wages. By correctly completing this form, you can adjust the amount of tax withheld to meet your tax liability. Failure to submit a properly completed Form G-4 will result in your employer withholding tax as though you are single with zero allowances.

Employers are required to mail any Form G-4 claiming more than 14 allowances or exempt from withholding to the Georgia Department of Revenue for approval. Employers will honor the properly completed form as submitted pending notification from the Withholding Tax Unit. Upon approval, such forms remain in effect until changed or until February 15 of the following year. Employers who know that a G-4 is erroneous should not honor the form and should withhold as if the employee is single claiming zero allowances until a corrected form has been received.

CRF-002 (Rev. 9/07)
GEORGIA DEPARTMENT OF REVENUE
REGISTRATION & LICENSING UNIT
P. O. BOX 49512
ATLANTA, GEORGIA 30359-1512
Fax: 404-417-4317 OR 404-417-4318
NEED HELP? CALL (404) 417-4490

E-MAIL: TSD-sales-tax-lic@dor.ga.gov
(PLEASE PRINT OR TYPE)

STATE TAX REGISTRATION APPLICATION
(Please Read Instructions Before Completing)

	IDENTIFICATION SECTION

1	IF YOU HAVE A STATE TAXPAYER IDENTIFIER (STI), ENTER HERE:

2 REASON FOR APPLICATION   ☐ New Business   ☐ Additional Tax Registration

☐ Application for a Master Number (4 or more Locations)   ☐ Change in Ownership Structure   ☐ Change in Alcohol Licensee*

☐ Change in Location Address (Alcohol Only)*

☐ New Location for a Master Sales Tax Account   Master Sales Tax Number :

3 FOR WHICH OF THE FOLLOWING ARE YOU APPLYING?

☐ Sales and Use Tax   ☐ Withholding Tax   ☐ Non-Resident Distribution

☐ Alcohol License *   ☐ Amusement License *   ☐ Tobacco License*

☐ Motor Fuel Distributor *   ☐ e-File/e-Pay Bulk Filer

Applications with an asterisk (*) require an additional application – See instructions for details

(If your business is a Sole Proprietorship – Your Name is the Legal Business Name)

4 LEGAL BUSINESS NAME

5 TRADE NAME / DBA NAME

6 TYPE OF OWNERSHIP   ☐ Sole Proprietorship   ☐ County Government   ☐ State Agency

☐ Estate   ☐ Partnership   ☐ Municipality   ☐ Federal Agency

☐ Fiduciary   ☐ Subchapter S Corp.   ☐ Professional Association   ☐ LLC

☐ Corporation   State of Inc. _____   Date of Incorporation   /   /

7 IF THE BUSINESS LISTED ABOVE HAS A "Federal Employer ID" NUMBER, ENTER HERE:

8 IF SEASONAL BUSINESS, STATE MONTHS BUSINESS WILL BE OPEN: Begin   Thru

9 WHAT IS THE LAST MONTH AND DAY OF YOUR ACCOUNTING YEAR: Month   Day

10 Which ACCOUNTING METHOD WILL YOU USE?   ☐ Cash Basis   ☐ Accrual Basis

11 IF THIS APPLICATION IS FOR A BUSINESS YOU PURCHASED, PROVIDE THE FOLLOWING INFORMATION REGARDING THE FORMER OWNER, IF KNOWN.

Legal Business Name   State Tax Identifier:

Georgia Sales Tax Number: Georgia Withholding Tax Number: Alcohol License:

	ADDRESS SECTION

12 PHYSICAL LOCATION ADDRESS, NUMBER AND STREET, SUITE/APARTMENT NUMBER (**YOU CANNOT** use a P.O. Box)
USING A POST OFFICE BOX FOR THIS ADDRESS WILL DELAY PROCESSING OF THIS APPLICATION.
NUMBER AND STREET ADDRESS

CITY   STATE   ZIP CODE   COUNTY   COUNTRY

13 PHONE   FAX   E-MAIL

14 IS THE ABOVE ADDRESS LOCATED WITHIN THE CITY LIMITS?   ☐ Yes   ☐ No

NOTE: To have correspondence and reporting forms sent to separate addresses, please complete Lines 15 and 16 and indicate the related tax type(s) for each. To list additional mailing addresses use Form CRF-003.

15 MAILING ADDRESS – IF DIFFERENT FROM THE LOCATION ADDRESS ON LINE 12 ABOVE.
(Please identify tax type(s) to be mailed to the address below.)

A ☐ Sales and Use   ☐ Withholding   ☐ Amusement   ☐ Alcohol   ☐ Tobacco   ☐ Motor Fuel Distributor

B ADDRESSEE (c/o) (If different from or in addition to the Legal Business Name)   E-MAIL ADDRESS

C NUMBER AND STREET, P. O. BOX or RFD NO.

D CITY   STATE   ZIP CODE   COUNTY   COUNTRY

E PHONE   FAX

16 ADDITIONAL MAILING ADDRESS – (Please identify tax type(s) to be mailed to the address below.)

A ☐ Sales and Use   ☐ Withholding   ☐ Amusement   ☐ Alcohol   ☐ Tobacco   ☐ Motor Fuel Distributor

B ADDRESSEE (c/o) (If different from or in addition to the Legal Business Name)   E-MAIL ADDRESS

C NUMBER AND STREET, P. O. BOX or RFD NO.

D CITY   STATE   ZIP CODE   COUNTY   COUNTRY

E PHONE   FAX

(Please Read Instructions Before Completing)

OWNERSHIP / RELATIONSHIP SECTION
(This section MUST be completed for your application to be accepted.)

17	CHECK ALL THAT APPLY	EFFECTIVE DATE ___/___/___

☐ Owner ☐ Officer ☐ Manager ☐ Tobacco Licensee
☐ Partner ☐ Managing Member ☐ Alcohol Licensee

A	BUSINESS NAME	STI or LICENSE NO. (If Applicable)
B	GA SALES TAX NO. (If Applicable)	GA WITHHOLDING TAX NO. (If Applicable)
C	LAST NAME	FIRST	M.I.	TITLE
	SOCIAL SECURITY NUMBER	Application will not be processed unless the social security number of an owner, officers, managing members or both partners is included. Reg. 560-1-1.18
D	ADDRESS	
E	CITY	STATE ZIP COUNTY COUNTRY PHONE

18	CHECK ALL THAT APPLY	EFFECTIVE DATE ___/___/___

☐ Owner ☐ Officer ☐ Manager ☐ Tobacco Licensee
☐ Partner ☐ Managing Member ☐ Alcohol Licensee

A	BUSINESS NAME	STI or LICENSE NO. (If Applicable)
B	GA SALES TAX NO. (If Applicable)	GA WITHHOLDING TAX NO. (If Applicable)
C	LAST NAME	FIRST	M.I.	TITLE
	SOCIAL SECURITY NUMBER	Application will not be processed unless the social security number of an owner, officers, managing members or both partners is included. Reg. 560-1-1.18
D	ADDRESS	
E	CITY	STATE ZIP COUNTY COUNTRY PHONE

(TO REPORT ADDITIONAL RELATIONSHIPS, USE FORM CRF-004)

SALES AND USE TAX SECTION

19	NATURE OF BUSINESS (If combination of two or more, list approximate percentages of receipts. Must equal 100%.)

☐ Retail ___% ☐ Manufacturing ___% ☐ Services (Specify) ___% _____
☐ Wholesale ___% ☐ Construction ___% ☐ Other (Specify) ___% _____

20	WHAT KIND OF BUSINESS WILL YOU OPERATE? (Be specific as to the product sold or service provided.)
21	DO YOU EXPECT TO REMIT MORE THAN $200 PER MONTH? ☐ Yes ☐ No
22	WILL YOU SELL ALCOHOLIC BEVERAGES? ☐ Yes ** ☐ No ** Additional Forms Required
23	WILL YOU SELL RETAIL TOBACCO PRODUCTS? ☐ Yes ** ☐ No ** Additional Forms Required
24	WILL YOU SELL GASOLINE AND/OR MOTOR FUEL? ☐ Yes ☐ No
	If "Yes", please specify the name of the dealer responsible for paying the tax on gasoline and/or motor fuel sales, if other than yourself.
	NAME _____ SALES TAX NO. _____
25	WHEN DID OR WILL YOU START SELLING OR PURCHASING ITEMS SUBJECT TO SALES TAX?
	Date ___/___/___
26	WILL YOU SELL LOTTERY AT THIS LOCATION? ☐ Yes ☐ No If "Yes", PLEASE PROVIDE YOUR RETAILER NUMBER _____
27	WILL YOU HAVE EMPLOYEES? ☐ Yes ☐ No If "Yes", complete the following WITHHOLDING TAX SECTION. If "No", stop here and complete the SIGNATURE SECTION.

WITHHOLDING TAX SECTION

28	WHO WILL BE RESPONSIBLE FOR FILING AND REMITTING THE PAYROLL TAXES FOR YOUR EMPLOYEES?
	☐ Applicant or Payroll Service Bureau ☐ Other
	If "Other", list the name and GA. Withholding No. of the business responsible for paying these taxes.
	NAME _____ GA. WITHHOLDING TAX NO. _____
29	DO YOU EXPECT TO WITHHOLD MORE THAN $200 PER MONTH? ☐ Yes ☐ No
30	HOW MANY EMPLOYEES DOES THIS BUSINESS HAVE OR WILL HAVE?
31	DATE ON WHICH WAGES WERE OR WILL FIRST BE PAID?

SIGNATURE SECTION

I HAVE EXAMINED THIS APPLICATION, AND TO THE BEST OF MY KNOWLEDGE IT IS TRUE AND CORRECT

_____ _____ _____
Signature Title Date

MUST BE SIGNED BY OWNER, PARTNER, MANAGING MEMBER, OR
CORPORATE OFFICER AS LISTED IN THE RELATIONSHIP SECTION (17 OR 18) ABOVE.

Rev. 09/07

INSTRUCTIONS FOR COMPLETION OF THE STATE TAX REGISTRATION APPLICATION
(PLEASE TYPE OR PRINT IN INK)

IDENTIFICATION SECTION

Line 1.   Enter your Georgia State Taxpayer Identifier Number. (If you do not have a number, leave blank.)

Line 2.   Indicate the reason for this application as follows:

    a.   **NEW BUSINESS** – If you are starting a new business or you have purchased an existing business, check here.

    b.   **ADDITIONAL TAX REGISTRATION** – If you are currently registered and have a tax ID number and you are applying for an additional tax registration number, check here.

    c.   **APPLICATION FOR A MASTER NUMBER** – If you currently have 4 or more locations within Georgia, check here. (**You are required by law to file your sales tax reports under a consolidated number.**)

    d.   **CHANGE IN OWNERSHIP STRUCTURE** (Example: proprietorship to corporation) – If your business is currently registered under one type of ownership and will be operating under a different type of ownership structure, check here.

    e.   **CHANGE IN ALCOHOL LICENSEE** – If current licensee has a Georgia Alcohol License and it is being changed to a new licensee, check here

    f.   **CHANGE IN LOCATION ADDRESS (ALCOHOL ONLY)**: If you are registered and have a current alcohol account and you are changing the location address, check here.

    g.   **NEW LOCATION FOR A MASTER SALES TAX ACCOUNT**: If you are adding a new location to your Master Sales Tax account, check here.

Line 3.   Check all tax license(s) and/or permit type(s) for which you are applying. Complete the CRF-002 and any of the following form(s) that apply to your registration.

Tax Type or License	Additional Form(s)	Form Name
Amusement License	CRF-013	Coin-Operated Amusement Machine Application
Motor Fuel Distributor	CRF-007	Motor Fuel Distributor Application
	FS-MFD-26	Motor Fuel Distributor's Bond (If Applicable)
Tobacco License	CRF-008	Tobacco License Application
Alcohol License Retail – Beer	CRF-009	State Alcohol License Application
Alcohol License Retail – Wine	CRF-009	State Alcohol License Application
Alcohol License Retail – Liquor	CRF-009	Alcohol License Application
	ATT-59	Retail Dealers & Retail Consumption Dealers Liquor Bond
	ATT-17	State Beverage Alcohol Personnel Statement
Alcohol Wholesale	ATT-104	Application for Brand and Label Registration and Designation of Sales Territory

Line 4.   If your business is registered with the Secretary of State, enter the name under which your business is legally registered. If your business is not registered, then enter the name under which you plan to operate.

Line 5.   Enter the trade name or doing-business-as (DBA) name of your business entity only if different from the Legal Business Name on Line 4.

Line 6.   Check the ownership structure under which your business is owned and operates. If the business is a "Corporation", enter the State and Date of Incorporation. (NOTE: If the business owners are a married couple, the ownership will presume to be a partnership.)

Line 7.   Enter your Federal Employer Identification (FEI) Number. If you have applied for an FEI number, write "APPLIED FOR." (Leave Blank If you do not have a current (FEI) number, and have not applied for one.)

Line 8.   If your business only operates seasonally, indicate the months you will conduct business, otherwise, disregard this line.

Line 9.   Enter the last month and day of your business' accounting year.

Line 10.   Check the accounting method you will use.
    Cash Basis – The seller reports the sale and remits the tax in the month that the tax is collected.
    Accrual Basis – The seller reports the sale and remits the tax in the month that the sale is made.

Rev. 09/07

Line 11.   If you purchased an existing business, enter the following information regarding the former owner if known: legal business name, State tax identifier number, Georgia Sales Tax Number, Withholding Tax Number, and/or Alcohol License Number.

ADDRESS SECTION

Line 12.   Enter the physical location address of your business including suite/apartment number. **(A post office box is not acceptable for a location address. If a P.O. Box is used, processing of your application will be delayed.)**

Line 13.   Enter the business phone number and e-mail address.

Line 14.   Check "yes" or "no" if your location address is within the city limits. (Disregard this line if business is not located in Georgia.)

Line 15.   Enter the mailing address of your business if different from the location address listed on Line 12.

    Line a.   Check all tax type(s) for the address you are entering. **(If you would like to have correspondence or reporting forms from any taxing unit sent to separate locations, please list these addresses on Lines 15 and/or 16, and indicate the tax type related to each. Use form CRF-003 for additional addresses.)**

    Line b.   If the addressee name is different from or in addition to the legal business name, enter the name as it should appear on a mailing label; otherwise, leave blank.

    Line c.   Enter the number and street address, P.O. Box or RFD Number.

    Line d.   Enter the city, state, zip code, county and country. (Note: enter only if address is located in Georgia)

    Line e.   Enter the phone number and e-mail address.

Line 16.   List any additional mailing address if necessary. Please refer to the instructions on Line 15 in completing this Section. **Use Form CRF-003 to list additional mailing addresses.**

OWNERSHIP/RELATIONSHIP SECTION

Line 17.   **The Department of Revenue requires that the following information be completed on all individuals or businesses to determine the relationship/ownership of the applying business.** This Section **MUST** be completed. **(If not completed your application will not be approved.** Complete one Section for each related business or individual, check all relationships that apply, and enter the effective date of that relationship. For all applications, provide information for the following:

    – **Owner** – If owner of the business, complete items C, D, and E.

    – **Partner** – If the business is a partnership, complete a separate RELATIONSHIP Section (C, D, and E) for each partner.

    – **Officer** – If the business is a corporation, complete a separate RELATIONSHIP Section (C, D, and E) for each corporate officer.

    – **Manager** – If manager of the business, complete items C, D, and E.

    – **Managing Member** – If the business is a LLC, complete a separate RELATIONSHIP Section (C, D, and E) for each managing member.

    – **Alcohol and Tobacco Licensee** – If the licensee is an individual, complete items C, D, and E. If the licensee is a Corporation, complete items A, B, D, and E.

For All Relationships:

    Line a.   If the relationship checked is a business entity, enter the name of that business entity and the State Taxpayer Identifier (STI) number or license number (if known).

    Line b.   If this business is registered for Georgia Sales Tax and/or Withholding Tax, enter its Sales Tax and/or Withholding Tax numbers (if known).

    Line c.   If the relationship checked is an individual, enter the individual's full name, title, and Social Security Number (Social Insurance Number if Canadian). **A Social Security number is required: Revenue Regulation 560-1-1-18.**

    Line d.   Enter the individual or business address here.

    Line e.   Enter the city, state, zip code, county and country. (Note: enter only if address is located in Georgia)

Line 18.   List any additional ownership/relationships. Please refer to the instructions on Line 17 in completing this Section. **Use Form CRF-004 to identify any additional ownership/relationship types.**

Rev. 09/07

SALES AND USE TAX SECTION

Line 19.   Identify the nature of your business. (If it is a combination of two or more businesses list percentages of receipts for each, total percentage must equal 100%)

Line 20.   Enter the kind of business you will operate, product(s) for sale, and/or service(s) to be provided. Examples of businesses are: grocery, restaurant, bakery, chain food store, department store, jewelry, hardware, service station, automobile dealership, furniture store, motel or hotel, warehouse, manufacturing plant, book store, etc. Specify if it is a combination of businesses.

Line 21.   Check "yes" if you expect to remit more than $200 per month; otherwise, check "no".

Line 22.   Check appropriate yes or no answers as to whether you will or will not sell alcoholic beverages. If "yes" complete the required additional form from line 3 of the application instructions.

Line 23.   Check appropriate yes or no answers as to whether you will or will not sell tobacco products. If "yes" complete the required additional form from line 3 of the application instructions.

Line 24.   Check appropriate yes or no answers as to whether you will or will not sell gasoline and/or other motor fuels. If "yes", specify the dealer responsible for paying tax on the gasoline and/or motor fuel sales and enter Sales Tax Number, if other than yourself.

Line 25.   Enter the date you actually started or will start selling or purchasing items subject to sales tax. (If this is an out-of-state business, enter the date of your first activity in Georgia.) **Do not indicate your date of incorporation for the answer to this question**. (Month/Day/Year required.)

Line 26.   Check appropriate yes or no answers as to whether you will or will not sell Lottery at this location. If "yes", provide your retailer number.

Line 27   Check appropriate yes or no answers as to whether you will or will not have employees. If "yes", complete the Withholding Tax Section. If "no", proceed to Signature Section.

WITHHOLDING TAX SECTION

Line 28.   Check "Applicant or Payroll Service Bureau" or "Other" to identify the party responsible for filing and remitting the required payroll taxes. If "Applicant or Payroll Service Bureau", your business will be assigned a withholding number. If "Other", list the name and a Withholding Number of the business responsible for paying these taxes. The name and number listed will be verified with our Registration records. If this information cannot be verified, a withholding number will be issued to the applicant.

Line 29.   Check "yes" if you expect to withhold more than $200 per month; otherwise, check "no".

Line 30.   Enter the number of employees hired or that you anticipate hiring once the business is started.

Line 31.   For Georgia Withholding Tax Purposes, enter the date of your first payroll. (Month/Day/Year required.)

SIGNATURE SECTION

This application must be signed by owner, partner, or corporate officer. This form will not be accepted unless signed by someone listed in the Relationship Section or on Form CRF-004. **Stamp signature(s) will not be accepted.**

If Sales and Use Tax was collected or Georgia Withholding Tax was withheld and due prior to the filing of this application, please complete and attach the appropriate tax return with separate checks and identify each check by tax type. (Combined tax payments are not acceptable and will delay the processing of your tax payments.)

The processing of this application will be delayed unless all applicable questions are answered; required information is provided, and application is properly signed. Please retain a copy of this application for your file.

PLEASE ALLOW 1 TO 2 WEEKS FOR PROCESSING OF APPLICATION.
MAIL OR FAX COMPLETED APPLICATION TO:

GEORGIA DEPARTMENT OF REVENUE
P. O. BOX 49512
ATLANTA, GA 30359-1512
FAX: 404-417-4317 or 404-417-4318

This page intentionally left blank.

0605704012

CRF-003 REV. 5/05
GEORGIA DEPARTMENT OF REVENUE
REGISTRATION & LICENSING UNIT
P. O. BOX 49512
ATLANTA, GA 30359-1512
404-417-4490
TSD-sales-tax-lic@dor.ga.gov

ADDITIONAL ADDRESS FORM
(Complete Only If Necessary)

(PLEASE PRINT OR TYPE)

FOR OFFICE USE ONLY	LEGAL BUSINESS NAME:

ADDITIONAL MAILING ADDRESS (Please identify tax type(s) to be mailed to the address below.)

☐ Sales & Use   ☐ Withholding   ☐ Alcohol
☐ Tobacco   ☐ Amusement   ☐ Motor Fuel Distributor

ADDRESSEE (C/O) (If different from or in addition to the Legal Business Name)   E-MAIL ADDRESS

NUMBER AND STREET, P. O. BOX, RFD NO.   FAX NUMBER
(   )

CITY   STATE   ZIP   COUNTY   COUNTRY   PHONE NUMBER
(   )

ADDITIONAL MAILING ADDRESS (Please identify tax type(s) to be mailed to the address below.)

☐ Sales & Use   ☐ Withholding   ☐ Alcohol
☐ Tobacco   ☐ Amusement   ☐ Motor Fuel Distributor

ADDRESSEE (C/O) (If different from or in addition to the Legal Business Name)   E-MAIL ADDRESS

NUMBER AND STREET, P. O. BOX, RFD NO.   FAX NUMBER
(   )

CITY   STATE   ZIP   COUNTY   COUNTRY   PHONE NUMBER
(   )

ADDITIONAL MAILING ADDRESS (Please identify tax type(s) to be mailed to the address below.)

☐ Sales & Use   ☐ Withholding   ☐ Alcohol
☐ Tobacco   ☐ Amusement   ☐ Motor Fuel Distributor

ADDRESSEE (C/O) (If different from or in addition to the Legal Business Name)

NUMBER AND STREET, P. O. BOX, RFD NO.

CITY   STATE   ZIP   COUNTY   COUNTRY   PHONE NUMBER
(   )

ADDITIONAL MAILING ADDRESS (Please identify tax type(s) to be mailed to the address below.)

☐ Sales & Use   ☐ Withholding   ☐ Alcohol
☐ Tobacco   ☐ Amusement   ☐ Motor Fuel Distributor

ADDRESSEE (C/O) (If different from or in addition to the Legal Business Name)   E-MAIL ADDRESS

NUMBER AND STREET, P. O. BOX, RFD NO.   FAX NUMBER
(   )

CITY   STATE   ZIP   COUNTY   COUNTRY   PHONE NUMBER
(   )

SIGNATURE SECTION

I HAVE EXAMINED THIS FORM, AND TO THE BEST OF MY KNOWLEDGE IT IS TRUE AND CORRECT.

_____   _____   _____
Signature   Title   Date

(MUST BE SIGNED BY OWNER, PARTNER, OR CORPORATE OFFICER AS LISTED IN THE RELATIONSHIP SECTION ABOVE.)

This page intentionally left blank.

ST-5 (REV. 05-00)

STATE OF GEORGIA
DEPARTMENT OF REVENUE
SALES AND USE TAX CERTIFICATE OF EXEMPTION
GEORGIA PURCHASER OR DEALER
EFFECTIVE JULY 1, 2000

To: _____   (MM/DD/YY) _____
            (SUPPLIER)   (DATE)

_____
(ADDRESS)

THE UNDERSIGNED HEREBY CERTIFIES that all tangible personal property purchased or leased after this date will be for the purpose indicated below, unless otherwise specified on a particular order, and that this certificate shall remain in effect until revoked in writing. Any tangible personal property obtained under this certificate of exemption is subject to the sales and use tax if it is used or consumed by the purchaser in any manner other than indicated on this certificate. (Check proper box.)

[   ]   1.   Resale, rental or leased only, including but not limited to the purchase for resale of gasoline and other motor fuels.

[   ]   2.   Materials for further processing, manufacture or conversion into articles of tangible personal property for resale which will become a component part of the property for sale, or be coated upon or impregnated into the product at any stage of its processing, manufacture or conversion and nonreturnable materials used for packaging tangible personal property for shipment or sale. Containers or other packaging materials purchased for reuse are not exempt.

[   ]   3.   Machinery used directly in the manufacture of tangible personal property for sale purchased as <u>additional, replacement or upgrade</u> machinery to be placed into an existing plant in this State.

[   ]   4.   Direct Pay Permit authorized under Regulation 560-12-1-.16. The holder of a Direct Pay Permit must pay the 3% Second Motor Fuel Tax to suppliers on purchases of gasoline.

[   ]   5.   For use by Federal Government, State Government, any county, municipality or public school system of this State, when supported by official purchase orders or for use by Hospital Authorities created by Article 4, Chapter 7, of Title 7, and County or City Housing Authorities created by Article 1, Chapter 3 of Title 8. The State of Georgia, counties, municipalities, public schools, Hospital and Housing Authorities of Georgia must pay the 3% Second Motor Fuel Tax to suppliers.
A Georgia Sales and Use Tax Certificate of Registration Number is not required for this exemption.

[   ]   6.   Aircraft, watercraft, motor vehicles and other transportation equipment manufactured or assembled, sold and delivered by the manufacturer or assembler for use exclusively outside this State, or delivery of the crafts is for the sole purpose of removing same under its own power when it does not lend itself more reasonably to removal by other means.
A Georgia Sales and Use Tax Certificate of Registration Number is not required for this exemption.

[   ]   7.   Aircraft, watercraft, railroad locomotives and rolling stock, motor vehicles and major components of each, which will be used principally to cross the borders of this State in the service of transporting passengers or cargo by common carriers and by carriers who hold common carrier and contract carrier authority in interstate or foreign commerce under authority granted by the United States government. Replacement parts installed by carriers in such craft or vehicles which become an integral part of the craft or vehicle are likewise exempt. Private and contract carriers are not exempt.

_____   _____
(TYPE OF BUSINESS ENGAGED IN BY THE PURCHASER)   (COMMODITY CODE)

I declare, under penalties of false swearing, that this certificate has been examined by me and to the best of my knowledge and belief is true and correct, made in good faith, pursuant to the sales and use tax laws of the State of Georgia.

_____   _____
(PURCHASER'S FIRM NAME)   (CERTIFICATE OF REGISTRATION NO.)

_____
(ADDRESS)

By _____   Title _____
            (SIGNATURE)   (OWNER, PARTNER, OFFICIAL)

A supplier is required to have only one certificate of exemption form on file from each purchaser buying tax exempt. The supplier must exercise ordinary care to determine that the tangible personal property obtained under this certificate is for the purpose indicated. Suppliers failing to exercise such care will be held liable for the sales tax due on such purchases. <u>For example, a supplier cannot accept a Certificate of Registration number bearing a "214" prefix since these are issued to a Contractor which has been deemed to be the consumer and is required to pay the tax at the time of purchase.</u>

This page intentionally left blank.

Form **ST-3** (Rev. 01/06)
Georgia Department of Revenue
Sales and Use Tax Division
P.O. Box 105296
Atlanta, Georgia 30348-5296

0702804013

Amended Return
Final Return
One Time Only Sale
EFT Payment

Name and Address

SALES AND USE #
COMMODITY CODE
COUNTY OF BUSINESS REGISTRATION

SALES AND USE TAX REPORT	USE THIS FORM ONLY FOR THE PRINTED PERIOD	To

Part A

1. Total Sales ....

2. Total Use ....

3. Total Sales and Use ....

4. Taxable State Sales & Use ....

5. Taxable MARTA Sales & Use ....

6. Taxable Local Option Sales & Use ....

7. Taxable Other Local Option Sales & Use ....

8. Taxable Special Purpose Sales & Use ....

9. Taxable Educational Sales & Use ....

10. Taxable Homestead Sales & Use ....

11. Total Tax from Tax Column ....

12. Excess Tax: Factor Amount .... +

13. Total Tax Amount ....

14. Vendor's Compensation .... -

15. Penalty (Use Penalty Worksheet) .... +

16. Interest (1% per month or fraction thereof) ..... +

17. Previous Prepaid Amount .... -

18. Current Prepaid Amount .... +

19. Credit (See instructions) ....

20. **Remit This Amount** ....

DEPARTMENT USE ONLY

Part B

---> Tax Rate

X .04 =

X .01 =

X .01 =

X .01 =

X .01 =

X .01 =

X .01 =

<--**Total**-->

TAX COLUMN

SCHEDULE OF TOTAL EXEMPTIONS / DEDUCTIONS

Part C

A. Total State ....

B. Total MARTA ....

C. Total Local ....

D. Total Other Local ....

E. Total Special ....

F. Total Educational ....

G. Total Homestead ....

268

0702804023

Part D

I certify that this return, including the accompanying schedules or statements, has been examined by me and is, to the best of my knowledge and belief, a true and

complete return made in good faith for the period stated. This _____ day of _____, _____

Return Prepared By_____Signature_____   _____ _____

Title   Phone Number

This return must be filed and paid by the 20th of the month following the period for which the tax is due to avoid loss of vendor's compensation and the payment of penalty and interest. **DEALERS AND CONTRACTORS MUST FILE A TIMELY RETURN EVEN THOUGH NO TAX IS DUE. DO NOT SEND CASH BY MAIL.**

Remittance by Electronic Funds Transfer (EFT) must be completed by 3:00 p.m. on the 19th. If the 20th is a Saturday, Sunday, Monday or a Federal Holiday the EFT must be completed before 3:00 p.m. on the preceding Friday.

Part E-County Distribution Schedule

S&U #

Enter the 1% tax reported for each county and tax type

County	Code	Homestead	Marta	Other Local Option
DeKalb	044			/////
Fulton	060	/////		/////
Rockdale	122		/////	/////
Towns	139	/////	/////	
City of Atlanta	060	/////	/////	
Total				

County	Code	Local	Special	Educational
DeKalb	044	/////	/////	
Fulton	060		/////	
Rockdale	122	/////		
Towns	139		/////	
Total				

COUNTY RATE CHART
EFFECTIVE April 1, 2007

CODE	COUNTY	RATE	TYPE		CODE	COUNTY	RATE	TYPE		CODE	COUNTY	RATE	TYPE
001	Appling	6	LS		058	Forsyth	7	LSE		115	Polk	7	LSE
002	Atkinson	7	LSE		059	Franklin	7	LSE		116	Pulaski	7	LSE
003	Bacon	7	LSE		060	Fulton	7	M L E		117	Putnam	7	LSE
004	Baker	7	LSE		061	Gilmer	7	LSE		118	Quitman	7	LSE
005	Baldwin	7	LSE		062	Glascock	7	LSE		119	Rabun	7	LSE
006	Banks	7	LSE		063	Glynn	6	LS		120	Randolph	7	LSE
007	Barrow	7	LSE		064	Gordon	7	LSE		121	Richmond	7	LSE
008	Bartow	7	LSE		065	Grady	7	LSE		122	Rockdale	7	SEH
009	Ben Hill	7	LSE		066	Greene	7	LSE		123	Schley	7	LSE
010	Berrien	7	LSE		067	Gwinnett	6	SE		124	Screven	7	LSE
011	Bibb	7	LSE		068	Habersham	7	LSE		125	Seminole	7	LSE
012	Bleckley	7	LSE		069	Hall	7	LSE		126	Spalding	7	LSE
013	Brantley	7	LSE		070	Hancock	7	LSE		127	Stephens	7	LSE
014	Brooks	7	LSE		071	Haralson	7	LSE		128	Stewart	7	LSE
015	Bryan	7	LSE		072	Harris	7	LSE		129	Sumter	7	LSE
016	Bulloch	7	LSE		073	Hart	7	LSE		130	Talbot	7	LSE
017	Burke	6	LS		074	Heard	7	LSE		131	Taliaferro	7	LSE
018	Butts	7	LSE		075	Henry	7	LSE		132	Tattnall	7	LSE
019	Calhoun	7	LSE		076	Houston	7	LSE		133	Taylor	7	LSE
020	Camden	6	LS		077	Irwin	7	LSE		134	Telfair	7	LSE
021	Candler	7	LSE		078	Jackson	7	LSE		135	Terrell	7	LSE
022	Carroll	7	LSE		079	Jasper	7	LSE		136	Thomas	7	LSE
023	Catoosa	7	LSE		080	Jeff Davis	7	LSE		137	Tift	7	LSE
024	Charlton	7	LSE		081	Jefferson	7	LSE		138	Toombs	7	LSE
025	Chatham	7	LSE		082	Jenkins	7	LSE		139	Towns	7	L E O
026	Chattahoochee	7	LSE		083	Johnson	7	LSE		140	Treutlen	7	LSE
027	Chattooga	7	LSE		084	Jones	7	LSE		141	Troup	7	LSE
028	Cherokee	6	SE		085	Lamar	7	LSE		142	Turner	7	LSE
029	Clarke	7	LSE		086	Lanier	7	LSE		143	Twiggs	7	LSE
030	Clay	7	LSE		087	Laurens	7	LSE		144	Union	7	LSE
031	Clayton	7	LSE		088	Lee	7	LSE		145	Upson	7	LSE
032	Clinch	7	LSE		089	Liberty	7	LSE		146	Walker	7	LSE
033	Cobb	6	SE		090	Lincoln	7	LSE		147	Walton	7	LSE
034	Coffee	7	LSE		091	Long	7	LSE		148	Ware	7	LSE
035	Colquitt	7	LSE		092	Lowndes	7	LSE		149	Warren	7	LSE
036	Columbia	7	LSE		093	Lumpkin	7	LSE		150	Washington	7	LSE
037	Cook	7	LSE		094	Macon	7	LSE		151	Wayne	6	LS
038	Coweta	7	LSE		095	Madison	7	LSE		152	Webster	7	LSE
039	Crawford	7	LSE		096	Marion	7	LSE		153	Wheeler	7	LSE
040	Crisp	7	LSE		097	McDuffie	7	LSE		154	White	7	LSE
041	Dade	7	LSE		098	McIntosh	7	LSE		155	Whitfield	6	L E
042	Dawson	7	LSE		099	Meriwether	7	LSE		156	Wilcox	7	LSE
043	Decatur	7	LSE		100	Miller	7	LSE		157	Wilkes	7	LSE
044	DeKalb	7	M EH		101	Mitchell	7	LSE		158	Wilkinson	7	LSE
045	Dodge	7	LSE		102	Monroe	7	LSE		159	Worth	7	LSE
046	Dooly	7	LSE		103	Montgomery	7	LSE		060	**City of Atlanta**	1	O
047	Dougherty	7	LSE		104	Morgan	7	LSE					
048	Douglas	7	LSE		105	Murray	7	LSE					
049	Early	7	LSE		106	Muscogee	7	LSE					
050	Echols	7	LSE		107	Newton	7	LSE					
051	Effingham	7	LSE		108	Oconee	7	LSE					
052	Elbert	7	LSE		109	Oglethorpe	7	LSE					
053	Emanuel	7	LSE		110	Paulding	7	LSE					
054	Evans	7	LSE		111	Peach	7	LSE					
055	Fannin	7	LSE		112	Pickens	7	LSE					
056	Fayette	6	LS		113	Pierce	7	LSE					
057	Floyd	7	LSE		114	Pike	7	LSE					

M = MARTA   L = LOCAL OPTION   S = SPECIAL PURPOSE   E = EDUCATIONAL   H = HOMESTEAD   O = OTHER LOCAL OPTION

IMPORTANT BULLETINS

COUNTY TAX RATE CHANGES EFFECTIVE
July 1, 2007

Code - County	Rate	Type
001 APPLING	7	LSE
048 DOUGLAS	6	LE
063 GLYNN	7	LSE
123 SCHLEY	6	LS
143 TWIGGS	6	LS

Instructions for Sales and Use Tax Form Preparation

Rev 1/06

Part A

Line 1 Total Sales. Enter total sales, leases, and rentals for the reporting period. Do not include collected sales tax. If none, enter "0" on Line 1.

Line 2 Total Use. Enter total <u>use</u> for the reporting period for items used in Georgia on which applicable tax was not paid at time of purchase. If none, enter "0" on Line 2.

Line 3 Total Sales and Use. Enter total of Lines 1 and 2. If none, enter "0".

Line 4 Taxable State. Enter the total State sales and use minus any state exemptions. Use the exemption worksheet to determine any sales and use not taxed.

Line 5 Taxable Marta. Enter the total Marta sales and use minus Marta exemptions. Use the exemption worksheet to determine any sales and use not taxed.

Line 6 Taxable Local Option. Enter the total Local Option sales and use minus Local Option exemptions. Use the exemption worksheet to determine any sales and use not taxed.

Line 7 Taxable Other Local Option. Enter the total Other Local Option sales and use minus Other Local Option exemptions. Use the exemption worksheet to determine any sales and use not taxed.

Line 8 Taxable Special Purpose. Enter the total Special Purpose sales and use minus Special Purpose exemptions. Use the exemption worksheet to determine any sales and use not taxed.

Line 9 Taxable Educational. Enter the total Educational sales and use minus Educational exemptions. Use the exemption worksheet to determine any sales and use not taxed.

Line 10 Taxable Homestead. Enter the total Homestead sales and use minus Homestead exemptions. Use the exemption worksheet to determine any sales and use not taxed.

Line 11 Total Tax from Tax Column (Line 4 through 10 of Part B). Enter total of Part B, Tax Column.

Line 12 Excess Tax. Enter the amount of tax collected in excess of the Total tax. If filing under an established representative Conversion Factor, calculate the excess tax by multiplying the taxable State sales and use (Line 4) by the printed Conversion Factor rate.

Line 13 Total Tax Amount. Enter the sum of Line 11 and Line 12.

Line 14 Vendor's Compensation. Please review the instructions on Vendor's Compensation located in this booklet.

Line 15 Penalty. Please review the instructions on Penalty calculations located in this booklet.

Line 16 Interest. Interest is calculated on 1% of tax owed by number of months (or fraction thereof).

Line 17 Previous Prepaid Amount. The amount of Estimated tax previously paid will be printed on this line.

Line 18 Current Prepaid Amount. The amount of Estimated tax due is calculated by the Department and printed on this line. This amount is updated annually.

Line 19 Credit. Enter the amount of credit from a credit memorandum **issued by the Department** and attach the credit memorandum to the ST-3. This amount should be deducted from the Total Tax Amount minus Vendor's Compensation, plus penalty **and interest** (if any), minus Previous Prepaid Amount, plus Current Prepaid Amount.

Line 20 Remit This Amount. This amount is equal to the Total Tax Amount minus Vendor's Compensation, plus Penalty (if any), plus Interest (if any), minus Previous Prepaid Amount, plus Current Prepaid Amount.

Part B - Tax Column
After entering the reported sales, multiply by the Tax Rate for each type (listed). The total is placed on line 11 of Part A and Part B.

Part C - Schedule of Total Exemptions/Deductions
These figures are transferred from the Exemptions/Deductions Worksheet.

Part D
The return must be signed and dated prior to submitting to the Department of Revenue.

Part E - Distribution Schedule
Enter the total taxes collected for each county and tax type. Enter the County Name in column one and the County Code in column two (located on the rate chart). These figures must balance to Part B, Tax Column.

Amended Returns
An amended return should be submitted on a ST-3, Sales & Use Tax form. The appropriate box should be checked and/or the taxpayer may write "amended" on the top of the return. An amended return should only be done if the taxpayer is making changes to the original figures (i.e. Total Sales, Distribution, and Exemptions). This return should not be

sent to Century Center but should be sent to P.O. Box 105296 Atlanta, GA 30348-5296.

Mailing Instructions
Please mail the return to one of the following addresses:

Return with check or money order:
State of Georgia
Department of Revenue
PO Box 105296
Atlanta, GA 30348-5296

Return with an Electronically Filed Payment (EFT):
State of Georgia
Department of Revenue
PO Box 740398
Atlanta, GA 30374-0398

Payment Voucher
The Payment Voucher must be returned with the ST-3 Sales and Use Tax Report and your payment in the same envelope.
- Do **not** mail the Payment Voucher if you file your payment electronically (EFT).
- Do **not** mail the Payment Voucher if you do not owe money/taxes.
- The Payment Voucher is **not** a substitute for the ST-3 Sales and Use Tax Report. Failure to file the ST-3 Sales and Use Tax Report may result in penalties.

If you need assistance in preparing this form or general tax information, please contact Customer Service or your local regional office listed below:

Customer Service	(404) 417-4477
Albany	(229) 430-4241
Athens	(706) 542-6058
Atlanta	(404) 968-0480
Augusta	(706) 737-1870
Columbus	(706) 649-7451
Douglas	(912) 389-4094
Lithia Springs	(770) 732-5812
Macon	(478) 751-6055
North East Metro	(404) 417-6605
Rome	(706) 295-6061
Savannah	(912) 356-2140

Additional forms and information may be obtained from:
Department of Revenue Website:
www.dor.ga.gov

Forms Facsimile Information
(Forms to your fax machine)
(404) 417-6011

Vendor's Compensation Formula

Vendor's Compensation rate on <u>collected taxes</u> (for State Tax, Marta Tax, Local Tax, 2nd Local Tax, Special Tax, Educational Tax, Homestead Tax, and Excess Tax) is three percent (.03) of the first $3,000 ($90.00) of <u>tax</u> plus one half of one percent (.005) on the <u>tax</u> above $3,000.

Example: Collected Taxes of $4500 would equal $97.50.

$$\$3,000.00 \times .03 = \$90.00$$
$$\underline{\$1,500.00 \times .005 = \$7.50}$$
$$\text{Total} \quad \$4,500.00 \qquad = \$97.50$$

In addition, Motor Fuel Dealers may also take a Vendor's Compensation on 2nd Motor Fuel Sales.

Vendor's Compensation rate on 2nd Motor Fuel <u>Sales</u> is calculated as follows: Total 2nd Motor Fuel <u>Sales</u> multiplied by the county of registration tax rate (see enclosed rate chart) multiplied by three percent (.03).

Example: 2nd Motor Fuel Sales of $5,000.00
$5,000 x .07 (as an example for Fulton County) x .03 = $10.50

Master Inserts

Any dealer with 4 or more locations is required to report on a consolidated Sales and Use Tax Form (ST-3). Consolidated reporting requires each individual location to be reported on a master insert declaring total gross motor fuel and non-motor fuel sales and use, exemptions and deductions, total tax due by tax type, and the calculation of Vendor's Compensation by locations. Failure to submit the master insert may result in the loss of Vendor's Compensation.

Penalty Worksheet for Delinquent Returns

Returns are considered timely filed if postmarked by the twentieth of the month following the close of the reporting period. Penalty is due on all returns filed after this date. Penalty should be calculated individually for each tax type.

	Tax Type	Tax Due	Penalty
1.	State Sales Tax, Motor Fuel, & Excess Tax		
2.	2nd Motor Fuel Tax		
3.	MARTA Tax		
4.	Local Option Tax		
5.	2nd Local Option Tax		
6.	Special Purpose Tax		
7.	Educational Tax		
8.	Homestead Tax		
	Enter Total Penalty Due on Line 17		

Penalty Formula

The penalty of five percent (.05) of the tax due or five dollars ($5.00), *whichever is greater*, for each tax type on any delinquent return. This is calculated for <u>each</u> month, or fraction of a month, when the return is delinquent. The penalty will not exceed twenty-five percent (.25) or twenty-five dollars ($25.00), *whichever is greater*.

rev. 01/03

Registration Change Form

For any change of Trade Name, Address, Ownership, or Telephone Number, check applicable boxes and provide information below. *Send completed form in a separate envelope to the address listed below:*

[ ] **New Business Location/ Trade Name**

Name _____

Address _____

City, State, Zip _____

Phone Number _____

County _____

[ ] **New Mailing Address**

Address _____

City, State, Zip _____

Phone Number _____

[ ] **Business Closed**

[ ] **Business Sold**

Date Sold/Closed _____

[ ] **Name, Address, and Phone Number of Owners**

Name _____

Address_____

City, State, Zip_____

Phone Number_____

SEND CHANGES TO:
Centralized Taxpayer Registration Unit
PO Box 49512
Atlanta, GA 30359-1512

This page intentionally left blank.

EXEMPTION/DEDUCTION WORKSHEET

THIS WORKSHEET MUST BE MAINTAINED FOR AUDIT PURPOSES

	STATE	1 % M/F	2ND MOTOR FUEL	MARTA	LOCAL OPTION	TOWNS COUNTY	SPECIAL	EDUCATIONAL	HOMESTEAD
1									
2									
3			No Motor Fuel Sales						
4									
5									
6									
7									
8									
9					Webster and Taliaferro Co. Only				
10									
11	Enter on Line A	Enter on Line B	Enter on Line C	Enter on Line D	Enter on Line E	Enter on Line F	Enter on Line G	Enter on Line H	Enter on Line I

SEE INSTRUCTIONS BEFORE COMPLETING

1. Sales for resale
2. Sales to Federal Government
3. Sales to State of GA., counties & municipalities thereof
4. Sales in bona fide interstate commerce
5. Sales and Use exempt from 1% Motor Fuel, 2nd Motor Fuel, MARTA, Local Option, Towns Co. 2nd L/O, Special, Educational, or Homestead Tax.
6. Purchases on which tax was previously paid
7. Taxable sales of gasoline and/or motor fuels for highway use
8. State Excise Tax (.075) on _____ gals. of Motor Fuel. Calculate only on taxable sales of Motor Fuel.
9. Exempt Food: State Tax - Oct. 1, 1998 - 100% State Tax, Homestead Tax in DeKalb (7/97) and Rockdale (4/02) Counties and the Local Option Tax in Taliaferro (10/98) and Webster (1/99) Counties.
10. Other Deductions authorized by law (specify)
    - - - - - - - - - - - - - - - - -
    - - - - - - - - - - - - - - - - -
11. Enter the total exemption amounts for each tax type on the front of the sales and use tax report form (ST-3) in Part C, Schedule of Total Sales and Use Exemption/Deduction.

This page intentionally left blank.

IRS Form 8300 (Rev. December 2004)
OMB No. 1545-0892
Department of the Treasury
Internal Revenue Service

Report of Cash Payments Over $10,000 Received in a Trade or Business

▶ See instructions for definition of cash.

▶ Use this form for transactions occurring after December 31, 2004. Do not use prior versions after this date.
For Privacy Act and Paperwork Reduction Act Notice, see page 5.

FinCEN Form 8300 (Rev. December 2004)
OMB No. 1506-0018
Department of the Treasury
Financial Crimes
Enforcement Network

1 Check appropriate box(es) if: **a** ☐ Amends prior report;   **b** ☐ Suspicious transaction.

Part I   Identity of Individual From Whom the Cash Was Received

2 If more than one individual is involved, check here and see instructions . . . . ▶ ☐

3 Last name	4 First name	5 M.I.	6 Taxpayer identification number

7 Address (number, street, and apt. or suite no.)	8 Date of birth . ▶ (see instructions)	M M D D Y Y Y Y

9 City	10 State	11 ZIP code	12 Country (if not U.S.)	13 Occupation, profession, or business

14 Identifying document (ID)   **a Describe ID** ▶ ....   **b Issued by** ▶ ....
c Number ▶

Part II   Person on Whose Behalf This Transaction Was Conducted

15 If this transaction was conducted on behalf of more than one person, check here and see instructions . . . . . ▶ ☐

16 Individual's last name or Organization's name	17 First name	18 M.I.	19 Taxpayer identification number

20 Doing business as (DBA) name (see instructions)	Employer identification number

21 Address (number, street, and apt. or suite no.)	22 Occupation, profession, or business

23 City	24 State	25 ZIP code	26 Country (if not U.S.)

27 Alien identification (ID)   **a Describe ID** ▶ ....   **b Issued by** ▶ ....
c Number ▶

Part III   Description of Transaction and Method of Payment

28 Date cash received M M D D Y Y Y Y	29 Total cash received $ .00	30 If cash was received in more than one payment, check here . . . ▶ ☐	31 Total price if different from item 29 $ .00

32 Amount of cash received (in U.S. dollar equivalent) (must equal item 29) (see instructions):

a U.S. currency $ _____ .00   (Amount in $100 bills or higher $ _____ .00)
b Foreign currency $ _____ .00   (Country ▶ _____)
c Cashier's check(s) $ _____ .00   Issuer's name(s) and serial number(s) of the monetary instrument(s) ▶
d Money order(s) $ _____ .00   ....
e Bank draft(s) $ _____ .00   ....
f Traveler's check(s) $ _____ .00

33 Type of transaction

a ☐ Personal property purchased
b ☐ Real property purchased
c ☐ Personal services provided
d ☐ Business services provided
e ☐ Intangible property purchased
f ☐ Debt obligations paid
g ☐ Exchange of cash
h ☐ Escrow or trust funds
i ☐ Bail received by court clerks
j ☐ Other (specify in item 34) ▶

34 Specific description of property or service shown in 33. Give serial or registration number, address, docket number, etc. ▶
....
....
....

Part IV   Business That Received Cash

35 Name of business that received cash	36 Employer identification number

37 Address (number, street, and apt. or suite no.)	Social security number

38 City	39 State	40 ZIP code	41 Nature of your business

42 Under penalties of perjury, I declare that to the best of my knowledge the information I have furnished above is true, correct, and complete.

Signature ▶ _____ Title ▶ _____
Authorized official

43 Date of signature M M D D Y Y Y Y	44 Type or print name of contact person	45 Contact telephone number ( )

IRS Form 8300 (Rev. 12-2004)   Cat. No. 62133S   **FinCEN Form 8300** (Rev. 12-2004)

278

Multiple Parties
(Complete applicable parts below if box 2 or 15 on page 1 is checked)

Part I   Continued—Complete if box 2 on page 1 is checked

3 Last name	**4** First name	**5** M.I.	**6** Taxpayer identification number

7 Address (number, street, and apt. or suite no.)	**8** Date of birth (see instructions) ▶	M M D D Y Y Y Y

9 City	**10** State	**11** ZIP code	**12** Country (if not U.S.)	**13** Occupation, profession, or business

14 Identifying document (ID)	**a Describe ID** ▶ -------------------------------------- **c Number** ▶	**b Issued by** ▶ ------------------

3 Last name	**4** First name	**5** M.I.	**6** Taxpayer identification number

7 Address (number, street, and apt. or suite no.)	**8** Date of birth (see instructions) ▶	M M D D Y Y Y Y

9 City	**10** State	**11** ZIP code	**12** Country (if not U.S.)	**13** Occupation, profession, or business

14 Identifying document (ID)	**a Describe ID** ▶ -------------------------------------- **c Number** ▶	**b Issued by** ▶ ------------------

Part II   Continued—Complete if box 15 on page 1 is checked

16 Individual's last name or Organization's name	**17** First name	**18** M.I.	**19** Taxpayer identification number

20 Doing business as (DBA) name (see instructions)	Employer identification number

21 Address (number, street, and apt. or suite no.)	**22** Occupation, profession, or business

23 City	**24** State	**25** ZIP code	**26** Country (if not U.S.)

27 Alien identification (ID)	**a Describe ID** ▶ -------------------------------------- **c Number** ▶	**b Issued by** ▶ ------------------

16 Individual's last name or Organization's name	**17** First name	**18** M.I.	**19** Taxpayer identification number

20 Doing business as (DBA) name (see instructions)	Employer identification number

21 Address (number, street, and apt. or suite no.)	**22** Occupation, profession, or business

23 City	**24** State	**25** ZIP code	**26** Country (if not U.S.)

27 Alien identification (ID)	**a Describe ID** ▶ -------------------------------------- **c Number** ▶	**b Issued by** ▶ ------------------

Comments – Please use the lines provided below to comment on or clarify any information you entered on any line in Parts I, II, III, and IV

_____

_____

_____

_____

Section references are to the Internal Revenue Code unless otherwise noted.

Important Reminders

- Section 6050I (26 United States Code (U.S.C.) 6050I) and 31 U.S.C. 5331 require that certain information be reported to the IRS and the Financial Crimes Enforcement Network (FinCEN). This information must be reported on IRS/FinCEN Form 8300.

- Item 33 box i is to be checked only by clerks of the court; box d is to be checked by bail bondsmen. See the instructions on page 5.

- For purposes of section 6050I and 31 U.S.C. 5331, the word "cash" and "currency" have the same meaning. See *Cash* under *Definitions* on page 4.

General Instructions

Who must file. Each person engaged in a trade or business who, in the course of that trade or business, receives more than $10,000 in cash in one transaction or in two or more related transactions, must file Form 8300. Any transactions conducted between a payer (or its agent) and the recipient in a 24-hour period are related transactions. Transactions are considered related even if they occur over a period of more than 24 hours if the recipient knows, or has reason to know, that each transaction is one of a series of connected transactions.

Keep a copy of each Form 8300 for 5 years from the date you file it.

Clerks of Federal or State courts must file Form 8300 if more than $10,000 in cash is received as bail for an individual(s) charged with certain criminal offenses. For these purposes, a clerk includes the clerk's office or any other office, department, division, branch, or unit of the court that is authorized to receive bail. If a person receives bail on behalf of a clerk, the clerk is treated as receiving the bail. See the instructions for Item 33 on page 5.

If multiple payments are made in cash to satisfy bail and the initial payment does not exceed $10,000, the initial payment and subsequent payments must be aggregated and the information return must be filed by the 15th day after receipt of the payment that causes the aggregate amount to exceed $10,000 in cash. In such cases, the reporting requirement can be satisfied either by sending a single written statement with an aggregate amount listed or by furnishing a copy of each Form 8300 relating to that payer. Payments made to satisfy separate bail requirements are not required to be aggregated. See Treasury Regulations section 1.6050I-2.

Casinos must file Form 8300 for nongaming activities (restaurants, shops, etc.).

Voluntary use of Form 8300. Form 8300 may be filed voluntarily for any suspicious transaction (see *Definitions*) for use by the IRS, even if the total amount does not exceed $10,000.

Exceptions. Cash is not required to be reported if it is received:

- By a financial institution required to file Form 104, Currency Transaction Report.

- By a casino required to file (or exempt from filing) Form 103, Currency Transaction Report by Casinos, if the cash is received as part of its gaming business.

- By an agent who receives the cash from a principal, if the agent uses all of the cash within 15 days in a second transaction that is reportable on Form 8300 or on Form 104, and discloses all the information necessary to complete Part II of Form 8300 or Form 104 to the recipient of the cash in the second transaction.

- In a transaction occurring entirely outside the United States. See Publication 1544, Reporting Cash Payments Over $10,000 (Received in a Trade or Business), regarding transactions occurring in Puerto Rico, the Virgin Islands, and territories and possessions of the United States.

- In a transaction that is not in the course of a person's trade or business.

When to file. File Form 8300 by the 15th day after the date the cash was received. If that date falls on a Saturday, Sunday, or legal holiday, file the form on the next business day.

Where to file. File the form with the Internal Revenue Service, Detroit Computing Center, P.O. Box 32621, Detroit, MI 48232.

Statement to be provided. You must give a written or electronic statement to each person named on a required Form 8300 on or before January 31 of the year following the calendar year in which the cash is received. The statement must show the name, telephone number, and address of the information contact for the business, the aggregate amount of reportable cash received, and that the information was furnished to the IRS. Keep a copy of the statement for your records.

Multiple payments. If you receive more than one cash payment for a single transaction or for related transactions, you must report the multiple payments any time you receive a total amount that exceeds $10,000 within any 12-month period. Submit the report within 15 days of the date you receive the payment that

causes the total amount to exceed $10,000. If more than one report is required within 15 days, you may file a combined report. File the combined report no later than the date the earliest report, if filed separately, would have to be filed.

Taxpayer identification number (TIN). You must furnish the correct TIN of the person or persons from whom you receive the cash and, if applicable, the person or persons on whose behalf the transaction is being conducted. You may be subject to penalties for an incorrect or missing TIN.

The TIN for an individual (including a sole proprietorship) is the individual's social security number (SSN). For certain resident aliens who are not eligible to get an SSN and nonresident aliens who are required to file tax returns, it is an IRS Individual Taxpayer Identification Number (ITIN). For other persons, including corporations, partnerships, and estates, it is the employer identification number (EIN).

If you have requested but are not able to get a TIN for one or more of the parties to a transaction within 15 days following the transaction, file the report and attach a statement explaining why the TIN is not included.

Exception: *You are not required to provide the TIN of a person who is a nonresident alien individual or a foreign organization if that person does not have income effectively connected with the conduct of a U.S. trade or business and does not have an office or place of business, or fiscal or paying agent, in the United States. See Publication 1544 for more information.*

Penalties. You may be subject to penalties if you fail to file a correct and complete Form 8300 on time and you cannot show that the failure was due to reasonable cause. You may also be subject to penalties if you fail to furnish timely a correct and complete statement to each person named in a required report. A minimum penalty of $25,000 may be imposed if the failure is due to an intentional or willful disregard of the cash reporting requirements.

Penalties may also be imposed for causing, or attempting to cause, a trade or business to fail to file a required report; for causing, or attempting to cause, a trade or business to file a required report containing a material omission or misstatement of fact; or for structuring, or attempting to structure, transactions to avoid the reporting requirements. These violations may also be subject to criminal prosecution which, upon conviction, may result in imprisonment of up to 5 years or fines of up to $250,000 for individuals and $500,000 for corporations or both.

Definitions

Cash. The term "cash" means the following:

- U.S. and foreign coin and currency received in any transaction.

- A cashier's check, money order, bank draft, or traveler's check having a face amount of $10,000 or less that is received in a designated reporting transaction (defined below), or that is received in any transaction in which the recipient knows that the instrument is being used in an attempt to avoid the reporting of the transaction under either section 6050I or 31 U.S.C. 5331.

Note. Cash does not include a check drawn on the payer's own account, such as a personal check, regardless of the amount.

Designated reporting transaction. A retail sale (or the receipt of funds by a broker or other intermediary in connection with a retail sale) of a consumer durable, a collectible, or a travel or entertainment activity.

Retail sale. Any sale (whether or not the sale is for resale or for any other purpose) made in the course of a trade or business if that trade or business principally consists of making sales to ultimate consumers.

Consumer durable. An item of tangible personal property of a type that, under ordinary usage, can reasonably be expected to remain useful for at least 1 year, and that has a sales price of more than $10,000.

Collectible. Any work of art, rug, antique, metal, gem, stamp, coin, etc.

Travel or entertainment activity. An item of travel or entertainment that pertains to a single trip or event if the combined sales price of the item and all other items relating to the same trip or event that are sold in the same transaction (or related transactions) exceeds $10,000.

Exceptions. A cashier's check, money order, bank draft, or traveler's check is not considered received in a designated reporting transaction if it constitutes the proceeds of a bank loan or if it is received as a payment on certain promissory notes, installment sales contracts, or down payment plans. See Publication 1544 for more information.

Person. An individual, corporation, partnership, trust, estate, association, or company.

Recipient. The person receiving the cash. Each branch or other unit of a person's trade or business is considered a separate recipient unless the branch receiving the cash (or a central office linking the branches), knows or has reason to know the identity of payers making cash payments to other branches.

Transaction. Includes the purchase of property or services, the payment of debt, the exchange of a negotiable instrument for cash, and the receipt of cash to be held in escrow or trust. A single transaction may not be broken into multiple transactions to avoid reporting.

Suspicious transaction. A transaction in which it appears that a person is attempting to cause Form 8300 not to be filed, or to file a false or incomplete form. The term also includes any transaction in which there is an indication of possible illegal activity.

Specific Instructions

You must complete all parts. However, you may skip Part II if the individual named in Part I is conducting the transaction on his or her behalf only. For voluntary reporting of suspicious transactions, see Item 1 below.

Item 1. If you are amending a prior report, check box 1a. Complete the appropriate items with the correct or amended information only. Complete all of Part IV. Staple a copy of the original report to the amended report.

To voluntarily report a suspicious transaction (see *Definitions*), check box 1b. You may also telephone your local IRS Criminal Investigation Division or call 1-800-800-2877.

Part I

Item 2. If two or more individuals conducted the transaction you are reporting, check the box and complete Part I for any one of the individuals. Provide the same information for the other individual(s) on the back of the form. If more than three individuals are involved, provide the same information on additional sheets of paper and attach them to this form.

Item 6. Enter the taxpayer identification number (TIN) of the individual named. See *Taxpayer identification number (TIN)* on page 3 for more information.

Item 8. Enter eight numerals for the date of birth of the individual named. For example, if the individual's birth date is July 6, 1960, enter 07 06 1960.

Item 13. Fully describe the nature of the occupation, profession, or business (for example, "plumber," "attorney," or "automobile dealer"). Do not use general or nondescriptive terms such as "businessman" or "self-employed."

Item 14. You must verify the name and address of the named individual(s). Verification must be made by examination of a document normally accepted as a means of identification when cashing checks (for example, a driver's license, passport, alien registration card, or other official

document). In item 14a, enter the type of document examined. In item 14b, identify the issuer of the document. In item 14c, enter the document's number. For example, if the individual has a Utah driver's license, enter "driver's license" in item 14a, "Utah" in item 14b, and the number appearing on the license in item 14c.

Note. You must complete all three items (a, b, and c) in this line to make sure that Form 8300 will be processed correctly.

Part II

Item 15. If the transaction is being conducted on behalf of more than one person (including husband and wife or parent and child), check the box and complete Part II for any one of the persons. Provide the same information for the other person(s) on the back of the form. If more than three persons are involved, provide the same information on additional sheets of paper and attach them to this form.

Items 16 through 19. If the person on whose behalf the transaction is being conducted is an individual, complete items 16, 17, and 18. Enter his or her TIN in item 19. If the individual is a sole proprietor and has an employer identification number (EIN), you must enter both the SSN and EIN in item 19. If the person is an organization, put its name as shown on required tax filings in item 16 and its EIN in item 19.

Item 20. If a sole proprietor or organization named in items 16 through 18 is doing business under a name other than that entered in item 16 (e.g., a "trade" or "doing business as (DBA)" name), enter it here.

Item 27. If the person is not required to furnish a TIN, complete this item. See *Taxpayer Identification Number (TIN)* on page 3. Enter a description of the type of official document issued to that person in item 27a (for example, "passport"), the country that issued the document in item 27b, and the document's number in item 27c.

Note. You must complete all three items (a, b, and c) in this line to make sure that Form 8300 will be processed correctly.

Part III

Item 28. Enter the date you received the cash. If you received the cash in more than one payment, enter the date you received the payment that caused the combined amount to exceed $10,000. See *Multiple payments* under *General Instructions* for more information.

Item 30. Check this box if the amount shown in item 29 was received in more than one payment (for example, as installment payments or payments on related transactions).

Item 31. Enter the total price of the property, services, amount of cash exchanged, etc. (for example, the total cost of a vehicle purchased, cost of catering service, exchange of currency) if different from the amount shown in item 29.

Item 32. Enter the dollar amount of each form of cash received. Show foreign currency amounts in U.S. dollar equivalent at a fair market rate of exchange available to the public. The sum of the amounts must equal item 29. For cashier's check, money order, bank draft, or traveler's check, provide the name of the issuer and the serial number of each instrument. Names of all issuers and all serial numbers involved must be provided. If necessary, provide this information on additional sheets of paper and attach them to this form.

Item 33. Check the appropriate box(es) that describe the transaction. If the transaction is not specified in boxes a–i, check box j and briefly describe the transaction (for example, "car lease," "boat lease," "house lease," or "aircraft rental"). If the transaction relates to the receipt of bail by a court clerk, check box i, "Bail received by court clerks." This box is only for use by court clerks. If the transaction relates to cash received by a bail bondsman, check box d, "Business services provided."

Part IV

Item 36. If you are a sole proprietorship, you must enter your SSN. If your business also has an EIN, you must provide the EIN as well. All other business entities must enter an EIN.

Item 41. Fully describe the nature of your business, for example, "attorney" or "jewelry dealer." Do not use general or nondescriptive terms such as "business" or "store."

Item 42. This form must be signed by an individual who has been authorized to do so for the business that received the cash.

Comments

Use this section to comment on or clarify anything you may have entered on any line in Parts I, II, III, and IV. For example, if you checked box b (Suspicious transaction) in line 1 above Part I, you may want to explain why you think that the cash transaction you are reporting on Form 8300 may be suspicious.

Privacy Act and Paperwork Reduction Act Notice. Except as otherwise noted, the information solicited on this form is required by the Internal Revenue Service (IRS) and the Financial Crimes Enforcement Network (FinCEN) in order to carry out the laws and regulations of the United States Department of the Treasury. Trades or businesses, except for clerks of criminal courts, are required to provide the information to the IRS and FinCEN under both section 6050I and 31 U.S.C. 5331. Clerks of criminal courts are required to provide the information to the IRS under section 6050I. Section 6109 and 31 U.S.C. 5331 require that you provide your social security number in order to adequately identify you and process your return and other papers. The principal purpose for collecting the information on this form is to maintain reports or records which have a high degree of usefulness in criminal, tax, or regulatory investigations or proceedings, or in the conduct of intelligence or counterintelligence activities, by directing the Federal Government's attention to unusual or questionable transactions.

You are not required to provide information as to whether the reported transaction is deemed suspicious. Failure to provide all other requested information, or providing fraudulent information, may result in criminal prosecution and other penalties under Title 26 and Title 31 of the United States Code.

Generally, tax returns and return information are confidential, as stated in section 6103. However, section 6103 allows or requires the IRS to disclose or give the information requested on this form to others as described in the Code. For example, we may disclose your tax information to the Department of Justice, to enforce the tax laws, both civil and criminal, and to cities, states, the District of Columbia, to carry out their tax laws. We may disclose this information to other persons as necessary to obtain information which we cannot get in any other way. We may disclose this information to Federal, state, and local child support agencies; and to other Federal agencies for the purposes of determining entitlement for benefits or the eligibility for and the repayment of loans. We may also provide the records to appropriate state, local, and foreign criminal law enforcement and regulatory personnel in the performance of their official duties. We may also disclose this information to other countries under a tax treaty, or to Federal and state agencies to enforce Federal nontax criminal laws and to combat terrorism.

The IRS authority to disclose information to combat terrorism expired on December 31, 2003. Legislation is pending that would reinstate this authority. "In addition, FinCEN may provide the information to those officials if they are conducting intelligence or counter-intelligence activities to protect against international terrorism."

You are not required to provide the information requested on a form that is subject to the Paperwork Reduction Act unless the form displays a valid OMB control number. Books or records relating to a form or its instructions must be retained as long as their contents may become material in the administration of any law under Title 26 or Title 31.

The time needed to complete this form will vary depending on individual circumstances. The estimated average time is 21 minutes. If you have comments concerning the accuracy of this time estimate or suggestions for making this form simpler, you can write to the Tax Products Coordinating Committee, Western Area Distribution Center, Rancho Cordova, CA 95743-0001. Do not send this form to this office. Instead, see *Where To File* on page 3.

This page intentionally left blank.

EMPLOYMENT AGREEMENT

THIS EMPLOYMENT AGREEMENT (the "Agreement") is made this _____ day of _____, 20___, between _____ a Georgia corporation, and its affiliates, current and future (collectively, the "Corporation") and _____ (the "Employee").

WITNESSETH

The Employee is a key employee of the Corporation and possesses an intimate knowledge of the business and affairs of the Corporation. The Corporation recognizes the Employee's potential for the growth and success of the Corporation and desires to assure to the Corporation the continued benefits of the Employee's expertise and knowledge. The Employee, in turn, desires to establish and continue in full-time employment with the Corporation on the terms provided herein.

Accordingly, in consideration of the mutual covenants and representations contained herein, the parties hereto agree as follows:

1. Full-time Employment of Employee

1.1 Duties and Status.

(a) The Corporation hereby engages the Employee as a full-time Employee for the period (the "Employment Period") specified in Section 4, and the Employee accepts such employment, on the terms and conditions set forth in this Agreement. During the Employment Period, the Employee shall exercise such authority and perform such Employee duties as are commensurate with the authority being exercised and duties being performed by the Employee for the Corporation immediately prior to the effective date of this Agreement. The Employee shall hold such position as assigned, being currently the position of _____, or such other titles or positions as are assigned to him by the corporation or its officers.

(b) During the Employment Period, the Employee shall (i) devote his or her full working time and efforts to the business of the Corporation and will not engage in consulting work or any trade or business for his or her own account or for or on behalf of any other person, firm or corporation which competes, conflicts or interferes with the performance of his or her duties hereunder in any way, and (ii) accept such additional office or offices to which he or she may be elected by Corporation, provided that the performance of the duties of such office or offices shall be consistent with the scope of the duties provided for in subsection (a) of this Section 1.1.

1.2 Compensation and General Benefits. As compensation for his or her services under this Agreement, the Employee shall be compensated as follows:

(a)   The   Corporation   shall   pay   the   Employee   an   annual   salary   of _____ Dollars ($___,000).

(b) The Corporation shall pay the Employee a one-time sign up bonus of $_____, which shall be payable at the time of the first paycheck issued to Employee.

(c) The Corporation shall provide other general benefits such as training, insurance, consistent with the benefits available to similarly situated employees and outlined in the Company Employee Manual.

2. Competition; Confidential Information. The Employee and the Corporation recognize that Employee has had access to and has acquired, will have access to and will acquire, and has assisted and may assist in developing confidential and proprietary information relating to the business and operations of the Corporation and its affiliates, including, without limiting the generality of the foregoing,

information with respect to their present and prospective products, systems, customers, agents, processes, and sales and marketing methods. The Employee acknowledges that such information has been and will continue to be of central importance to the business of the Corporation and its affiliates and that disclosure of it to, or its use by, others could cause substantial loss to the Corporation. The Employee accordingly agrees as follows:

2.1 **Non-Competition.**

(a) The Employee agrees that during his or her employment by the Corporation and for a period of **TWENTY-FOUR (24) months** following the Employee's termination of such employment or the Corporation's termination of such employment for cause (as defined in section 4.1 below), he or she will not (except on behalf of or with the prior written consent of the Corporation) within the "Area" and "Industries" defined below, either directly or indirectly, on his or her own behalf or in the service or on behalf of others engage in any business which sells products or services that are competitive with the products or services provided by the Corporation (any business carrying on such activities being herein called a "Competing Business") in any capacity similar to the capacity or capacities in which the Employee was employed by the Corporation. For purposes of this Agreement the "Area" shall be defined as the State of Georgia, and the "Industries" shall be defined as including 1) _____ and 2) _____. **For purposes of this Agreement "Business of the Company" shall mean: the business of the Company, and the business of its affiliates, current or future. Collectively such businesses shall be referred to as the "Company."**

(b) The Employee further agrees that during his or her employment by the Corporation and for a period of **TWENTY-FOUR (24)** months following the Employee's termination of such employment or the Corporation's termination of such employment for cause (as defined in section 4.1 below), he or she will not (except on behalf of or with the prior written consent of the Corporation), either directly or indirectly, on his or her own behalf or in the service or on behalf of others, (i) solicit or divert or appropriate to a Competing Business, or (ii) attempt to solicit, divert or appropriate to or for any Competing Business, any person or entity whose customer account with the Company was sold or serviced or pursued by or under the supervision of Employee during the term of his or her employment with the Corporation.

(c) The Employee agrees that during his or her employment by the Corporation and for a period of **TWENTY-FOUR (24)** months following the Employee's termination of such employment or the Corporation's termination of such employment for cause (as defined in section 4.1 below), he or she will not, either directly or indirectly, on his or her own behalf or in the service or on behalf of others solicit, divert or entice, or attempt to solicit, divert or entice, to any Competing Business any person employed by the Corporation, whether or not such employee is a full-time employee or a temporary employee of the Company, and whether or not such employment is pursuant to written agreement and whether or not such employment is for a determined period or is at will. The foregoing shall not apply to solicitation of former employees that have been separated from the Corporation for 6 months or more.

2.2 **Confidential Information.**

(a) "Confidential Information" shall mean any and all data and information relating to the Business of the Company which is not a Trade Secret, as hereinafter defined), (i) which is or has been disclosed to the Employee, or of which the Employee became aware as a consequence of or through his or her employment relationship with the Corporation; and (ii) which has value to the Corporation or the Company and is not generally known by competitors; provided (iii), that no information will be deemed confidential unless such information has been reduced to writing and marked clearly and conspicuously as confidential information, or such information is otherwise treated by the Corporation as confidential, or such information failed to be properly identified and protected as a result the Employee's omission in performing such functions. The Employee, as a key employee of the Corporation, shall have a duty to identify and protect such Confidential Information on behalf of the Corporation.

(b) The Employee agrees that during the term of his or her employment by the Corporation and for ten (10) years thereafter, he will not disclose or make available, directly or indirectly, any

Confidential Information to any person, concern or entity, except in the proper performance of his duties and responsibilities hereunder or with the prior written consent of the Corporation. This restriction shall not apply to information generally available to the public or to any information properly obtained from a source completely independent from the Corporation. The Employee, as a key employee of the Corporation, shall have a duty to identify its Confidential Information and to keep secret and to otherwise protect such Confidential Information on behalf of the Corporation.

2.3 Trade Secrets.

(a) "Trade Secrets" shall mean and include the whole or any portion of any technical or nontechnical data, formula pattern, compilation, program, device, method, technique, drawing, process, financial data, lists of actual or potential customers, lists of actual or potential suppliers, or other information which derives economic value, actual or potential, from not being generally known to, and not being readily ascertainable by proper means by, other persons who can obtain economic value from its disclosure or use.

(b) The Employee agrees that during the term of his or her employment by the Corporation and for ten (10) years thereafter, he will not disclose or make available, directly or indirectly, any Trade Secrets to any person, concern, or entity, except in the proper performance of his or her duties and responsibilities hereunder or with the prior written consent of the Corporation. This restriction shall not apply to information generally available to the public or to any information properly obtained from a source completely independent from the Corporation or the Company. The Employee, as a key employee of the Corporation, shall have a duty to identify its Trade Secrets and to keep secret and to otherwise protect such Trade Secrets on behalf of the Corporation and the Company.

2.4 Intellectual Property.
Promptly upon request by the Corporation, the Employee will assign permanently to the Corporation exclusive rights to any patents, design patents, copyrights, trademarks, service marks, and other intellectual property rights awarded to him or her on the basis of (i) ideas developed in whole or in part by the Employee during the term of his employment with the Corporation and its affiliates; and (ii) ideas developed by the Employee within **SIX (6) months** following the termination of his or her employment by the Corporation, which are related to or result from such employment.

3. Corporation's Remedies for Breach.
It is recognized that damages in the event of breach of Section 2 by the Employee would be difficult, if not impossible, to ascertain, and it is, therefore, agreed that the Corporation, in addition to and without limiting any other remedy or right it may have, shall have the right to an injunction or other equitable relief in any court of competent jurisdiction, enjoining any breach, and the Employee hereby waives any and all defenses he may have on the ground of lack of jurisdiction or competence of the court to grant such an injunction or other equitable relief. The existence of this right shall not preclude any other rights and remedies at law or in equity which the Corporation may have.

4. Employment Period, Equity Options, etc.

4.1 Period of Employment.
The Employment Period shall commence on the date of this Agreement and shall continue indefinitely on an at-will basis until terminated by either party via written notice to the other, **but such termination shall not be effective until 14 days after giving written notice.** The foregoing notwithstanding, the Corporation may terminate the Employee's employment hereunder for "cause" and such termination shall be effective immediately and without regard to when notice of same is given the Employee. The term "cause" means (i) fraud, misappropriation, or intentional material damage to the property or business of the Corporation; (ii) commission of a felony; (iii) continuance of failure by the Employee to perform his or her duties in compliance with this Agreement after written notice to the Employee by his or her supervisor; (iv) a violation of Section 2 of this Agreement, (v) incompetence; (vi) incapacitation for a period of 14 days or more; or (vii) Employee's bankruptcy, assignment for the benefit of creditors, becoming subject to execution on a judgment, or insolvency.

4.2 Survival of Covenants.
Termination of the Employee's employment hereunder shall in no way diminish the Employee's duty to fully honor the covenants of Section 2 herein. Further, no purported or actual breach of this Agreement by the Corporation shall in any way diminish the Employee's duty to fully honor the covenants of Section 2 herein.

5. **Notices.** Any notices, requests, demands, or other communications provided for by this Agreement shall be sufficient if in writing and shall be deemed given when delivered personally or when sent by registered or certified mail to the Employee at the last residence address he has filed in writing with the Corporation or, in the case of the Corporation, at its principal Employee offices.

6. **Binding Agreement.** This Agreement shall be effective as of the date hereof and shall be binding upon and inure to the benefit of the Employee, his or her heirs, personal and legal representatives, guardians and permitted assigns. The rights and obligations of the Corporation under this Agreement shall inure to the benefit of and shall be binding upon any successor or assignee of the Corporation.

7. **Entire Agreement.** This Agreement constitutes the entire understanding of the Employee and the Corporation with respect to the subject matter hereof and supersedes any and all prior understandings written or oral. This Agreement may not be changed, modified, or discharged orally, but only by an instrument in writing signed by the parties.

8. **Tolling.** In the event that Employee shall breach any or all of the covenants set forth in Section 2 hereof, the running of the restrictions set forth in such Section breached shall be tolled during the continuation(s) of any such breach or breaches by Employee, and the running of the period of such restrictions shall commence or commence again only upon compliance by the Employee with the terms of the applicable Section breached.

9. **Waiver.** The waiver by the Corporation of any breach of this Agreement by the Employee shall not be effective unless in writing, and no such waiver shall operate or be construed as the waiver of the same or another breach on a subsequent occasion.

10. **Governing Law.** This Agreement shall be governed by and construed and enforced in accordance with the laws of the State of Georgia.

11. **Severability.** The invalidity or unenforceability of any provisions hereof shall in no way affect the validity or enforceability of any other provision.

IN WITNESS WHEREOF, the parties have executed, sealed and delivered this Employment Agreement as of the date first above written.

CORPORATION:

By: _____ (seal)
_____, Pres.

[corporate seal]

EMPLOYEE:

_____ (seal)
_____, Individually

Index

C

C corporation, 165, 170, 178
capital, 8, 15, 37, 39, 40, 43, 46, 73, 143
cash, 41, 42, 117, 121, 134, 139–143, 180
check, bad, 140
check, 84, 121, 133, 139–143, 166
checking account, 9, 10
child labor law, 112, 115
Children Online Privacy Protection Act of
    1998 (COPPA), 83
Code of Federal Regulations (C.F.R.), 90,
    91, 115, 123–125, 132, 134, 143, 154
collection law, 139, 141, 143, 145
commerce, 24, 31, 57, 85, 91, 111, 120,
    127, 184
consideration, 59, 60, 140
Consumer Product Safety Commission
    (CPSC), 91, 92
contract law, 59, 61–63
Controlling the Assault of Non-Solicited
    Pornography and Marketing Act of
    2003 (CANSPAM), 130
copyright, 74, 75, 81, 83, 149–151
corporation, 8–11, 14, 17–22, 24, 26, 39,
    43, 50, 51, 62, 65, 66, 68, 69, 72, 73, 82,
    128, 144, 165, 167, 168, 170–173, 177,
    178, 183
counteroffer, 61
court, 11, 17, 20, 22, 43, 54, 60, 61, 63, 72,
    79, 94, 101, 105, 108, 110, 112, 122,
    128, 133, 140, 141, 145, 148, 159, 183
credit card, 10, 12, 15, 42, 84, 139,
    142–145
customer, 3, 4, 8, 26, 28–34, 36, 40, 48, 49,
    59–61, 63, 68, 77, 78, 82, 84, 135,
    140–144, 146, 150, 185

D

Davis-Bacon Act, 117
Department of Homeland Security (DHS),
    157
Department of Revenue (DOR), 12, 70,
    176–178, 184
Department of Transportation, 91
Determination of Worker Status (IRS
    Form SS-8), 103
discrimination, 97, 99, 105, 106, 108, 119,
    120, 148
domain name, 15, 22, 23, 71–73, 75
drug test, 99
duty to open, 50

E

earned income credit, 173
email, 10, 21, 78, 81, 82, 84, 130, 187
employee, 1–4, 12, 14, 18, 26, 30, 32–34,
    36, 37, 40, 49, 66–70, 73, 89, 90, 93, 94,
    96–122, 133, 153, 167, 171–174, 177,
    179, 184
Employee Polygraph Protection Act, 99
Employee Retirement Income Security
    Act (ERISA), 114
employer, 66, 89, 90, 93, 94, 97, 99–101,
    103, 105–113, 115–121, 171, 172, 177,
    179, 180
employer identification number (EIN), 12,
    171
employment agreement, 100, 101
employment at will, 120
Employment Eligibility Verification (form
    I-9), 115
Encyclopedia of Associations, 5, 27